Leslie J. Harris is Assistant Professor of Communication at the University of Wisconsin, Milwaukee.

State of the Marital Union

State of the Marital Union

Rhetoric, Identity, and Nineteenth-Century Marriage Controversies

Leslie J. Harris

BAYLOR UNIVERSITY PRESS

Waco, Texas 76798-7363

Cover Design by Nita Ybarra Design

Library of Congress Cataloging-in-Publication Data

Harris, Leslie J., 1978–
State of the marital union : rhetoric, identity, and nineteenth-century marriage controversies / Leslie J. Harris.
223 pages cm
Includes bibliographical references and index.
ISBN 978-1-4813-0051-3 (hardback : alk. paper)
1. Marriage—United States—History—19th century. I. Title.
HQ535.H37 2014
306.81097309'034--dc23
2013048779

Printed in the United States of America on acid-free paper with a minimum of 30% post-consumer waste recycled content.

To John, Anna, and James

Contents

Acknowledgments

I find writing an acknowledgment a difficult task, in part because there are so many people to whom I owe gratitude, and I fear that any expression of gratitude will be inadequate. The University of Wisconsin–Milwaukee has provided significant institutional support through a Faculty Arts and Humanities Travel Award, Graduate School Research Committee Award, and University of Wisconsin Libraries Research Fellowship. I have been fortunate to have research support from amazing undergraduate and graduate students, including David Nawrocki, Semra Schneider, and Stephanie Gille. My colleagues at UWM have been incredibly encouraging in innumerable ways, including talking about ideas and reading drafts. In particular, I believe that this project has been improved by support from William Keith, Kathryn Olson, John Jordan, Kathryn Fonner, Mike Allen, and Sang-Yeon Kim.

I don't think that it is possible to name everyone who has influenced me in writing this book. Mary Stuckey, Bonnie Dow, Rena Hassian, Sarah VanderHaggen, Louise Knight, Elizabeth Benacka, Lisa Corrigan, and Ebony Utley have all read chapters and given me feedback that has made this book better. I am grateful to have been assisted by some wonderful librarians and archivists. Luis Acosta from the Law Library in the Library of Congress was especially kind in helping me sort through a confused history and truly going beyond what was necessary in helping with additional research and questions. Several University of Wisconsin–Milwaukee librarians were tremendously helpful, especially Linda A. Kopecky. Finally, I am very appreciative of Carey Newman, Gladys Lewis, and everyone at Baylor University Press for their assistance, support, and advice. I am also appreciative of the advice and support from David Zarefsky and Angela Ray at the early stages of this manuscript.

I have presented parts of this research at annual National Communication Association conventions, the Rhetoric Society of America Convention, the Central States Communication Association Conference, the Organization for the Study of Communication, Language, and Gender Conference, and two National Communication Association/American Forensics Association Summer Conferences on Argument. I am grateful to panel respondents and conference participants whose ideas, comments, and questions have made this project better. I am also thankful for opportunities to present this research at colloquiums for the Center for Print Culture at the University of Wisconsin–Madison and the Department of Communication at the University of Wisconsin–Milwaukee.

My family has been essential through every step of this process. My partner, John, and children, Anna and James, have tolerated large piles of research scattered throughout our home and my absences for research and writing. My mother-in-law, Lynne, is a wonderful reader, and my mother, Terry, provided enthusiasm and encouragement.

INTRODUCTION

Marriage and the Nation

In a 1905 speech to the National Congress of Mothers, President Theodore Roosevelt argued,

> In the last analysis the welfare of the state depends absolutely upon whether or not the average family, the average man and woman and their children, represent the kind of citizenship fit for the foundation of a great nation; and if we fail to appreciate this we fail to appreciate the root morality upon which all healthy civilization is based.[1]

In this speech, Roosevelt articulated a vision of public life in which family and marriage were critical, and "average" people synecdochically represented the state of the nation as a whole.[2] Roosevelt's expression of the relationship between family and state was not new. This book traces the public fixation with the seemingly private sphere of the family through five nineteenth-century marriage controversies. Each of these controversies remained in the spotlight for a significant part of the century and came to be implicated in some of the most heated issues of the time. In considering these controversies, this book begins with the following questions: What were the ways in which Americans attempted to negotiate and regulate a public concept of marriage, and what were the implications of public understandings of marriage for the myths of American public identity?

Nation is a rhetorical fiction. That is, the concept of nation as a device for organizing and forming identity, entailing values, priorities, and norms, is rhetorically constituted and constructs understandings of both self and Other.[3] In the United States, national identity is constituted through a variety of rhetorical modes and sources: myths of the nation's history, the election of public representatives, the words of the presidents, acts of public protest, and much more.[4] Occasionally a person, such as a president, or an object, such as the flag, represents "the" concept of nation, yet we know that any symbolic representation is, at best, incomplete. This book is about one important yet often hidden aspect of national identity—marriage. Rather than being about the joy, pain, or complexity of individual marriages or the $161-billion wedding industry, this book is about the *public* conception of marriage.[5] In particular, this book concerns the ways that Americans attempt to negotiate and regulate this public concept of marriage and the implications of the understandings of marriage on American public identity.

State of the Marital Union is not a comprehensive history of marriage.[6] Rather, through a rhetorical analysis of public marriage controversies, the text argues that marriage is a public institution unlike any other. It works to structure relationships between citizens and the state, constituting lines between American and Other while functioning in a space between (or at odds with) traditional conceptions of civic republicanism and liberal individualism. Public marriage controversies thus participate in constituting symbolic womanhood, a mythic yet powerful conception of public identity that both constrains and enables public action. Symbolic womanhood constitutes women as containers of the culture, values, and morals of the nation, and regulation of marriage as a public institution enables an enforcement of the line between civilization and barbarism.

SYMBOLIC WOMANHOOD

In the nineteenth-century United States, the power of the American woman was commonly considered to be in the home, which was her "sphere." Writers such as Catherine Beecher explained that women in their capacities as wives and mothers could shape the "destinies of a nation."[7] Correspondingly, both the law and social norms of the nineteenth-century United States limited women's access to the public sphere, substituting "married women's obligations to their husbands for obligations to the state."[8] The years between 1820 and 1860 have been identified as the heyday of the "cult of true womanhood," which called for women to be pure, pious, domestic, and submissive.[9] However, from persistent appeals to women's chastity in fiction to the social purity crusades of the Women's Christian Temperance Union, many of these norms persisted throughout the century.[10]

Marriage and motherhood were commonly represented as the ultimate achievements for a woman, and public rhetoric represented those roles of wife and mother as important to the nation as a whole. Although there were significant shifts over the course of the century, public discourse and policy persistently connected women's public identities to marriage, family, and home, providing both obligation and unique qualification to women.[11] Indeed, these connections are not limited to the nineteenth century as there is evidence of associations between womanhood and family in the eighteenth-century conception of Republican Motherhood and in the early twentieth century, when Theodore Roosevelt called on women to serve the nation through their role in the home.[12] In this sense and despite a rhetoric that suggests otherwise, throughout much of American history the home has been a public space (or at least a quasi-public space).

Women, however, defied expectations of domesticity and femininity in a variety of ways.[13] Women protested, petitioned, spoke publicly, and wrote, all of which challenged expectations of domesticity and subservience. Through attempts to enter into public space, women challenged and appropriated expectations of proper womanhood. Yet cultural expectations of symbolic womanhood remained influential and often were reinforced through law.

In the nineteenth century, laws enforced women's limited access to what is traditionally understood as the public sphere, and laws of marriage were inextricably bound to laws of coverture. Coverture, the political and legal "covering" of wives under the male head of household, created the basis for women's limited participation in the public.[14] In describing what coverture meant to American women, many nineteenth-century judges and legal scholars cited William Blackstone's influential treatise on the laws of England, in which he wrote, "By marriage, the husband and wife are one person in law: that is, the very being or legal existence of the woman is suspended during the marriage, or at least is incorporated and consolidated into that of the husband: under whose wing, protection, and *cover*, she performs every thing."[15] While the United States was no longer governed by the laws of Great Britain, the principle of coverture remained tremendously influential in the nineteenth-century United States.[16] This seemingly static legal principle came to function as a means of disciplining conceptions of proper citizenship.

In attempting to make sense of the concept of coverture, judges and legal scholars employed a metaphor of family-as-government. This was a controlling metaphor that shaped the meanings and implications of coverture in the nineteenth-century United States; the metaphor reflected ways of thinking about the relationship between family and law, enabling material action.[17] This metaphor conceived of the family as an insular governing unit headed by the husband/father: in turn, the head of the family government represented the family to the outside world. The metaphor of family government was often used to insulate the family from public scrutiny and limit women's rights, including suffrage.[18] This framing of family was also used across the country in judicial decisions to justify the right of wife whipping, to allow the father to avoid bills for goods delivered to his children without his consent, to permit the father to punish his children as he saw fit, and to require a husband to pay his wife's debts.[19] As a controlling metaphor, family-as-government was present in both judicial and deliberative discourse, and it reflected ways of thinking about family and its relationship to the state.

Despite women's material exclusion from many areas of public life, symbolic representations of womanhood were an important part of a mythic American identity in the nineteenth-century United States. Indeed, women have always been an important part of American public identity, but when people are trained to see the public sphere through the lens of political participation, women appear to be conspicuously absent. This book suggests that a symbolic womanhood existed in the same cultural space as rationality, strength, fraternity, and masculinity as markers of American public identity.[20] Public debates about marriage were not simply about marriage laws, but were also important sites of negotiating the meanings and significance of symbolic womanhood.

In nineteenth-century marriage controversies, women were represented as containers of the culture and purveyors of public morality. These representations posited womanhood as a critical part of the larger cultural milieu. Public debates over marriage were about protecting women and preventing contamination of both women's bodies and morals, each of which came to represent an important part of what made Americans "civilized" in contrast to a barbarous Other. Therefore, the symbolic category of womanhood functioned as a lens for understanding and regulating public morality, a necessarily sticky and ambiguous concept. Through rhetorical analysis of marriage controversies, particular conceptions of symbolic womanhood and, thus, public morality emerge.

Purity, although often connected to monogamy, was a controlling value that limited the public possibilities for "good" marriage and a "good" nation. There were at least two dimensions to public understandings of purity that linked the sacred and the secular, physical and metaphysical. Racial purity was represented in the values, ethics, and biology of the culture at large and resided in women's bodies. To regulate women's bodies, particularly women's sexuality, enabled a regulation of racial purity. Nonetheless, this conception of race was rhetorical and depended on perceived lines between civilized and barbarian, and although these lines often mapped onto whiteness or lack thereof, the public imagination inextricably linked moral and physical purity, creating a circular logic that helped sustain existing power hierarchies. If public morality was understood as the "right" people behaving in the "right" ways, deviation could simply be explained away, and both physical and metaphysical purity needed to be carefully guarded against corruption.

Marriage operates both as synecdoche for the moral condition of the nation and as a literal determinate of public status. Through concerns over the family, Americans attempted to make sense of tremendous political, cultural, and even geographical change. The seeming obsession over marriage reflected a larger concern over public morality, and the public rhetoric tended to locate this morality in the home. The country was shifting, and the family unit, because of its symbolic importance, became a site of negotiation and regulation. As a result, marriage controversies are critical places to uncover the hidden assumptions of American identity, especially as public identity pertains to public morality. Indeed, public morality is sticky business, and few controversies illustrate the malleability and inconsistency of public morality as do controversies over marriage. Public morality was frequently articulated through rhetorics of Christianity and science, but analysis of marriage controversies also suggests that these rhetorics were often symbolically located in women's bodies.

At the same time, marriage had very practical implications on people's lives. Because of their marriages, some women were tortured in their homes with no legal remedy, polygamists lost many of their legal rights, and many women lost property and financial security. These literal connections between marital status and public status were intimately connected to the synecdochical relationship between the family and the nation. As marriage functioned as a litmus test for the moral condition of the nation as a whole, marriage enforced idealized notions of womanhood through both law and culture. Even as women's public status continued to change, with women attaining property rights and eventually voting rights, the nineteenth-century rhetoric of marriage remained tremendously influential, participating in a rhetorical logic that limited women's participation in public.

RHETORIC OF MARRIAGE

Careful inquiry into the rhetoric of marriage reveals patterns of values, norms, and expectations of nation. Because marriage confers a sense of normality, its presumptions are often invisible and taken for granted. Accordingly, norms are most visible in moments of disruption. Rhetorical analysis of these moments of controversy enables a deep account of persuasive mechanisms and an analysis of the ways in which discourse constitutes public norms. As a critical framework, rhetorical analysis calls for a dialectical interaction between text and context that can make the hidden assumptions of marriage controversies visible. A metaphor, for example, is often not a mere flourish of language, but it reflects ways of thinking and structures a logic that can have material implications.

This book begins with the assumption that "rhetorical action is a complex business that occurs simultaneously at many levels, some of them extending far beyond the artistic representation located in a single case."[21] Critical analysis of rhetorical texts is important in revealing the rhetorical economy and persuasive mechanisms of a text, as well as issues of power. Thus, rhetorical criticism can productively address controversy through examining rhetorical patterns across a particular controversy and considering individual texts as representative of a larger controversy.[22] This book moves between the analyses of specific discrete texts that function as representative antidotes of a controversy and intertextual fragments that participate in larger patterns of meaning making. The analysis looks inward in an attempt to unpack the persuasive economy of texts and examines the success and failure of persuasion in marriage controversy. However, rhetorical criticism also enables an outward concern for the ways in which rhetoric constitutes the realities of American identity. This dual movement can make rhetorical history and criticism valuable.[23] By understanding citizenship as a rhetorical process that shapes material possibilities and marriage as an important lens through which citizenship is rhetorically constituted, this study contributes to a fuller understanding of both American citizenship and marriage—for our historical understanding and possibilities for the future.

In many ways, life of the nineteenth-century United States may seem like a quaint anachronism. Yet marriage retains it public significance. Celebrity divorces are national news, Americans are riveted by stories of polygamous families, and states debate (and courts adjudicate) the marriage of same-sex couples. In some ways little has changed, and the American obsession with marriage continues. This book attempts to answer the question of *why* marriage matters so much—why Americans can't leave it alone. The nineteenth-century United States provides a unique window to understand the ways in which marriage continues to function as a lens through which to view American identity and its relation to gender, race, and class.

[1]

Abuse, Murder, and Discipline in Marriage

In 1836 a woman who was beaten with a horsewhip by her husband and locked in a cellar was told by a judge to "return to a path of duty."[1] If she would behave herself, the judge told her, her husband would have no need for discipline. Yet just a few years later a husband doused his "pure" and "innocent" wife with cold water while cursing at her, and the judge in that case reprimanded the husband for being "unmanly."[2] That judge granted the wife a divorce on the grounds of her husband's cruelty. Such accounts of domestic violence and the dramatically inconsistent interpretations of that violence were common throughout much of the nineteenth century. Judges were called to determine when family violence was unacceptable, and communities were forced to grapple with that violence when it became severe enough that it could no longer be hidden behind the walls of the home.

Once it entered into public space, nineteenth-century domestic violence forced a tension between individual rights and the rights and obligations in marriage. Any attempt to resolve this tension was inextricably tied to social norms of manhood and womanhood and implicated in attempts to regulate not only individual behavior but also public expectations of gender. The legal debate attempted a public negotiation between justified correction and unmanly violence, creating a legal and cultural understanding of the rights and responsibilities in marriage. At the same time, newspapers both sensationalized and trivialized domestic violence, publicly reaffirming frames of race, class, and gender that were present in legal rhetoric. Even public attempts to curtail violence against women were grounded in many of the same assumptions that justified abuse. Through each of these spaces, the rhetoric of nineteenth-century gendered violence often functioned as a means of understanding and regulating the perceived future of civilization in the United States.

JUDICATING CORRECTION OR CRUELTY

Under the logic of family government, the legal status of the wife was similar to that of a minor child. Although the husband had a legal duty to maintain his wife, the wife owed her husband obedience and services.[3] If a wife failed in her duty, the husband, as head of the family government, had a moral and legal responsibility to correct that behavior. The 1868 decision in *State v. Rhodes* illustrated the family-as-government metaphor as it was utilized in the nineteenth-century United States. This decision derived from an attempt to convict a husband of criminal charges after he beat his wife with a switch, and the decision addressed an appeal of the husband's acquittal in a North Carolina trial court. In this decision, the judge used the phrase "family government" to describe the relationship between family and state, justifying limited state involvement in the family. Justice Reade argued that the "family government is recognized by law as being as complete in itself as the State government is in itself."[4] While the authority of the family was posited as subordinate to the state, the state had an obligation to interfere in the family only when necessary. In this case, domestic violence was portrayed as trivial because it occurred in the context of the home, and the judge conceded that if the context were different, the act of whipping a woman would be assault. The home was insulated through a federalism-like argument where the husband was head of the family government. In that role, the husband had vast discretion over the "laws" and discipline of the family.

In a legal context, spousal abuse was framed as pragmatically arising from the structure of the family government. That is, because the husband represented the wife to the outside world, he was also legally responsible for his wife's conduct. As a result, many nineteenth-century courts and legal scholars posited "correction" as not only a right but also a necessity. Joel Bishop, foremost nineteenth-century legal authority on family law, insisted that there were "limits" to the husband's power and "lawful and unlawful methods" of discipline.[5] However, as late in the century as 1896 one legal scholar maintained that those "limits" and "lawful and unlawful methods" were legally contested and remained "shadowy and undefined."[6] This ambiguity resulted in dramatically inconsistent interpretations of the law in both divorce trials and trials resulting from criminal assault charges.[7]

Judges were often tasked with assessing actions within the family government as legitimate correction or unlawful cruelty. The most commonly deployed legal definition of "cruelty" included "permanent injury" or "excessive violence . . . as indicates malignity or vindictiveness."[8] A frequently cited New Hampshire decision argued that extreme cruelty was "willful misconduct of the husband, which endangers the life or health of the wife."[9] Later decisions built on this precedent to argue that cruelty necessitated more than one act of violence, such that there was a continued bodily threat,[10] and under some conditions "the subtle torture of mental anguish" could be considered cruelty if accompanied by physical violence.[11] Throughout the century, lawyers and judges struggled to establish a consistent and clear legal principle.

The rhetorical challenge was one of naming or defining.[12] To name an action as "correction" not only made the action legally permissible but also naturalized the cultural assumptions behind the act of naming. For example, if a judge were to define actions as "cruelty," those actions would be deemed outside of culturally appropriate bounds and could function as legal grounds for divorce or perhaps even criminal charges. While legal decision making appeared wildly inconsistent, even within the same period and region, representations of class and gender performance in the *obiter dicta* of frequently cited upper court case law proffer a somewhat consistent distinction between impermissible cruelty and permissible chastisement.[13]

The legal rhetoric of divorce and criminal trials suggests that the degree of permissible violence was often dependent on the character of the participants in the marriage, and judges frequently read women's characters through the lens of proper womanhood, demanding that women behave in ways deemed good and pure. In an 1847 Alabama decision, throwing water on the wife's head and cursing at her was cruelty, in part because, the court explained, the "proof shows that the wife was kind, dutiful and obedient."[14] By all reports, the wife fit within norms of delicate and refined womanhood, so the comparatively mild violence of her husband was seen as particularly harmful. An 1882 Illinois decision argued, "There is nothing that inflicts so deep and cruel a wound upon a pure wife as a false accusation of a want of chastity."[15] Accusations of adultery were framed as cruel only because the woman involved was deemed to be chaste, and in equating a threat to purity with physical violence, the court posited women's purity as a core marker of identity. In other words, sullying a pure woman's character was considered "cruel, barbarous, and inhumane."[16] If the woman were not already "pure," such accusations would have been truth, not cruelty.

On the other hand, there were cases across the country that illustrated what the courts deemed as acceptable levels of violence in marriage. That violence was not acceptable because of the intrinsic nature of the action but because of the behavior of the woman in the marriage. The frequently cited 1836 *Poor* decision described the distinction in terms of the abused woman's behavior toward her husband. Rather than being "meek and quiet," Mrs. Poor was described by the court as having a "high, bold, masculine spirit" that would not "submit . . . to the legitimate authority of her husband."[17] The court used a war metaphor that built from an idea of familial federalism. The wife, the court argued, "went out in open rebellion against the known will of her husband" and attempted to "take his castle [home] by storm."[18] Although the court described the husband's violence (whipping his wife with a horse whip, locking her in the cellar, and hitting her with a crowbar) as "unmanly," the violence was ultimately framed as justifiable "chastisement" as a result of Mrs. Poor's "improper conduct."[19] The judge suggested that Mrs. Poor "return to the path of duty." If she were to conduct herself, the judge continued, "towards her husband with that sweetness and goodness which belong to the true character of wife, we think she will have no reasonable ground to apprehend any further injury to her person,"[20] implying that there was a conceivable "reasonable ground" to beat a woman with a crowbar. The husband was called to remember his duty such that his reason would prevent him from engaging in violence despite his wife's provocations.

The *Poor* decision drew on the family-as-government metaphor in positing the husband as head of the family government and his wife's actions as "rebellion" against that leadership. Yet this metaphor makes sense only in the context of specific gender expectations. The judges justified the violence against Mrs. Poor because as a wife she was expected to be meek, submissive, and sweet. The language in the decision appealed to religion to naturalize these expectations of gender, emphasizing the "gentle spirit of the gospel." At the same time, the judges expected the actions of the husband, as head of the family government, to be governed by rationality, not passion. His violence was permissible if it arose from a rational need to correct his wife's improper behavior, rather than the passion of anger. Thus, the gender expectations of the *Poor* decision were also tied to cultural expectations of rationality and religion.[21]

On many of the occasions when the courts condoned or ignored violence against women, they deployed a rhetoric of class. The courts appeared to be more inclined to simply tell couples of lower classes to resolve their differences without court intervention. According to an 1855 Alabama decision, "Between persons of education, refinement, and delicacy, the slightest blow in anger might be cruelty; while between persons of a different character and walk in life, blows might occasionally pass without marring to any great extent their conjugal relations, or materially interfering with their happiness."[22] The judge continued:

> There may, as we have intimated, be cases where the offer to personal violence to a female might properly be regarded as an act of barbarous and unmanly cruelty; but we must discriminate—we must not be so unjust as to put all of the sex on the same level; and if a woman chooses to unsex herself, and forget that she is a female, she should not complain if others do not always remember it.[23]

In other words, violence against a proper woman was portrayed as "unmanly," but if a woman failed to behave properly, she became "unsexed" and violence was justifiable. This "unsexing" was rhetorically posited as a sign of barbarism, and the barbaric were simply assumed to be violent. An 1856 Wisconsin case, for example, described the husband as a "man of coarse nature" and "very reprehensible and improper, yet [the conduct] of the wife," the judge continued, "appears to us to be more so."[24] The wife, the judges argued, brought on the abuse because her "conduct has been most wonton, most wicked, and most disgraceful,"[25] and the main evidence of this unwomanly behavior was from events that occurred before her marriage. When Mrs. Skinner, the woman in question, was about eighteen she was reported to have "cut off her hair, dressed herself in men's clothes, and [gone] on a boat from Milwaukee to Cleveland."[26] This ultimate act of desexing functioned as *de facto* justification for abuse, even though the abuse occurred years after this woman's act of rebellion. The rhetorical framing of women's proper behavior was necessarily connected to perceptions of status and class. The judges built their conclusions on logically tenuous argumentative ground, constructing violence as a marker of barbarism, and passionate violence was then dismissed as the norm of the barbaric. However, violence was legally impermissible when it extended to the upper classes (those perceived as proper men and women).

While the actual rules evoked in these cruelty trials were fairly consistent (some "correction" of the wife was permissible in marriage while violent "cruelty" functioned as grounds for divorce or criminal assault charges), the rhetoric in the *obiter dicta* of the decisions suggested that the line was drawn based on an understanding of status and the connections between status and gender. Men and women were marked as civilized when they performed proper gendered behavior; women were expected to behave within the parameters of proper womanhood, and men were expected to protect proper women. Deviation from proper gendered expectations marked people as barbaric, providing legal justification for violent "correction" on the part of men or divorce on the part of women.

In upholding a criminal conviction of a husband, an 1874 decision argued that courts had "advanced from barbarism" to make beating a wife impermissible, but the judge also warned that courts will not listen to "trivial complaints."[27] By the end of the century, courts were unlikely to condone violent abuse (such as in the *Poor* decision), but judges continued to trivialize or ignore violence against many wives.[28] As masculine rationality emerged as a sign of civility, courts increasingly condemned "excessive" violence within marriage. Yet conceptions of home as a private refuge remained, and ambiguous notions of what was considered "excessive" or simply a "trivial complaint" helped normalize and hide domestic violence from public scrutiny.

MAKING SENSE OF SPOUSAL MURDER

While under certain circumstances the courts condoned domestic violence, it was never permissible to murder a spouse. Indeed, spousal murder was an ultimate betrayal of marital and social expectations. Chicago provides a useful case study. In over eleven thousand murder arrests in Chicago between the years 1870 and 1930, about four hundred were instances of spousal murder, 3.6 percent.[29] Yet these numbers account only for arrests and actual murders by a spouse. There were likely many more cases of domestic violence that did not result in murder and instances of spouses who were never arrested for intentional murder. Nonetheless, newspapers often reported on horrific and sensational cases of wife murder, and narratives of spousal murder in newspaper reporting constituted frames for making sense of the senselessness of murder.[30]

Analysis of police records reveals that there were no significant differences in race, ethnicity, immigrant status, or class among men who were arrested for murdering their wives.[31] Nonetheless, newspaper reports tended to fit within at least one of three general frames for understanding wife murder, all of which rhetorically marked the murderers as Other. The first and perhaps most dominant frame positioned the family involved in the murder as low-status, which naturalized violence in a seemingly different world from the newspapers' readers. Such murders were described as occurring in a "hard section of country"[32] or, perhaps most telling for Chicago readers, the Maxwell Street District.[33] The area was located on the near west side of Chicago, and it was known as an area of excessive immigration, crime, and poverty. Simply labeling the crime as occurring in the Maxwell Street or Near West Side area marked the participants as low-class and probably immigrant.[34]

In addition to the description of physical location, intemperance and immigrant status marked wife murderers as low-status. In many of the murders, poverty, intemperance, and abuse went hand in hand, positioning the wife murder as a natural conclusion to what was represented as a culture of laziness and violence. These murdering husbands were described in newspapers as "intemperate, shiftless, and cruel,"[35] "unsteady, unreliable, and generally worthless,"[36] "unquestionably a degenerate,"[37] "ne'er-do-well,"[38] or "ruffian" immigrant.[39] Such descriptions were represented as innate characteristics of flawed or lesser men. Wife murderers violated expectations of good manhood in their failure to support their families, lack of self-control evidenced by intemperance, and crossing from permissible correction to unrestrained violence against the women they were obligated to protect. In other words, these were not good men; they were represented as a barbarous Other.

While the newspapers portrayed wife murderers as lower-class and inherently different men, the murders were often represented as shameful, although unsurprising, spectacles occurring among those who brought it on themselves. Josephine McNamara, for example, died slowly after an 1882 incident when her husband delivered a blow to the neck that severed her spine.[40] The brief newspaper reporting of the incident focused on the character of those involved. According to the physician who treated the wife, "She seemed to be a hard-working woman, and ran the house there, letting rooms and paying expenses while her husband was carousing around spending his wages in having a good time."[41] The silently suffering wife was a common theme in this frame of spousal murder. Indeed, the wife's failure to seek help or attempt to escape abuse was praised in one incident as "wife-like."[42] Of James McNamara the papers reported, "In his sober senses McNamara seems to have been a decent sort of fellow, but was completely changed when under the influence of liquor."[43] McNamara's seeming lack of self-control both explained and naturalized his long history of violence, and police failed to get involved until Josephine McNamara had died from the abuse.

There were several other similar instances. A man named Walsh who beat his wife to a "pulpy mass" (because, as he explained, he was enraged when she was drunk)[44] was described by the newspapers as a regular drunk, which "transformed him into a fiend in human form."[45] He and his wife were described as living in "squalid apartments," creating a setting where such violence may have seemed commonplace.[46] Yet when the judge sentenced Walsh to thirty-five years in prison (about nineteen years with good behavior), the judge said, "The testimony proves to my satisfaction that prior to the murder you had borne, perhaps deservedly, the reputation in this community of a peaceable, quiet, orderly, and industrious man, engaged in honorable vocations, and making a livelihood for yourself and family."[47] The long history of violence against his wife did not appear to negate the perception that Walsh was a respectable member of his community, positioning domestic violence as private, publicly insignificant, and a commonplace of low-class communities.

Another frame for making sense of spousal murder relied on justification, rather than naturalization. In these cases, newspaper reporting not only portrayed violence as a continuous part of life but also represented it as a part of life that the murdered women created. The Kings, for example, were both portrayed as quarrelsome and "hard drinkers."[48] When the judge sentenced Thomas King for murdering his wife, the judge explicitly considered the wife's "bad temper" and "provocation," sentencing King to only twenty-five years in prison.[49] The issue of provocation was also significant in the Walsh case, where the couple's young daughter was called to challenge the testimony of the husband and local bar owner that characterized Mrs. Walsh as a drunk.[50] Similarly, Mrs. Geist, a recent German immigrant, was represented as having a "quarrelsome nature," and her husband was sentenced to only sixteen years in prison for her murder.[51] The abuse of a quarrelsome or bad wife was portrayed as simply less egregious than similar actions perpetrated against the prototypical good wife.

While the nature of some wives appeared to mitigate the harm of murder, some wives so defied cultural expectations of femininity that their murders were portrayed as justified. Newspapers typically framed the murder of a truly deviant wife as an act of "emotional insanity" by an otherwise upstanding man. Although John Condon, for example, admitted to killing his wife, the newspapers depicted him as an "unfortunate old fellow" who was driven insane by an unscrupulous and conniving young wife.[52] Neighbors testified that the wife was planning on killing her husband for his money and was seen to "pick men up on the street."[53] John Condon's actions were justified by his wife's deceptiveness and apparent impurity.

The defense of "emotional insanity," the legal argument that murder was excused because of a husband's jealousy of his wife's apparent infidelity, gained national attention in the 1870 McFarland-Richardson trial. This trial relied on the "unwritten" law that a husband could be excused for murdering his wife's seducer or rapist.[54] The assumptions that backed this unwritten law hinged on a man's supposed right to protect his property and, as a result, protect his wife and family. Suppositions of the husband's apparently uncontrolled passion and jealousy could excuse the murder if it occurred at the moment of discovering a wife's infidelity.[55] The McFarland-Richardson trial gained national notoriety for extending the husband's right to murder when Daniel McFarland was acquitted of Albert Richardson's murder. At the time of the murder, McFarland had known about the supposed affair between his wife and Richardson for years, and McFarland had already shot and wounded Richardson once before. Indeed, by the time of the murder, McFarland was divorced from his wife, Abby. To extend the unwritten law, McFarland's lawyers relied on tropes of honorable manhood and a loose conception of insanity that was represented as deriving from his wife's betrayal.[56] The extension to the justified murder of a wife (not only the wife's seducer) was also grounded in these tropes of honorable manhood and emotional insanity.

However, claims of "emotional insanity" were presented in newspapers as persuasive only when the husband otherwise embodied the myth of ideal masculinity. A German "ruffian" was described by the newspapers as "feigning both insanity and illness."[57] A brass finisher with a long history of violence was reportedly aware of previous cases of emotional insanity and was simply attempting to "play off crazy" when he killed his wife.[58] Similarly, a New York man with a history of intemperance who had abandoned his wife many years prior claimed emotional insanity after murdering his long-estranged wife. The newspaper did not believe the claim, framing it as a "pretense" for the murder and arguing, "The man clearly understood that for such a murder he had only to plead marital infidelity, or the suspicion of it."[59] Murder of a wife was justified only if a husband truly loved his wife. In a case with a good and loving husband, the act of wife murder was simply represented as an outgrowth of honorable masculinity. One article, reprinted from the *Cincinnati Commercial*, satirically reflected on the trend of justified wife murder, suggesting, "At any rate, whenever the modern husband puts his arm around his wife's waist, squeezes her affectionately, and, with his eyes full of tears, says: 'God bless you, I love you,' it will not be a bad idea for the wife to keep one eye on him, lest at that moment he be preparing to make her an angel."[60] Nevertheless, such reflexivity was rare.

A final frame for making sense of wife murder was both the rarest and the most sensationalized. Here the seemingly upstanding citizen was revealed to be a monster in disguise. Although this frame may initially appear socially destabilizing in suggesting that anyone could be a wife murderer, public rhetoric positioned the identity of the murderer as inherently different; the murderer was never truly part of the class in which he represented himself. In Chicago, the Luetgert murder was the best example of this frame. Just days before Adolph L. Luetgert's sausage factory was foreclosed upon, his wife, Louisa Luetgert, went missing, although the disappearance was not reported to the police until a week later. The newspapers initially reported a suspicion of suicide.[61] In these initial reports Adolph Luetgert was the hardworking "Sausage King."[62] The Luetgerts were said to live in a "comfortable home," and Adolph Luetgert even offered a $200 reward for any information leading to his wife.[63] The reward, home, and industrious factory owner were all markers that the Luetgerts were of a respectable class, justifying front-page newspaper coverage, unlike the vast majority of reporting on wife murders.

Nevertheless, it was not long before Adolph Luetgert came under suspicion. Luetgert was arrested seventeen days after his wife's disappearance, and, at that point, representations of Luetgert began to shift dramatically. Accounts of the murder were chilling. Luetgert reportedly lured his wife to the sausage factory under false pretenses, immobilized her, threw her into a vat of acid, and disposed of the remaining parts of her body in the smokehouse and furnace. With his arrest, Luetgert's representation changed from successful businessman to a large, unrestrained, German immigrant. One article described him as follows:

> Luetgert's appearance is that of a butcher. . . . For years he has overeaten and overdrunk. . . . Luetgert's sensuous mouth is nearly concealed by his yellow beard, but his eyes are a good index to his character. They are narrow, oblique, and restless. . . . Luetgert became a gourmand after he went into the sausage-making business. He ate meat excessively. On some days he practically gave himself up to eating and drinking. After a debauch of that sort, for which he paid by acute attacks of dyspepsia and indigestion, he kept to his bed in the office and his wife, a pigmy compared with this giant, served him like a slave.[64]

Luetgert's indulgence to excess marked him as someone who was unrestrained and, therefore, unrefined. He entered into the sausage-making business after a career as a saloonkeeper, and newspapers portrayed Luetgert as never far from his working-class and distinctly German roots. While Luetgert's ethnicity was not mentioned in the early days of his wife's disappearance, once he was arrested Luetgert's identity as German was inseparable from understandings of his guilt. One writer portrayed Luetgert as having a "ruddy Teuton flush,"[65] describing the scene thus: "On the eve of his trial this hale German joyously puffed away at mediocre cigars and joked with prisoners, guards, and visitors alike."[66] Luetgert's German ethnicity marked him as different from refined Americans and evoked images of brutishness and arrogance. In short, Luetgert's business success initially masked his true brutish nature, which emerged most clearly when his love letters to the wealthy widow Christina Feldt were read in court. The newspapers reported, "Adolph L. Luetgert's eyes bulged out with terror and thick drops of greasy sweat formed on his flabby cheeks and neck yesterday when he saw Mrs. Christine Feldt, in whose hands he had declared his life lay, on her way to the witness stand to testify against him."[67] The moment of "terror" was represented as a moment of truth where Luetgert shed his mask of refinement to reveal a brute.

Each of these frames of understanding spousal murder posited the events as unimaginable for civilized men and women. Either the murderer was a brute (although he was occasionally a brute in disguise) or the victim brought the murder on herself through her misbehavior. Either way, spousal murder was represented as a spectacle, and those involved were to be pitied or admonished but certainly not identified with. Newspaper representations of wife murder naturalized violence against women for some people whose identities were simply thought to be violent. As a result, ways of making sense of wife murder enforced cultural blindness to domestic violence because only brutes were assumed to be subject to this violence, and in their cases, the violence was thought to be unavoidable. By extension, representations of spousal murder assumed away the possibility that refined and civilized people could engage in violence, masking the possibility of domestic violence in many homes. In representing violence against women as a condition of the Other, newspaper reporters participated in normalizing and sustaining that violence.

RESPONDING TO VIOLENCE

Reformers often identified violence against women as a significant problem necessitating some sort of intervention. The issue was highlighted throughout nineteenth-century women's movements.[68] The 1848 Declaration of Sentiments, the document that arose from the prominent Seneca Falls Woman's Rights Convention, noted the problem: "In the covenant of marriage, she is compelled to promise obedience to her husband, he becoming, to all intents and purposes, her master—the law giving him power to deprive her of her liberty and to administer chastisement."[69] The detached language of the Declaration represented the threat of violence as a denial of individual liberty, although the phrase "administer chastisement" risks obfuscating that the "chastisement" could be in the form of violent brutality. Other rhetors, however, drew on the visceral outrage of violence and emphasized a broad social interest in eliminating violence in marriage. Lucinda Chandler, for example, defiantly stated in the *Woman's Tribune*, "The abolition of the legal power and right of the husband over the person of the wife, will lay the foundations for an abatement of born criminals and a social purity that alone can save the race."[70] Among the supposedly civilized there was little question that violence against women was harmful. There was, however, disagreement on the extent of the problem and its remedies. Responses to domestic violence reflected a larger conflict over the role of violence in a civilized country, which had implications for types of responses to violence as well as public understandings of womanhood and manhood.

If violence was publicly understood as a sign of barbarity, the question became one of how to civilize the barbarians. However, there was little public action that attempted to address directly domestic violence. Legislation in Maryland was an exception. In March of 1882, the Maryland General Assembly adopted "AN ACT to inflict Corporal Punishment upon Persons found guilty of Wife-beating."[71] The legislation permitted anyone who "brutally assault[ed] or beat his wife" to be sentenced to a whipping of up to forty lashes, up to one year in prison, or both. Mr. Keilholtz of the House of Delegates proposed the legislation after serving on a grand jury where he saw several instances of domestic violence with women protecting their abusers. Keilholtz expressed a desire to "thrash the barbarians" who would lift their "arm to strike a woman."[72] Newspaper reports suggested that the legislation was at least somewhat controversial, with debate in the Maryland Senate extending an evening session past midnight before opposition was worn down enough for the bill to pass.[73] While the debate never appeared to question that wife beating was a harm, there was significant disagreement on the remedy for the harm. Proposed amendments included one by Mr. Lloyd to punish abusive wives in a similar manner, but under the proposed amendment "any man allowing his wife to beat him shall receive double the regular whipping."[74] Comments such as Lloyd's, even in its seeming opposition to domestic violence, perpetuated the assumption that men were the agents of families and required to discipline their wives, ensuring that a husband does not "allow" his wife to use violence against him. Nonetheless, serious opposition was silenced. For example, when a recently married Mr. Mudd expressed opposition, Mr. Johnson of Baltimore County ridiculed Mudd by asking, "Does the gentleman desire the privilege of whipping his wife?"[75]

Those who supported whipping as a response to domestic violence argued that it would decrease costs and function as a deterrent because the offender would not need to be housed in a "comfortable" jail cell for an extended period of time.[76] Delaware was consistently evoked as a success story for public whipping as crime prevention.[77] Some advocates suggested that whipping was better for the family, not only because it would deter domestic violence, but also because the family would not be without the husband's wages while he was in jail.[78] Public humiliation provided an additional attractiveness to the punishment. One advocate from the religious community argued, "Humiliation and the pain that accompanies it is the merit of the application."[79] Advocates answered the argument that public whipping was brutish by asserting that "flogging is not half so barbarous as wife beating," and humanitarians that opposed public whipping were simply dismissed as disconnected from reality.[80]

Once the Maryland legislation passed, the sentence of corporal punishment for wife whipping was infrequently utilized, and the punishment of white men was much more widely reported than of black men.[81] Frank Pyers was reportedly the second man sentenced under the 1882 legislation and probably the first white man to receive the punishment. His whipping was vividly described by the *Baltimore*

Sun. Pyers was reported to have said, " 'That was a d— hard punishment for a white man' . . . and as he spoke tears came in his eyes, caused by the relaxation of his nervous system and probably by the realization of his degradation."[82] The *Baltimore Sun* reported the second whipping sentence of a white man to have been in 1896.[83] In that case John Boots brutally beat his wife, Mary Boots, and Mary Boots "came running into town, the blood flowing from the wounds in her face."[84] There had apparently been enough previous instances of abuse to prompt Mary Boots to move out of state to escape her husband, but in this specific instance Mary Boots fled to town, making the violence public and punishment necessary. Newspapers made the race of the whipped men explicit, and that they did not extensively report on the whipping of black men signaled a public acceptance of punishing black men in this manner.

Opposition to corporal punishment tended to emphasize the brutishness of the act of whipping as a relic of the past. For example, one opponent argued that public whipping would "demoralize" the public rather than "elevate."[85] Another critic of the practice suggested that whipping was simple cruelty and the function of punishment should be justice rather than vindictiveness.[86] The public nature of whipping was represented as particularly objectionable. In its explanation of the declining popularity of whipping as a punishment, the *Washington Post* argued, "But it is believed that the spectacle of a public flogging, or even the existence of a statute authorizing such an exhibition, is degrading to a community and because of its effect on the public generally, not on the recipient, legislative bodies decline to set up the whipping-post."[87] Indeed, John Boots, a Maryland man who was sentenced to whipping, was reported to be most distressed not by the whipping itself but by the public embarrassment.[88] Further, a later reported whipping sentence was done "within the privacy of the jail walls" and "as merciful[ly] as possible."[89] The criticism of corporal punishment questioned the civility of a punishment that inflicted public violence. Thus, much like the domestic abuse that was being punished, legally sanctioned whipping made violence a public act and was, therefore, brutish in itself.

The connections between slavery and public whipping were also inescapable. The scarred back and red bleeding welts of the slave were a common trope of the abolitionist movement. The *Baltimore Sun* reported that before the 1882 law, no white man had been legally whipped in Maryland since 1809. However, until 1864 slave owners could whip their slaves, and constables had the right to round up and whip any black people (slave or free) that they suspected of congregating with "rebellious intentions."[90] Virginia had public whipping as a punishment until 1879, when the law was reportedly repealed because "it was naturally in bad odor with the darkies."[91] Thus, public whipping was degrading not only because it exposed the brutishness of the abusive husband, but also because it marked the wife beater with the scarred back of the unruly slave, receiving the punishment of the perceived brutish Other. Just as the slave was thought to be of an irrational and lesser race and, thus, in need of whipping, the wife beater became framed as someone so brutish and uncontrolled that he needed whipping to correct his behavior.

Following Maryland's adoption of the corporal punishment statute, both New York and Washington, D.C., began seriously debating similar statutes. At the same time, Delaware considered repealing its long-time corporal punishment statute, which was used to punish several petty crimes in addition to wife beating. The Washington, D.C., debate on public whipping for domestic violence and petty crimes began in 1895, when a grand jury expressed frustration over the extent of these crimes and recommended public whipping as an effective deterrent.[92] The debate in New York gained traction when it was supported by Commodore Gerry, a wealthy lawyer and advocate for the New York Society for the Prevention of Cruelty to Animals and the Society for the Prevention of Cruelty to Children.[93] Indeed, whipping-post legislation unanimously passed the New York Senate, but wife beaters were excluded from the legislation out of fear that a public whipping of a husband would damage the possibilities for marital reconciliation.[94] Nevertheless, whipping as a punishment for domestic violence lost public favor as it became associated with brutishness and civil regression.

More frequently, however, domestic violence functioned as a catalyst for other reform movements, such as those for temperance, divorce, free love, and humane treatment of animals. In each of these instances, domestic violence was treated as a sign of barbarity, and reformers attempted to civilize the wife beaters in an effort to civilize the country. Humane societies, for example, began in England in the

1820s and spread to the United States by the second half of the nineteenth century as private organizations that often worked in cooperation with local police and government officials. The primary goal of humane organizations was the protection of animals through legislation and education, but many organizations expanded their mission to include children in an effort to both popularize the organizations and maintain ideological consistency.[95] The moves toward ideological consistency occasionally led humane organizations to include women in their folds (although most often they did so informally). Reverend David Swing, speaking before the Illinois Humane Society, argued, "There is [*sic*] few mental phenomena more inexplicable than the passion . . . of cruelty."[96] Cruelty, he argued, was a "last remnant of the barbaric period."[97] Based on this rationale, cruelty against a horse, a child, or a woman was a remnant of a barbaric age.

The mission of humane societies involved both the prevention of cruelty (installing water fountains to keep horses hydrated, intervening in cases of suspected child abuse) and education. Humane society officials would hand out information on animal cruelty to an individual mistreating a horse or dog before taking steps to ticket and fine offenders. These advocates found education to be especially important for children. In his annual report, president of the Illinois Humane Society John G. Shortall explained, "The child who learns his duty toward its dog, its cat or its horse, and does it, cannot choose but be kind and dutiful to father and mother, brother and sister, playmate and teacher; and when it rises to the dignity of citizenship may be safely entrusted with his sacred rights."[98] Shortall adopted a commonly appropriated logic that framed individual humane behavior as begetting humanity in general and, thus, the foundation for proper citizenship.

However, humane societies were only tangentially involved in violence against women. Chicago newspapers reported that neighbors would occasionally call on the Illinois Humane Society in instances of continued and severe domestic violence, but the Humane Society was only inconsistently involved, often requiring abused women to come to its offices for aid before any intervention. Clearly, the Humane Society did not delay in its intervention of animal or child abuse, but abuse of women was considered more complicated. Many women were thought to participate in the conditions that created their abuse, and organizations were often hesitant to become involved in this type of familial relationship. Nevertheless, the abuse of women and the abuse of children were often difficult to separate. In Boston, for example, 34 percent of cases brought to child protection officials also involved wife beating.[99] President Shortall of the Illinois Humane Society commented on the broadly interpreted mission of the Illinois Humane society when he noted, "The name Humane is interpreted in its broadest sense by hundreds of ignorant, helpless persons who apply to the office and go away, I think, feeling better for their coming, and (when we can not aid them directly,) with information and instruction that usually prove beneficial."[100]

While there were hundreds of societies for the protection of animals and children, there were shockingly few organizations that sought to protect and aid battered wives and women who were raped. Indeed, the Protective Agency for Women and Children, founded in Chicago in 1886, may have been the only such organization in the nineteenth-century United States.[101] Because the Chicago Women's Club was particularly large and respectable, it spearheaded the creation and initial running of the agency in cooperation with the Woman's Christian Temperance Union (WCTU), the Illinois Woman's Press Association, the Cook County Suffrage Association, the Moral Education Society, the Illinois State Industrial School for Girls, the Woman's Homeopathic Medical Association, and the Woman's Christian Association.[102] The organization's activities included acquiring legal assistance for women, providing "the presence of a delegation of reputable women, women of social position and influence . . . [to change] the moral tone of a police court," and providing moral support. It worked to aid women hounded by scam artists and disreputable debt collectors, and the organization also engaged in political activism.[103] In its first year, for example, the agency successfully campaigned to raise the age of consent for girls in Illinois from ten to fourteen (although it had advocated for eighteen).[104]

The agency consistently moved between moralistic and legalistic language (occasionally merging the two) in descriptions of its mission. The original Protective Agency Constitution defined the primary objective of the organization as the protection of women and children's "morality and virtue" and the extension of "wholesome moral support."[105] At the same time, the agency was created to fill what it viewed as a major hole in providing "*justice* in behalf of women and children."[106] The agency used a legalistic frame in its description of women's "rights" and "justice." Indeed, the Protective Agency modified its constitution in 1891 to read, "Its objects are to secure justice for women and children, to give legal counsel free of charge, and to extend moral support to the wronged and to the helpless."[107] Rather than emphasizing morality and virtue, the agency eventually came to represent its focus as "justice." One manifestation of the conflict between moral and legalistic frames was a consistent hesitancy to use divorce as a remedy for domestic violence. The Annual Reports included statements of a "firm determination" to avoid breaking up families and that the "agency rather plumes itself upon being an anti-divorce institution." Yet early in the agency's existence it found that many families plagued with domestic violence and abuse could not be safely reunited. In these cases, justice seemed to require reconciliation with morality, prompting a suggestion in the Annual Reports that these families were not real families in the first place.[108]

The Woman's Christian Temperance Union (WCTU) not only was one of the early supporting organizations of the Protective Agency, but also drew on domestic violence as part of its rhetorical justification for temperance.[109] The WCTU journal, the *Union Signal*, occasionally included accounts of abusive husbands who reformed once abstaining from alcohol, and "home protection," for the WCTU, was synonymous with temperance.[110]

Through the 1880s and 1890s the WCTU amassed huge numbers of women under the banner of temperance, maternity, and purity, and eventually the group attained tremendous political sway. Frances Willard, influential president of the WCTU, argued in an 1889 speech, "Over 800 papers printed in foreign languages circulate constantly through the nation, a majority of which contain ideas concerning home and women, temperance and the Sabbath, that are European and revolutionary, not American and Christian."[111] Willard represented a common association for many Americans: immigrants, unless Americanized, were a threat because of the propagation of intemperance, radicalism, and violence. The first ethnic riot that occurred in Chicago came to be known as the Lager Beer Riot of 1855 and reinforced the perceived connections between immigration, intemperance, and violence. The riot occurred when German immigrants protested against Sunday closing laws, laws that prohibited the selling of alcohol on Sundays.[112] While many Americans viewed alcohol as an evil, one that was especially problematic on Sundays, a day that was thought to belong to God, many immigrants viewed bars and beer gardens as important to their communities and resented closing these establishments on workers' one day off work. The WCTU drew off popular associations between immigration, barbarity, and intemperance to suggest that violence and intemperance not only went hand in hand but also were grounded in barbarity. By drawing on mythical conceptions of symbolic womanhood in an attempt to curtail violence, the WCTU and other organizations relied on the same ideological divisions that were used to justify or ignore violence against women.

Rather than domestic violence representing an evil in itself, many organizations that attempted to address the problem of domestic violence tended to treat it as a sign of a larger cultural problem. The best-publicized responses to domestic violence (such as the whipping post and temperance) did not frame violence against women as a violation of individual liberty, a stance that would have necessarily presupposed women as citizens with equal standing before the law as men. Instead, violence against women was represented in these instances as a sign of cultural barbarity, and the debates about that violence became debates about methods of civilizing the barbaric (through whipping or removing alcohol, for example). Grounding opposition to domestic violence in the supposed dichotomy between civilized and barbarian was based in the assumption that civilized men protect and care for pure women, simply reifying the gender norms that disempowered women within the family government and, thus, the state. This frame also condoned some violence, especially violence against those who did not meet expectations of civility; and, circularly, the frame also hid some violence by seeming to support the assumption that those who were already civilized did not abuse women.

FAMILY VIOLENCE AND BARBARITY

Uncontrolled violence against women was not supposed to happen in a civilized country like the United States. Women, through their status as women, were assumed to be refined, delicate, and in need of protection. However, when violence against women left the seemingly sacred space of the home and became publicly visible, Americans were forced to reconcile the incongruity between the myths of the revered woman in a civilized nation and the reality of violence against women. Rather than challenge these myths, the public rhetoric of domestic violence reified myths of nation and womanhood while scapegoating a violent Other.

Within the cultural myths of the nineteenth-century United States, civilized men were expected to behave rationally. While legitimate "correction" of a wife was framed as a rational act, violence was represented as a sign of uncontrolled passions and, thus, barbarism. Therefore, domestic violence came to be understood through a lens of supposed intrinsic cultural difference. The public controversy over violence in the home illustrates inextricable connections between gendered violence and racial violence. Through a feat of circular reasoning, the public rhetoric tied violence to barbarism. Therefore, not only did violence mark one as barbaric, but also if an individual was already deemed to be civilized because of that person's race or class, that individual was assumed to not be violent. This rhetoric led to a public emphasis on family violence among lower classes, immigrants, or racial and ethnic minorities, while the violence of the presumably civilized was hidden behind a veil of familial privacy.

Occasionally, women publicly deviated from social expectations of womanhood, and, in these instances, judges and public opinion (at least the public opinion commonly expressed in newspapers) not only condoned violence but also represented violence against individual women as necessary to protect the myth of the symbolic woman—a myth tied to civilized American identity. With very few exceptions, the public rhetoric of family violence obfuscated women's individual rights and condoned (or challenged) violence through women's status, a status that tied women's roles in families to women's roles as citizens. Thus, the rhetoric of family violence functioned as one thread of a tapestry binding gender performance to national identity.

Although individual families lived with violence, the public meaning of that violence was not about individuals; it was about the nation as a whole. The public controversy over spousal abuse and murder uncovers many of the assumptions that formed the basis for marriage controversies in the nineteenth century. Controversy over marriage violated norms of the family government by opening the insular governing unit of the family to public scrutiny, consequently challenging seemingly clear structures of authority and representation. In a context that understood the future of the nation in terms of a conflict between the civilized and the brute, marriage functioned as a lens for viewing the state of civilization and the nation.

[2]

Constituting the Divorced Citizen and Saving the Nation

For most Americans in the nineteenth century, divorce was something to be feared. In one of his best-known speeches, Abraham Lincoln drew on a biblical verse, declaring that a "house divided against itself cannot stand." By utilizing the metaphor, Lincoln appealed to this fear of divorce, and the Civil War became a realization of the ultimate consequences of familial rupture. Just as with the divorce of a nation, the anxiety about the divorce of families created an ongoing national melodrama complete with heroes, villains, and innocent victims. At least two stages for the melodrama of divorce existed: the public conflict over the laws of divorce and salacious entertainment generated from public divorce trials. In both of these stages, divorce was a lens through which gender was performed, contested, and regulated. Yet the regulation of gender wasn't simply about performance of identity; it was a debate about public status.

In the nineteenth-century United States, few shifts in legal or cultural status were more dramatic than the shift to or from being a married woman. Marriage had profound implications for women. While unhappy marriages were nothing new, the emergence of divorce as a significant public issue in the mid-nineteenth century challenged then dichotomous understandings of women's status by creating a cultural space between the single (*femme sole*) and married (*femme covert*) woman. The public identity of the divorced woman created a lens through which to negotiate public conceptions of identity in a changing American landscape.

DIVORCE AS SPECTACLE

Divorce was risky for the individuals involved, especially because all divorce required assignment of fault. A convicted wife risked losing her family, social status, and economic support.[1] On the other hand, divorce allowed an innocent spouse to escape the "moral contamination" of a guilty spouse.[2] Yet understandings of guilt and innocence were in flux in the second half of the nineteenth century, and public divorce trials functioned as ways of making sense of cultural changes in the family. Americans voraciously consumed sensational accounts of divorce. In one sense these public divorces functioned as an entertaining yet salacious public spectacle, but they also became ways to understand divorce and its cultural implications.

With divorce rates steadily increasing (by 1860 1.2 in 1,000 marriages ended in divorce), there was no shortage of "sensational" divorce cases in the nineteenth century.[3] Newspapers were consistently publishing and republishing accounts of particularly shocking divorces, and occasionally publishers would take advantage of what seemed to be a national obsession by issuing cheap books of the most scandalous divorces. Despite the seeming triviality of the public entertainment of these divorce trials, they participated in the national melodrama of divorce, constituting proper performances of gender even while seeming to defy the cultural expectations of womanly propriety.[4]

Two very different but similarly sensational public divorce trials illustrate ways in which the divorce controversy constituted proper performance of gender even as women seemed to be stepping away from their expected role as wife. The 1860 Beardsley divorce occurred in New York, where the issue of divorce was fiercely contested. In 1860, New York divorces were allowed only on the grounds of adultery and desertion, but a separation of bed and board, which did not allow the parties to remarry, was allowed on broader grounds, although it was still fairly rare.[5] On the other hand, the Ticknor divorce occurred in 1867 in Illinois, which was typically lumped in with the western states that were thought by many to have "lax" divorce laws, prompting what critics characterized as a rash of people to travel west in order to procure easy divorces.[6] These two cases illustrate representative ways in which performance of gender was negotiated in the context of sensationalized divorce trials.

The Beardsley Divorce

The 1860 Beardsley divorce trial was both sordid and convoluted. Alfred Beardsley accused his wife, Mary Elizabeth Beardsley, of seducing and marrying another man, Dr. Thomas Francis Mahan, while still married to Alfred Beardsley. According to Alfred Beardsley, his wife was an adulteress and bigamist, and she deceived both men while she lived a double life. Mary Elizabeth Beardsley countered these accusations by saying that it was Alfred Beardsley who had committed adultery. According to Mary Elizabeth Beardsley, Alfred Beardsley had committed adultery with various women throughout their marriage, but the conflict in their marriage escalated when he had an affair with Mary Elizabeth Beardsley's friend Mary Elizabeth Greenwood. Alfred Beardsley orchestrated the charges of bigamy, according to Mary Elizabeth Beardsley, when he got his lover, Greenwood, to marry Mahan in order to frame Mary Elizabeth Beardsley for bigamy.

The Beardsley trial kept New Yorkers riveted in such a way that it received extensive newspaper coverage by the *Brooklyn Eagle*, the *New York Times*, and the *New York Tribune.*[7] New York publisher Robert M. DeWitt eventually published a transcript of the trial in a book called *Report of the Beardsley Divorce Case.* By 1860 DeWitt had already published what he labeled as "reliable" accounts of several "very interesting" and "important trials" including *The Burch Divorce Case* (sold at the price of twenty-five cents) and *The Forrest Divorce Case* (sold at the price of fifty cents).[8] Even though DeWitt's account claimed to include the complete and unedited transcript of the trial, DeWitt's melodramatic editorializing and mass marketing of the trial worked rhetorically to frame and regulate gender expectations through the seemingly innocuous construction of divorce as public entertainment.

According to DeWitt, Alfred Beardsley's lawyer framed Mary Elizabeth Beardsley as an evil seductress who tricked both her husband and an Irish physician. The problem, according to Richard Busteed, Alfred Beardsley's lawyer, began with Mary Elizabeth Beardsley's deviation from the role of proper wife. He argued, "Mrs. Beardsley, it would seem, . . . was fonder of promenading [on] Broadway and visiting places of amusement without her husband than was consistent with wifely propriety."[9] The very act of "promenading" without her husband was represented as a deviation from the role of a good Christian wife, and that deviation made the next step of the story, Dr. Thomas Francis Mahan's seduction, appear more plausible. Mary Elizabeth Beardsley was said to have winked at Mahan and dropped a rosebud to entice him to follow her. Mahan followed Beardsley and her female companion, and when he introduced himself, Mary Elizabeth Beardsley supposedly assumed a "romantic" false name and claimed to be the daughter of a rich sea captain. While Mahan was portrayed as an inevitable victim of seduction, Mary Elizabeth Beardsley was portrayed as the agent of seduction who "captured" the innocent doctor.[10]

Alfred Beardsley's lawyers claimed that Mary Elizabeth Beardsley married Thomas Mahan in December of 1855, and after she consummated her bigamous marriage, she returned home to her first husband and child.[11] This narrative portrayed both Thomas Mahan and Alfred Beardsley as innocent victims of Mary Elizabeth Beardsley. DeWitt noted that Mary Elizabeth Beardsley seduced Mahan, who was "an Irishman naturally susceptible to female charms."[12] Similarly, Alfred Beardsley was framed as an innocent victim of his wife. In his closing arguments, Richard Busteed, Alfred Beardsley's lawyer, proclaimed, "There he [the plaintiff] sits and has sat during the most painful revelations that can be made to a human being; a dishonored husband with the first blush of health and youth upon his brow. . . . A father! A son! A brother! Oh God, that he should be a husband!"[13] In short, Alfred Beardsley was portrayed as a man with whom any of the men in the jury could identify, and he was represented as a faithful husband who did his duty as defined by gender expectations. Within this version of the melodramatic narrative there is little doubt that Alfred Beardsley embodied the good and innocent victim. Alfred Beardsley's lawyer represented Mary Elizabeth Beardsley as the villain, and her bigamous marriage was portrayed as the catalyst that destroyed a family.

Mary Elizabeth Beardsley's supposed guilt was represented as primarily manifest in her deviation from gender expectations. Not only was she represented as an evil seductress driven by hypersexual lust, but also Alfred Beardsley's lawyer concluded his closing arguments by saying, "I have no fears as to your verdict. You are left without alternative. It must be guilty against this faithless wife, this wicked woman, this unnatural mother, this impudent bawd! Honor demands it—decency claims it—truth requires it."[14] He also called Mary Elizabeth Beardsley the "harlot of the nineteenth century," framing her as antithetical to a good and proper woman, and in the context of the dichotomization demanded in melodrama, Mary Elizabeth Beardsley must have been either a heroine or harlot—there was no middle ground.[15] Instead of being devoted, loving, nurturing, and pure, Mary Elizabeth Beardsley was a "faithless," "wicked," and "unnatural" "harlot." Further, this constructed identity worked circularly because these characteristics functioned as evidence of her guilt, but her guilt functioned as evidence for these characteristics (she was guilty because she was a "harlot," but she was represented as a "harlot" because she was guilty).

Mary Elizabeth Beardsley's appearance was also constructed to embody her guilt. DeWitt described her entrance into the courtroom on the second day of the trial:

> She was attired in a dark dress, wearing a black cloth light bodied cloak, known to the ladies as "The Washington Jacket;" it was trimmed with black beads and bugles. She wore a handsome white silk bonnet, and a heavy black laced veil, which she slowly raised, and gave a good many eager eyes an opportunity of gazing on a countenance as fresh and blooming as that of a maiden of dashing sixteen, and an eye too bright and beautiful for even age to dim. She was pronounced at once a showy woman, that might play the dence [*sic*] with a more susceptible heart than that which Dr. Mahan, or any other son of the Emerald Isle, might possess.[16]

Mary Elizabeth Beardsley's appearance functioned rhetorically as *de facto* proof for her guilt by seeming to illustrate that she was a "showy woman" who was capable of seducing and marrying a man while still married to another. While DeWitt framed Mary Elizabeth Beardsley's bright eyes as evidence of her guilt, it was her cloak, bonnet, and veil that seemed to represent her seductive personality.[17] Beardsley's clothes were just one element of her body being rhetorically appropriated and placed in competition with expectations of proper womanhood. Her clothes were used to illustrate that she was showy, her eyes made her capacity for seduction demonstrable, and it was the lustful urges of her body that supposedly motivated her to commit this crime. In each of these instances, the representations of Mary Elizabeth Beardsley's body overwhelmed any possible attempt for her to be viewed as a good woman. This description of clothing focused attention on appearance and, thus, worked as part of a melodramatic trope that configured morality and circumscribed gender.

Mary Elizabeth Beardsley's defense, on the other hand, portrayed her as the innocent victim of Alfred Beardsley, who seduced and betrayed her. In Mary Elizabeth Beardsley's narrative, she supposedly fell in love with and married Alfred Beardsley only to find that he squandered their money, and the couple was forced to live with Mary Elizabeth Beardsley's parents, relying upon their support. Her lawyer, Chauncey Shaffer, explained, "There he stayed [on his father-in-law's support] until in visiting harlots he stained his physical manhood; he bought their favors with means of his injured brother-in-laws, and sullied the purity of his young wife with his leprous touch."[18] Thus, this account represented Alfred Beardsley as the villain, but his performance of gender was intimately connected to this representation. Alfred Beardsley's primary failure was framed as a failure to support his family financially. It was not his visiting of "harlots" that was problematic, but that he "sullied the purity of his young wife" with a sexually transmitted disease and had to borrow money to do so.[19]

Shaffer reframed the same events that were described by Alfred Beardsley's lawyers within the context of women's frailties, thus placing Mary Elizabeth Beardsley as both a proper woman and an innocent victim. For example, if Mrs. Beardsley did wink at Mahan, she did so only because women cannot help but wink at men; she was simply acting as a woman. Rather than being enticed, Mahan hounded the women, and, rather than "promenading," Mary Elizabeth Beardsley was going to Barnum's museum, a respectable place to study zoology.[20] Alfred Beardsley, then, was portrayed as the truly evil character in the story, seducing other women and plotting against his wife, and Mary Elizabeth Beardsley's proper performance of gender was portrayed as evidence of her innocence. Both sides of the story relied on Mary Elizabeth Beardsley's performance of gender to make the story plausible. In Alfred Beardsley's version, Mary Elizabeth

Beardsley could have committed those acts only if she were the "harlot of the nineteenth century," an aberration of proper womanhood. Mary Elizabeth Beardsley's lawyer, on the other hand, placed her squarely within the sphere of proper womanhood, and her failings were simply represented as the failings of all women.

The Beardsley trial was certainly entertaining. The trial provided a morally appropriate space to publicly talk about sex and seduction, and it allowed Americans voyeuristically to watch the drama of a family that was both similar to and yet very different from that of many American observers. Nonetheless, the Beardsley trial was not simply entertainment. The public drama created space to understand gender performance in the context of divorce and the disrupted American family. Divorce challenged cultural expectations of proper womanhood while introducing a new public figure of the divorced woman. Mary Elizabeth Beardsley synecdochically represented the divorced woman, and the public trial functioned as a way to understand the cultural meanings of this new public figure. While Mary Elizabeth Beardsley was either a victim of an evil husband or the "harlot of the nineteenth century," other trials introduced additional ways of understanding the divorced woman.[21]

The Ticknor Divorce

In 1867 Chicago, the legal context of divorce was significantly different from that of New York, but the sensationalism surrounding popular divorce trials was surprisingly similar. The Ticknor divorce and child custody trial participated in the social controversy over divorce and, like the Beardsley trial, obtained an extraordinary level of press coverage. The trial received daily coverage in the *Chicago Republican* and *Chicago Tribune*, prompting one *Tribune* reader to criticize the paper for its coverage of the scandal and publishing what he labeled as "disgusting details."[22] The *Tribune* editor even stated, "The public have been sufficiently nauseated with the case already."[23]

After nine years of marriage, Susan Ticknor filed for divorce from her husband, Aurora Ticknor, on the grounds of "extreme and repeated cruelty." Aurora Ticknor responded by charging Susan Ticknor with adultery with his former business partner. The details of the case were developed daily in the newspapers and became increasingly sordid and confusing as the twelve-day trial progressed, with each side attempting to frame the situation in dichotomous melodramatic terms. Susan Ticknor testified first, and she was represented as an innocent victim. She said that the abuse began on their wedding tour, where "Mr. Ticknor's friends took every occasion to ill-treat her, and on one occasion he abused her because she asked him not to drink any more liquor."[24] From this first instance, Susan Ticknor was portrayed as both an innocent victim of undeserved abuse and a model of domesticity—a woman who attempted to save her husband from the evils of liquor. According to Susan Ticknor, the abuse became increasingly horrific. On a few occasions, Aurora Ticknor hit her and pushed her to the ground, and one evening he invited an acquaintance, Helen Blair, into their bedroom and committed adultery without allowing his wife to leave the room.[25] Perhaps the most shocking allegation was that he allowed his nephew Lewis to remain in his house after Lewis abused the Ticknors' young daughter, Isabelle.[26]

These events characterized Aurora Ticknor as clearly evil and Susan Ticknor as a wholesome mother who attempted to protect her morality and her children. Even the judge appeared to support this image when Aurora Ticknor's lawyers objected to allowing the children to huddle and sob around their mother while she was testifying. The judge was quoted as replying to the objection by saying that "the children had no place to go to, and perhaps Ticknor had better put them in jail or some other convenient place. If the counsel insisted on making the witness cry he had no right to complain of the effect of his own actions."[27] The judge and newspapers characterized Susan Ticknor as the natural guardian of the children who had "no place to go to" and an innocent victim who was bullied by her husband and her husband's lawyers.

While the frames of purity and innocence were consistent in the Ticknor and Beardsley trials, coverage of the Ticknor trial created an image of the divorced woman that highlighted her role as mother. Deliberative debates about divorce also drew on this rhetorical construction. For example, Robert Dale Owen, in his exchange with Horace Greeley in the *New York Tribune*, wrote of the degradation of the "girl's heart" who marries and finds herself in an abusive relationship.[28] Owen asked, "Will he beat her—the mother of his children, the one he has sworn to love and protect? Likely enough."[29] Owen and the newspaper coverage for the Ticknor trial constructed the public image of the divorced woman in similar ways. For both, the divorced woman was a symbol of good motherhood. Her heart was broken, her purity was sullied, and she attempted to protect her children at all costs. The proper role of the husband, then, was to protect his wife and children, and the only reason the divorced woman sought a divorce, based on this image, was to protect her children from an evil husband. Thus, the public image of the divorced woman fit within the cultural myth of proper womanhood, but she was also publicly shamed by making her private family concerns public through a divorce trial.

A few days into the Ticknor trial, the defense presented its case against Susan Ticknor. The defense introduced witnesses who said that the couple was "always pleasant toward each other" until Susan Ticknor began having an affair with her husband's former business partner, Eugene Fishborn.[30] Despite Fishborn's denials—he claimed that all of his interactions with Susan Ticknor had been gentlemanly and usually consisted of escorting her when they met on the street—the defense had several witnesses supporting the allegations. Aurora Ticknor further claimed that Lewis (the nephew) remained in the house after Isabelle's abuse because Susan Ticknor requested that he stay.[31]

The jury quickly decided for Susan Ticknor, and they granted her a divorce on the grounds of "extreme and repeated cruelty."[32] Jury members were evidently not persuaded by evidence of Susan Ticknor's adultery, even though she may have been guilty of an affair because she married Fishborn about six months after the divorce.[33] Nevertheless, the newspapers framed Susan Ticknor's innocence as the natural conclusion.

The melodramatic narrative of the popular trial may help explain this framing. Melodrama demands a dichotomy between characters, so either Aurora Ticknor or Susan Ticknor must be completely guilty; there is no shared or partial guilt. This need to ascribe absolute guilt to one person explains why the decision appears to be such an oversimplification of the issues in this case.[34] During the trial, Susan Ticknor embodied the role of mother when she comforted her sobbing children, and her lawyer continually framed her within the context of motherhood. Susan Ticknor's role as the ideal mother was never meaningfully contested, and the extension of this logic suggested that if Susan Ticknor was an ideal mother, she must have also been an ideal wife. Thus, Aurora Ticknor remained to be configured as the clearly evil husband.[35] As in the Beardsley trial, the woman's innocence was dependent on the proper performance of gender.

The melodrama in the Ticknor divorce was not exceptional. Other divorce trials received substantial attention and were equally scandalous.[36] In the same month as the Ticknor scandal, there were also Quimby and Wright divorce scandals in Chicago papers. Mr. Quimby had the police break down a hotel door and put his wife in the Armory for adultery (but only after she accused him of having an affair with her mother), and Mr. Wright had his eleven-year-old son testify to his mother's adultery.[37] Charles Cowley, a Massachusetts lawyer, even published *Browne's Divorce and Its Consequences*, a melodramatic account of the purportedly true story of the ill-fated marriage and "foreordained" divorce of Jeannie and George Browne, "which broke up a family, delivered a disordered [and insane] wife to the lewd beds of a succession of libertines and swindlers, and sent five children on the road to vice and ruin."[38] Newspapers also listed numerous divorces every day, and taken together, these trials illustrate that divorce was a kind of shameful spectacle, prompting a writer calling himself or herself "The Spirit of the Jail, Confidential Secretary" to compare Chicago to Sodom.[39]

Divorce also functioned as the central melodramatic feature in sensational murder cases, and the Walworth murder was perhaps the most infamous example. On June 4, 1873, *Chicago Republican* readers woke to the headlines "PISTOLED. / The Bloody Reign of King Revolver. / . . . A Father Deliberately Murdered by His Son in a Prominent New York Hotel. / The Cause of Trouble—The Antecedents of the Family. / Cool Conduct of the Young Ruffian After the Deed. / . . . Gotham's Latest Horror."[40] As these headlines suggest, nineteen-year-old Frank Walworth lured his father, prominent writer Mansfield Tracy Walworth, into a New York hotel room and shot him multiple times. Frank then turned himself in to police. The paper, however, did not portray Frank as a "young ruffian," but, instead, he was a hero who had attempted to protect his mother. The Walworths were divorced, but Mansfield Walworth's abuse of his wife reportedly continued.[41] After Mansfield Walworth threatened to murder his former wife, their son Frank claimed that he felt compelled to protect her, and he committed the murder in his mother's defense, saying that "there were bounds beyond which [he] would not allow any man to go," framing his actions within the proper performance of gender roles.[42] This case was represented as a classic melodrama—the characters were dichotomously good and evil, and there was a struggle among irreconcilable virtues—and as such, Mansfield Walworth's murder was portrayed as necessary for good to prevail.

In each of these instances, divorce was the framework on which gender was publicly performed. The prominence of divorce as a frame suggests that divorce coverage was about more than public voyeurism; it was a way of regulating gender and understanding social conflict. As a result, the account of the Mansfield Walworth murder holds interest because it attempted to understand that murder through the context of the Walworths' earlier divorce. Thus, the divorce trial was more than popular entertainment; it was a way of enforcing gender expectations through publicizing the consequences of gender deviation and figuring the discursive and social constraints for how the divorced identity could be understood. These trials illustrate that the nineteenth-century divorced woman existed in a liminal space between the married and single woman. While the divorced woman could never regain the innocence of the unmarried woman, proper performance of gender (especially mothering) could allow her to assume the role of victim rather than harlot.

The close association between gender performance and guilt in these divorce trials sent a powerful message about women's deviation from gender expectations. In this context, there was not a legitimate or acceptable deviation from norms of proper womanhood; any deviation created a presumption of guilt because if a woman did not perform proper womanhood in one case, it was more likely that she would deviate in another. The sensationalism of these trials transformed indecent and entertaining accounts of adultery, bigamy, and seduction into appropriate negotiations of public morality. The divorce trial, then, used entertainment as a pervasive way to regulate gender in public culture and constituted the new public figure of the divorced woman, and while this new public figure had the potential to transform women's role in the public sphere, mass media coverage of popular divorce trials simply reified traditional gender roles and created a mechanism of disciplining gender. More significantly, however, the reiteration of gender norms in media coverage of these trials functioned as a means to negotiate public morality and worked to stabilize the newly emerging identity of the divorced woman in the nineteenth-century American social imaginary.

DIVORCE AS POLITICAL CONTROVERSY

At the same time as Americans consumed entertaining and salacious accounts of public divorces, many were also debating the laws of divorce and, thus, the future of the American family. Although legally formalized divorce was rare in the Colonial Era, most colonies allowed divorce for adultery and desertion, and colonial Connecticut was unusually lax, allowing divorce for several other grounds.[43] By the nineteenth century the rate of divorce in the United States was increasing, and it continued to increase steadily before 1860.[44] This boost, in part, can be attributed to the liberalization of divorce laws. Between 1820 and 1860 many states initiated new divorce legislation, which resulted in an increase in the number of states that allowed divorce for reasons such as habitual drunkenness or cruel and inhuman treatment. Connecticut, Indiana, Illinois, North Carolina, Rhode Island, Maine, Iowa, and the Utah territory even included an omnibus clause that gave courts vast discretion in granting divorces. The state of South Carolina was on the other end of the extreme, having the distinction of being the only state not to allow any divorce whatsoever. It is, however, important to note that the absence of legal divorce did not ensure happy marriages. South Carolina was often accused of being a state with legal concubinage, and every state had examples of desertion that resulted from the inability to procure a legal divorce.[45]

In one sense, divorce laws were highly localized. In early America, most states allowed divorce only by legislative decree and were inconsistent in execution. By the mid-nineteenth century, however, all states (except South Carolina) had passed some sort of divorce legislation and moved individual decision making to the courts. Despite the localized nature of divorce legislation, divorce became a national controversy, especially with reports of divorce mills in states such as Indiana and Illinois.[46] Some citizens in states with restrictive divorce laws expressed fear that people would shop around for a divorce in another state with more liberal laws, and, at the same time, some citizens in states with liberal divorce laws expressed fear that people would take advantage of their state because of a desire for an easy divorce.[47] Because divorce legislation in one state had the potential to impact citizens in other states, seemingly local debates took on a national importance. As with the typical melodrama, debates about divorce tended to be reduced to two dichotomous positions, each of which posited the fate of the nation at stake.

Opposition to Divorce

The opposition to expanding grounds for divorce tended to presuppose idealized American identities. For women, proper behavior was characterized by public invisibility and legally sustained by coverture, the concept where husbands legally and politically represented their wives. For men, optimal public status was characterized by autonomy within the home. To seek a divorce or even have the possibility of divorce challenged the public status of both married men and women because the insular family became open to outside regulations over legitimate or illegitimate actions within marriage. The common tropes in the opposition to divorce initially emerged through disparate voices in newspapers, pamphlets, and books until the creation of the National Divorce Reform League in 1885, when opposition to expanding divorce became part of the federally sanctioned narrative.

In 1867 Auguste Carlier, a French author who wrote about the United States and was often compared to Tocqueville, published an English translation of his book *Marriage in the United States*. The book underwent at least four editions and was praised for its "objective" account that was thought to come only from a foreigner, but the book was also highly criticized because of its disapproving account of the state of American marriage.[48] Carlier expressed concern over what he estimated to be more than three thousand divorces annually in the United States.[49] Similarly, Theodore Woolsey, president of Yale College, who later founded the National Divorce Reform League, wrote his treatise on divorce because of his concern over the growing number of divorces in the United States, and he noted, "There is an impression in the mind of many persons . . . that in a certain stratum of society—shall we call it Protestant society?—the feeling of the sanctity of marriage is passing away; that the highest crimes against that covenant . . . are either excused . . . or laughed at."[50] The rhetoric of Woolsey's criticism suggests that the public concern over divorce was grounded in a moral/religious framework. While an individual divorce may have been painful for those involved, that individual family synecdochically represented a much larger cultural problem, disrespect for a covenant with God.

The opposition to divorce often began with a definition of marriage that posited the public identity of married persons as permanent. Perhaps the most widely circulated example of this position came from an exchange in the *New York Tribune* between the paper's publicly active editor Horace Greeley, anarchist Stephen Pearl Andrews, free love advocate Robert Dale Owen, and author Henry James. Andrews later republished the exchange in book form, including letters that were excluded from the *Tribune*. Like many who opposed the expansion of divorce, Greeley grounded his arguments in definition, which were often tied to interrelated understandings of nature and religion. For example, Horace Greeley stated in the *New York Tribune*, "For what *is* Marriage? . . . Dr. Webster's great dictionary says: 'MARRIAGE: The act of uniting a man and woman *for life*; wedlock; the legal union of a man and woman *for life*. Marriage is a contract both civil and religious, by which the parties engage to live together in mutual affection and fidelity *till death shall separate them*.' "[51] Greeley continued to ask sarcastically, "There may be something better than Marriage; but nothing *is Marriage* but a solemn engagement to live together in faith and love *till death*. Why should not they who have devised something better than old-fashioned Marriage give their bantling a distinctive *name*, and not appropriate ours?"[52]

A similar debate over definition occurred in the 1860 Woman's Rights Convention in New York.[53] The state legislature had recently passed married woman's property rights legislation, and woman's rights leader Elizabeth Cady Stanton became active in a campaign to expand New York's restrictive divorce laws. When Stanton raised the issue at the convention, Antoinette Brown (later Blackwell), a reverend and prominent woman's rights advocate, objected, arguing that marriage was a permanent union between two individuals. In her 1860 speech, Antoinette Brown (Blackwell) used a similar definition of marriage to Greeley's. She argued, "Resolved, That marriage is the voluntary alliance of two persons of opposite sexes into one family, and that such an alliance, with its possible incidents of children, its common interests, &c., must be, from the nature of things, as permanent as the life of the parties."[54] These understandings of marriage functioned as arguments *from* definition; the arguments about marriage reasoned from the starting premise of an incontrovertible and immutable definition.[55] In both cases the definition of marriage was posited as an absolute because meaning came from God. There was no debate about what marriage should be; rather the definition of marriage was a given and functioned as implicit support for the authors' claims about divorce. Additionally, both of these definitions of marriage were gender-specific and permanent, creating an implicit limitation to both public identity and agency.

Several commentators developed explicitly religious consequences to divorce. In reference to the New Testament, Woolsey stated, "The wife and husband are bound by a covenant. To put a wife away is to break that covenant, to act treacherously or faithlessly. This is what God hates."[56] Divorce, then, was portrayed as not simply a deviation; it angered God. Part of the problem derived from the assumed religious foundation of marriage.[57] These advocates posited man and woman as designed by God to be together, and divorce was a challenge to that perfect union. The production of children was assumed to be one element of that perfect union.[58] Thus, the demands of procreation naturalized the assumed religious foundation of marriage.

Constructing marriage as permanent and immutable meant that when women entered into marriage they became publicly absent or hidden, losing their public voice and ability to define acceptable behavior within marriage. If a woman was, for example, beaten in her marriage, she had little legal recourse because the act was construed as private, becoming invisible to the legal system and public scrutiny. The transformation between crime (beating a woman outside of marriage) and a trivial disagreement (beating a woman inside of marriage) occurred at the point where women's political subjectivity shifted away from citizen to wife.[59] Constructions of marriage as permanent and immutable created a religious and natural foundation for women's public identities to be characterized by absence.

Dichotomous characterizations of man/woman and good/evil positioned divorce as a danger to the country. Any deviation from the "natural" understanding of marriage was thought to threaten the moral underpinnings of the nation. This line of reasoning was typically articulated as a slippery-slope argument (or argument of direction).[60] While some opponents of divorce alluded to the possibility of polygamy once the institution of marriage became degraded, most referred to social morals more generally.[61] For example, American author Elisah Mulford argued, "It is the degradation of the family, and the lower apprehension of its obligations, that is represented alike by all her annalists and her satirists, as the cause and circumstances of the ruin of Rome."[62] In that sense, an intimate connection was thought to exist between the family and the moral foundation of the nation—the destruction of one was thought to risk the destruction of the other. Critics of divorce engaged in a subtle rhetorical move that associated the moral worth of a nation with the nation's survival. The moral worth of the nation was determined through citizens' relationship with God, and, in turn, marriage (and proper roles within marriage) was implicitly framed as an important part of that individual relationship with God. Thus, opponents of divorce framed proper performance of public identity, even if that identity was defined through absence, as a laudable act of citizenship and necessary to the "moral foundation of the nation."

By the 1880s divorce was consistently perceived as a national issue, as each individual divorce in different states with different laws came to reflect on the condition of the nation as a whole. Popular American magazines and newspapers expressed concern over rising divorce rates and lamented the potential decline of the family.[63] One marker of the escalation of divorce into a national issue came with the creation of the National Divorce Reform League in 1885. This organization derived from the New England Divorce Reform League, created in 1881 by Theodore Woosley, and was one of many groups that participated in constituting divorce as a national crisis.[64]

In 1889 the United States Bureau of Labor issued the first federally sponsored report on marriage and divorce in the United States. On the surface, the report appeared to be simply informative rather than persuasive, reporting on the status of marriage in the nation. Nevertheless, the way in which the report constituted divorce as a national problem was persuasive. The report derived from "influential petitions" that were sent to Congress in 1884, and these petitions were a direct result of work by the National Divorce Reform League. The petitions were explicit in intent, stating that the report was necessary to assess the "magnitude of these evils [divorces]."[65] The presentation of facts and the need to collect those facts rhetorically constituted divorce as a significant national problem. Within this frame there was no acceptable level of divorce, and when Congress authorized and funded the report, it *de facto* established divorce as a social evil.[66] Further, Rev. Samuel W. Dike, secretary of the National Divorce Reform League, was influential in getting federal support for the report, aided in the investigation to create the report, and extensively utilized the report once it was released.[67] The seemingly objective report was heavily influenced by an organization created for the explicit purposes of limiting divorce. Additionally, the report presented the crisis of divorce as not grounded in the behaviors of people within marriage, but in the act of divorce itself. The actions that could lead to divorce, such as adultery and abuse, were not framed as problems. Instead, the report represented the fact of divorce as the national problem. By highlighting the number of divorces instead of the reasons for divorce, the report made the concerns of the home public (or visible) only when that home legally dissolved.

Although the perceived problem of divorce led some activists to call for nationally uniform divorce laws prior to the federal report, the publication of the report provided the impetus for renewed efforts. The push for uniform divorce laws took two basic forms. The first was in the form of federal legislation. Although Oregon senator Joseph N. Dolph and others argued that the federal government had the power to legislate marriage and divorce,[68] it was far more common for people to insist that federal legislation required a constitutional amendment.[69] An alternative to federal action entailed attempts to get individual states to agree to uniform marriage and divorce laws.[70] Perhaps needless to say, attempts to get states to agree on a single divorce law were ineffective. Yet initiatives such as these kept divorce and questions over the legitimate grounds for divorce in the spotlight for years.

Support for Expanding Divorce

Just as opposition to divorce extended a seemingly individual drama to the nation as a whole, advocates for expanding the grounds for divorce positioned the stakes as similarly high. In this context, however, advocates rhetorically posited traditional laws of marriage as a threat to women. The woman's rights movement used the metaphor of slavery to characterize the relationship between women and traditional marriage. For example, the 1848 Seneca Falls Declaration of Sentiments stated,

> He has made her, if married, in the eye of the law, civilly dead. . . . In the covenant of marriage, she is compelled to promise obedience to her husband, he becoming, to all intents and purposes, her master—the law giving him power to deprive her of her liberty, and to administer chastisement. He has so framed the laws of divorce, as to what shall be the proper causes, and in case of separation, to whom the guardianship of the children shall be given, as to be wholly regardless of the happiness of women—the law, in all cases, going upon a false supposition of the supremacy of man, and giving all power into his hands.[71]

The Seneca Falls Declaration of Sentiments framed the laws of marriage in terms of slavery, positioning the husband as "master" over the civilly powerless wife. Divorce, then, was like an escape from slavery, but restrictive divorce laws and women's lack of custody of their children made escape nearly impossible.

The slavery metaphor became a longtime characteristic of the woman's rights movement, and in 1851 abolitionist and early woman's rights advocate Angelina Grimké was explicit in arguing for the similarities between slave laws and the laws for married women.[72] After the abolition of slavery the metaphor gained additional traction, highlighting the disjunction between the freed bondsman and the women who were still "enslaved." To illustrate, in 1890 Mary Livermore made a similar association, characterizing the married woman as a slave in saying, "A wife and mother should always be mistress of herself, and never the slave of another, not even when that other is her husband and the slavery is founded on her undying love."[73] In this sense, the slavery of marriage was represented as more insidious than the slavery of men and women of African descent.[74]

Some advocates insisted that the way to empower women was to redefine marriage—shifting the institution from a natural and immutable state to a simple contract.[75] Defining marriage as a contract was significant because it removed marriage from the divine to the secular realm and, thus, made it open to human intervention. This reasoning suggested that if humans created marriage, then humans could change marriage, and if marriage was a contract, contracts could be broken or declared invalid. The contract argument in support of divorce reform was an argument that configured identity within marriage as essentially a status as citizen with individual rights and privileged human agency to modify or change marriage to meet the needs of citizens. The choice to divorce or the possibility for divorce constituted women as public agents and citizens in that the private roles for women were intimately connected to women's public identities. Just as divorce was an issue of personal violation and personal justice, it was also a public act in that it made acceptable actions within marriage a shared concern (people could see those violations and their real victims), and divorce framed the personal violation as a social evil. As a result, divorce created new understandings of deviations in marriage as a civic problem, making women's voices and experiences public.

Those in favor of expanding divorce legislation countered religious arguments in two principal ways. First, some challenged the legitimacy of religious considerations in relation to the marriage contract.[76] Thus, while proponents of divorce expansion argued for a new definition of marriage, they also explicitly countered the religious definition of marriage, which moved definition from functioning implicitly to an explicit argument about definition. Further, by contesting the definition of marriage, those in favor of expanding divorce legislation also implicitly contested the limited conceptions of citizenship entailed in traditional definitions of marriage.

Additionally, several activists appropriated religion, arguing that expanding causes for divorce was more moral and closer to religious ideals. Robert Dale Owen argued in the *New York Tribune* in reference to Indiana divorce laws, "Are these lax principles? . . . You have elopements, adultery, which your law, by rendering it indispensable of release, virtually encourages; you have free-love, and that most terrible of all social evils, prostitution. . . . I think that we are justified in His sight, rather than you."[77] Here, Owen frames the lack of access to divorce as creating more moral problems than having the possibility of divorce. The imperfection of marriage, according to Owen and others, functioned as proof of its lack of divinity, and only when people were free to divorce could the family exist in harmony necessary for the divine.

Some advocates further secularized marriage by conceptualizing it as a right rather than a sacred covenant. Stanton insisted, for example, "The best interest of the community never can require the sacrifice of one innocent being—of one sacred right."[78] And, "It is the inalienable right of all to be happy."[79] The language of rights created a competing value to the value of religion, and here, rights were not simply attached to the ability to marry and divorce. Rather, Stanton echoed the Declaration of Independence to argue for a right to happiness in general. Stanton's framing of women's personal and familial identity in terms of the public rights of citizenship worked to reframe implicitly private enactments of gender as public acts of citizenship.

Just as with those who opposed expanding divorce laws, advocates of expanding legal grounds for divorce argued that the failure to do so would result in dire consequences. However, while the consequences on the other side were essentially public, the arguments by proponents of divorce drew from private examples and often argued inductively from the individual experience of people hurt by restrictive marriage laws. Stanton claimed to have developed her strong feelings on divorce from the "sufferings of a friend from my girlhood."[80] Owen called for the audience to think of the "worthy girl" who is a "single captive" in an unhappy marriage.[81] In a letter to the editor of the *Woman's Herald* one woman used typical language, arguing,

> What morality can be urged in defense of a case such as the following?—and such cases are not rare: A well-brought up woman, a devout Catholic, lying on a miserable bed dying; her lord and master upon whose brutal face is written only too plainly the vicious life he leads, enters—drunk; walking, or staggering rather, to the bedside of the woman he has sworn to love, he picks up a jug of water standing on a chair beside her, and with blood-curdling oaths empties it upon the poor creature. For eight years thus has this so-called husband treated his unhappy wife, until at last she obtained peace beyond the gates of death.[82]

These types of arguments promoted identification by allowing the audience to place themselves or loved ones in the position of those suffering in an unhappy marriage and challenged the assumption on the other side of the debate that those who divorced were attempting to destroy the American family.

While arguments restricting divorce placed the limited political subjectivities of women as a starting premise, attempts at expanding divorce worked to bring the line between public and private to the forefront. For Owen, the "worthy girl" transformed from a private, suffering individual to a public symbol. While this transformation did not necessarily shift or redraw the line—the suffering of the "worthy girl" was always part of her political subjectivity—it made the line more apparent, implicitly challenging a politics that condoned the "worthy girl's" suffering. Rather than understanding marriage in terms of a relationship with God, advocates of expanding grounds for divorce fundamentally changed the public rhetoric to be about individual citizens. The shift in public rhetoric shaped the possibilities for argument from status as a woman in a Christian family to the status as an individual citizen in a democratic nation. Such a rhetorical shift was vitally important because it shaped value hierarchies, expectations of gender roles, and the assumed relationship between the individual and the state. In short, the arguments justifying expanded divorce laws framed divorce and actions taken to break the bonds of marriage as enactments of citizenship, suggesting that only by gaining the right to divorce did women and men really gain the right to marry.

THE DIVORCED CITIZEN

When Lincoln appealed to the metaphor of divorce in speaking about the state of the nation just prior to the Civil War, he was drawing on a widespread fear about the changing nature of family in the United States. Just as the cultural ideal of the stable and permanent union of marriage came to be challenged by increasing divorce rates, the nation itself faced the possibility of divorce. Yet the cultural anxiety about divorce was not simply about dissolution of what once seemed enduring; it was also about the moral hierarchy created in that dissolution.

Although the practice of marriage may have been about love or economics, legally and politically nineteenth-century marriage was about status and public identity. Divorce resulted in a radical transformation of public identity. It meant that a man had failed in his familial role, but, perhaps more significantly, divorce created a new public space for women beyond the dichotomy of *femme sole* and *femme covert*. As much as the divorce debates were about the laws of divorce and the entertainment of the masses, they were also about constituting the public identity of the divorced woman and assessing the future of the American family. These new roles entailed moral judgments such that the divorced woman would be understood as a harlot, an innocent victim, or something in between. The very possibility of divorce made seemingly private behavior within families open to public scrutiny, and divorce changed seemingly individual family tragedy into public melodrama that came to reflect the state of the nation as a whole. Thus, as Americans debated about divorce and the future of the American family, they were also debating about the quintessential American citizen and the future of the nation.

[3]

Polygamy and the Relics of Barbarism

For some, it was a revelation from God; for others, it was the epitome of sinfulness.[1] Regardless of label, the announcement of the doctrine of polygamy by the Latter-Day Saints in 1852 began a battle over religion, citizenship, and sex that changed the American cultural milieu.[2] The configuration of households in the far western territories precipitated as much, if not more, outrage than the institution of slavery. Statehood, and thus full citizenship of thousands, became predicated on abandoning what some individuals called a fundamental principle of their religion. The federal government formally defined the institution of marriage, and men and women across the country organized to "save" women, many of whom claimed that they were not oppressed and had no desire to be saved. Thus, the controversy over Mormon polygamy became a controversy over the image of the American family and the identity of the nation itself. Both literally and figuratively, proper performance of gender and race constituted the line between American citizen and the seemingly barbarous Other.

The long and complicated controversy over Mormon polygamy emerged through the rhetoric of male and female Mormons, the popular press, courts, Congress, women's movements, popular lectures, and novels. Despite the widely divergent rhetorical forms, each of these locations of controversy illustrates that much more was thought to be at stake than the lives of some families in Utah. The polygamy controversy functions as an indispensable part of the larger puzzle illustrating the role of marriage as a lens through which the identity of "citizen" and the symbolic woman was negotiated. Although polygamy would seem to be a fundamental challenge to the institution of marriage as it was then known, neither side of the controversy contested traditional conceptions of marriage. Rather, the controversy hinged on which marriage was the better instantiation of traditional patriarchal marriage. Thus, the polygamy controversy became a major site of conflict over public morality and the limits to individual liberty.

MORMONS AND MARRIAGE

Young America had no shortage of neophyte spiritual leaders and ideas. One of those unlikely leaders was Joseph Smith Jr., founder of the Latter-Day Saints (LDS) Church. The LDS Church came to be implicated in some of the most significant controversies of the young nation, including slavery, federalism, women's rights, and westward expansion. In each case, polygamy was a catalyst for public dispute.

Joseph Smith Jr. was born in Vermont in 1805 into an impoverished family that moved to Palmyra, New York, in 1816. While Smith's mother frequently experimented with different religious sects, cults, and visions, Smith's father consistently failed in business, and father and son eventually sought income by using a divining rod to search for hidden treasure.[3] By 1820, when Smith was fifteen, the Second Great Awakening was sweeping upstate New York, and the Smith family actively participated in camp meetings and revival services of the Presbyterian Church. During this period, Smith claimed that he experienced his first visions calling existing religions false, and he created the basis for a new church. According to LDS theology, Smith was directed by an angel to discover golden plates that contained what would become the *Book of Mormon*, and Smith became known by some as a prophet.

The *Book of Mormon* told the story of two families that came to the Americas before the birth of Jesus, and church leaders framed the LDS Church as the true manifestation of Christianity and the *Book of Mormon* as the true word of God. LDS theology postulated that God was a material being who progressed from manhood to godhood through various stages in celestial life, and men could replicate this celestial progression.[4] Further, the tenets of the religion were considered to be somewhat fluid because God spoke through the true living prophet, and the Mormons entered into a covenant with God that involved the continual process of becoming more godlike.

Joseph Smith was a charismatic figure. The *Book of Mormon* was published in 1830, and after its publication the LDS Church grew rapidly. Looking for Zion and a location to continue to expand, Smith and his followers moved to Missouri. After being run out of Missouri and Ohio, the Mormons settled in Navoo, Illinois, in 1839. Within five years Navoo became the second-largest city in the state, and while the Saints were initially welcomed, animosity quickly mounted because of their centralized political and economic power, aggressive proselytizing, and rumors of sexual irregularities.[5] In 1844 Joseph Smith was arrested and sent to the Carthage jail. Shortly after his arrest, an angry mob stormed the jail, killing Smith and his brother Hyrum.

No clear successor to Smith existed, and in the midst of confusion and uncertainty, Brigham Young emerged as the new prophet and leader of the LDS Church. Young told his followers that he received a revelation from God that the Saints must move west in order to avoid persecution, and, by 1847, the Mormons had begun moving west, across desert, plains, and mountains, outside of US territory, searching for a new Zion. The Salt Lake Valley seemed like an unlikely location; it was declared by many to be desolate and uninhabitable. However, that isolation likely contributed to the choice of the valley as the new settlement for the Saints. Young became the religious, political, and economic leader of what the Saints then called the State of Deseret.

In the 1830s, the Federal Bill of Rights was not necessarily thought to apply to state and local government; it was commonly understood as exclusively applying to the federal government. As a result, as long as Mormons remained in the United States, they could not be ensured federal protection from local harassment.[6] The LDS Church took advantage of this same principle once members settled in Salt Lake City. With Utah's consideration for US territorial status in 1849, the church almost immediately applied for statehood, recognizing that because a territory had an ambiguous legal status the Mormons could ensure greater autonomy with statehood.[7] Congress denied statehood to the proposed State of Deseret, and a prolonged fight between the quickly growing LDS Church and the federal government began.

Although rumors of polygamy circulated around the Mormons for years, prior to 1852, the church vigorously denied those rumors. Not until 1852 did the leaders of the church publicly announce Joseph Smith's 1843 revelation calling for polygamy. Many reports suggested that Smith was practicing polygamy well before his 1843 revelation, but the official church history names 1843 as the date when Smith wrote that he was demanded by a sword-wielding angel to accept the doctrine.[8] Despite his initial resistance, Smith was said to have accepted the revelation, telling only a select number of leaders in the church while declaring the revelation too controversial to be made known publicly at that time. Early in the church's history, polygamy came to be equated with the concept of marriage as celestial—marriage for eternity with "sealing and binding in both heaven and earth."[9] Polygamy, then, created the possibility for greater procreation, fulfilling the "duty" of men and women on earth.[10] With greater perfection and fulfillment of "duty," men were thought to become gods. Thus, marriage became closely tied to one's progress through celestial kingdoms in heaven.

Because plural marriages were performed by the church and records were never made public, it is difficult to know how many Mormons were actually in a plural marriage at any given time. It is likely that only community and church leaders practiced polygamy because even though the principle was preached to all, only the most pure and pious could enter into a plural marriage.[11] The estimates of how many members of the church practiced polygamy vary widely, from less than 2 percent to well over 30 percent.[12] Regardless of the actual numbers involved in the practice, plural marriage was vigorously defended as a central tenet of the LDS religion.

In 1852 Orson Pratt, who became the "church's chief defender of 'the principle'" publicly announced the doctrine of polygamy, commonly called "plural marriage," "celestial marriage," or "the Principle" by church members and leadership.[13] Between 1852, when Pratt made his announcement, and 1884, when the last public defenses of polygamy appeared, Mormon authors published about twenty pamphlets in defense of polygamy.[14] The official rhetoric in support of plural marriage tended to be grounded in at least one indistinct category: religious, legal, or pragmatic. The religious justification for plural marriage was based in an understanding of a celestial kingdom beyond earthly bounds. A celestial marriage was thought to extend beyond life and to allow people, as a family, to become closer to God. In an 1869 sermon, Pratt argued that celestial marriage was a "biblical doctrine and part of the revealed religion of the Almighty," and he frequently relied on examples of polygamy in the Old Testament.[15]

Mormon leaders represented love and sexuality between men and women as a gift from God that could be expressed only within marriage.[16] This is because, as Pratt explained, "He gave to man, whom he created, a helpmeet," and within this role women were expected to be a "joy and a comfort" to men and fulfill what was represented as women's most noble purpose, propagation of the species.[17] As long as women's identity was framed through the lens of helpmate and procreator, women's sexuality was both permitted (in the context of marriage) and necessary to become closer to God. The Mormon justification of polygamy built on this understanding of women's identity as designed by God to argue that the more celestial wives a man had, the greater his kingdom in heaven, and women's salvation resided in becoming and properly performing the role of wife. In addition to saving women's souls, the Saints justified polygamy as pragmatically and comparatively better for women because no woman would need to remain unmarried.[18] These unmarried women, according to Pratt, were denied not only salvation but also financial support and their "right" to have children. The result, as Pratt explained in a different sermon, was that in Gentile communities women were pushed into prostitution, and men had license to act on lustful urges outside of marriage.[19] Thus, polygamy was framed as more moral than monogamy. The final category of justification for polygamy was legal, and polygamy advocates reminded audiences that the US Constitution ensured religious protection.[20]

POLYGAMY IN THE POPULAR IMAGINATION

The announcement of polygamy was not quietly received. Much of the outrage derived from the assumed status of women under polygamy. By the 1850s, Americans had become heavily invested in the home as a moral sanctuary, and the state of the home reflected the moral status of the nation. The perceived morality of the nation was grounded in a tenuous balance between liberty and license; Americans valued their freedoms but desired those freedoms to remain in morally appropriate bounds derived from cultural understandings of civic advancement. Thus, much American rhetoric framed the supposed corruption of women under polygamy as licentiousness and a sign of barbarity. Opponents of polygamy conceptualized barbarity within American borders as a threat to civilization and the nation itself.

Some of the earliest public responses to polygamy came in the form of popular literature, including novels, short stories, and magazine articles. Indeed, over the next half century, nearly one hundred novels and over two hundred newspaper and magazine stories occupied the genre of antipolygamy literature.[21] Antipolygamy fiction tended to fit into the generic pattern distinctive of antislavery literature, and authors commonly invoked the metaphor of slavery, representing polygamy as a moral battle with women as the slaves.[22] Much like antislavery literature, antipolygamy literature drew on sentimental forms, evoked the trope of the sexually degraded woman, and appealed to other women as the only hope of rescue.[23] Fanny Stenhouse's novel, *Tell It All: The Tyranny of Mormonism or an Englishwoman in Utah*, illustrated the connection. Fanny Stenhouse and her husband, Thomas B. H. Stenhouse, converted to Mormonism while in Britain and came to Salt Lake City in 1859. Although they became prominent members of the Mormon community in Salt Lake City, their resistance to plural marriage and economic grievances led to the couple's excommunication from the church in the early 1870s.[24] Harriet Beecher Stowe's preface to Stenhouse's novel made the comparison between antislavery and antipolygamy literature explicit. Stowe asked, "May we not then hope that the hour is come to loose the bonds of a cruel slavery whose chains have cut into the very hearts of thousands of our sisters—a slavery which debases and degrades womanhood, motherhood, and the family?"[25] In other words, polygamy was represented as a particularly egregious slavery because it was a slavery to which any woman could be subject. The analogy is significant because it enabled white Americans to identify with Mormon women in a way that may have been more difficult with race-based slavery. Whereas white Americans could imagine themselves, their wives, their mothers, or their daughters tricked or forced into polygamy, identification with slaves of African descent was limited by assumptions of intrinsic racial difference.

Those assumptions of difference gave the slavery analogy rhetorical power because women's position in polygamy was framed as that of debased and barbaric Other. Such a position was a far cry from predominate cultural rhetoric that revered women as proprietors of cultural morality and virtue. Thus, the rhetoric of slavery posited that polygamists were debasing the symbol of the nation's morality.

In 1873 Ann Eliza Young became the newest voice in the antipolygamy movement with her public divorce from Brigham Young, antipolygamy speaking tour, and book. Young's notoriety kept her and the subject of Mormon polygamy in the spotlight for nine years.[26] Although it is difficult to assess the extent of Young's influence, one account describes it as follows:

> Armed with letters of introduction, . . . we reached Washington, where we got into the speaker's room and she [Ann Eliza Young] sent her card to speaker Blaine. . . . There was a stampede on the floor [of Congress], and she held an ovation for two hours. Everybody wanted to see and hear her. Two days after that she did tell her story in Washington. Forty-eight hours later the Poland bill for the relief of the oppressed in Utah was a law.[27]

Ann Eliza Young was born into the Mormon Church in 1844 and traveled with her family on the arduous journey west into Utah. Ann Eliza Young's first marriage ended in divorce, which was occasionally permitted by the church, and in 1869 she reluctantly married Brigham Young. Young called herself Brigham Young's nineteenth wife, but because the church did not make records public, that number is difficult to verify.[28] Ann Eliza Young escaped Salt Lake City in 1873, immediately began a speaking tour, and filed a divorce suit against Brigham Young.[29]

Ann Eliza Young's book *Wife No. 19, or The Story of a Life in Bondage, Being a Complete Expose of Mormonism, and Revealing the Sorrows, Sacrifices and Sufferings of Women in Polygamy* is unambiguous in its message and heavily relied on Young's experiences in polygamy, especially her experiences as "Brigham Young's Apostate Wife." Throughout the book, Young assumed a reluctant persona of a woman who spoke only because she was called to speak the "truth." In her introductory message to the wives of Brigham Young, Ann Eliza Young stated, "I was driven to the course I am pursuing by sheer desperation."[30] Young's motivation, she continued, was to vindicate and save her "companions and . . . sisters in tribulation."[31] Young not only wrote from her experience as an oppressed woman but also framed that experience of oppression as a public concern. She was not writing about unhappy wives—a matter commonly understood to be both trivial and private. Rather, she wrote about the oppression of citizens—a violation of national ideals.

Much like earlier novels condemning polygamy, Young's book challenged polygamy through demonstrations of its evil effect on the family. She told the stories of many women, including her own mother, destroyed by polygamy. To illustrate that no woman could be happy in polygamy, Young recounted the story of a woman named Delia Dorr Curtis, who claimed to enter into polygamy happily but was clearly deluded because, as Young explained, just a few years later she died. According to Young, "She was another victim to polygamy, that horrible system which crushes women's hearts, kills their bodies, and destroys their souls."[32] Even women believing that they freely entered into polygamous marriages, according to Young, slowly became crushed under the oppression of polygamy.

Ann Eliza Young's descriptions of oppression were laced with examples of depravity. Rather than portraying Brigham Young as a saintly prophet, she represented him as violent, lustful, and power hungry. The doctrine of blood atonement and the Mountain Meadows Massacre served as examples of Brigham Young's violence in protection of his power.[33] Ann Eliza Young vividly recounted Brigham Young's failure to pay debts and to support his wives adequately, and she described the lust that motivated him to marry so many women that he could not remember all of his wives.[34] The depravity, however, extended beyond Brigham Young to the entire Mormon community. According to Young, "relatives intermarried in a manner that would shock even the most lax-moralled [*sic*] community. . . . [It] was a very common thing [for example] for a mother and daughter to have the same husband."[35] Young also noted that during the height of religious fervor, marriages of girls as young as thirteen were common.[36] The unrelenting depiction of moral depravity was rhetorically significant. First, the salaciousness fit well into the rhetorical culture of the time, making Young's descriptions both entertaining and familiar enough to be believable. Further, her book framed the primary evil of polygamy through the lens of feminine virtue. Thus, the issue of polygamy was of public importance as a violation of the cultural expectations of femininity. These violations of feminine virtue captured a recognizable fear for most Americans.

The scene for Ann Eliza Young's book and speaking tour was set by the wildly popular lyceum speech, "Whited Sepulchres," by Anna Dickenson in 1869 and 1870. Anna Dickenson was one of the most popular lyceum lecturers of the 1860s and early 1870s, and she rose to national acclaim during the Civil War with her speeches supporting the Union cause.[37] "Whited Sepulchres" was developed for the lyceum after Dickenson and her brother took a trip west on the newly built Pacific Railroad and stopped in Salt Lake City. Being both "educational and entertaining," the "Whited Sepulchres" became Dickenson's major speech of the lecture season.[38]

After introducing listeners to the natural beauty of the Salt Lake Valley, Dickenson argued, "Fair indeed to the eye, pleasant to the traveler who knoweth not that the dead are there, and that her inhabitants are in the depths of Hell."[39] By creating a dissociation between the appearance and reality of Salt Lake City, Dickenson set the context for a second appearance/reality dissociation not grounded in a place but in the consciousness of the "oppressed."[40] She argued,

> "These women are satisfied, they are . . . contented; they not only desire no change but they laugh at and ridicule and sneer at their so-called emancipators." That is what can be said to me in Salt Lake City, that is what can be said to me here, and being said to me, I answer, "Granted; it is true; but what is proven thereby? That there are human beings too ignorant to know they are wronged, too debased to feel, too careless to inquire, too happy in servitude to know that freedom holds aright better for them—all this I grant you, but not that wrong is right." The very argument urged *for* is the strongest *against*, since there was no more hideous feature of slavery than the degradation that hugged the chain; discontent was its noblest attribute.[41]

The circularity of Dickenson's argument made any counter nearly impossible, and Dickenson reinforced her conclusion through specific examples of women whom she was able to enlighten enough so that they realized their own oppression. The initiation of each story began with the exclamation, "Contented!," which functioned to highlight the distinction between the appearance and reality of contentment in the minds of the oppressed as Dickenson implicitly asked her audience to question what the reality of contentment looked like.

While Mormon polygamy entered into the American imagination under the guise of entertainment, it quickly became an ongoing public controversy. Much of the public debate mirrored literature and speeches, arguing that polygamy was based in corruption and that most Mormons did not truly like the corrupting force of the institution. Much like Anna Dickenson's lecture, this knowledge was often represented as emerging through travel to Salt Lake City and experience with the Mormons.[42] The structure of the travel narrative both privileged personal observation and suggested that Salt Lake City was an exotic location or geographic space where the Other resided. To illustrate the pervasiveness of understanding Mormons as exotic Others, some writers of travel narratives expressed surprise over how much the Mormons resembled those on the east coast of the United States. Nevertheless, those same writers universally condemned polygamy, and for many the resemblance to other Americans simply masked the moral depravity of the LDS Church.[43]

The opposition to polygamy was commonly constructed as inevitable and natural given the perception of inherent corruption of the LDS religion. For example, "Mormonism is founded upon ignorance and licentiousness,"[44] and, "Adultery, fornication, prostitution, incest, are not changed in nature by calling them something else."[45] A Utah judge argued that Mormonism "enforces the systematic degradation of women, not only permits, but orders, the commission of the vilest lusts, in the name of Almighty God himself, and teaches that it is a sacred duty to commit the crimes of theft and murder."[46] Within this frame, the freedom of religious practice needed to be balanced with public good (liberty and license), and public good was often represented through the trope of home, a symbol of purity and sanctuary. One author reported, "Mother and daughter are often wives of the same man. The jealousies between the wives, make inevitable discords in the polygamous family. The children breathe a vitiated air; there is no privacy—no oneness of sentiment—no home."[47] Critics expressed concern over polygamy as outrage about sexual deviation, extending sentimental tropes of the novel to newspaper reports and public framing of the controversy.

Just as the raw emotion surrounding polygamy seemed to be the driving force of the public controversy, the evidence of harm was also grounded in descriptions of Mormons' corporeality that were used to support the construction of LDS followers as a lesser race. Based on personal observations, descriptions of Mormon women and children's behaviors and bodies functioned to legitimize the moral outrage about polygamy. One reporter explained, "The women, however, with very few exceptions, are coarse-featured, and wear a careworn, if not dissatisfied expression, which indicates a spirit-within totally at variance with the creed of polygamy, and which nothing but masculine authority supported by the power of 'the Church' could effectually curb."[48] Similarly, in its account of a lecture delivered by Mrs. C. V. Waite, the *Chicago Tribune* reported, "Mormon wives were the most miserable and heart-broken women she [Mrs. Waite] ever saw. Their fate was awful. The children were coarse and ignorant; young men were gamblers and drunkards, and the young women were looking out for a good match in the person of some other woman's husband."[49] These descriptions assumed not only that the outward body was a reflection of the inside (a decrepit body was evidence of a decrepit soul), but also that the bodies of individual women synecdochically represented the moral decay of the religion as a whole and the threat of national corruption.

Each of these depictions—immoral practices, decrepit bodies, abused women, the exotic place—participated to rhetorically constitute the Mormons as Other. The public controversy about polygamy was about more than pity over miserable women and children; it came to symbolize a conflict between the civilized world and the barbarous Other. While the Republican Party called polygamy (along with slavery) one of the "twin relics of barbarism," the theme of the barbarous Other also manifested in newspaper coverage over the controversy. The Mormons were labeled as "ignorant and stupid people"[50] and heathens,[51] and were described as practicing "no other or higher order of bestiality than any other form of indiscriminate lust."[52] Critics conceptualized the harm as an epic struggle that extended beyond individual Mormon families. One newspaper explained, "All history shows that the fundamental distinction between different grades of mankind, the savage, barbarous, and civilized, grows out of the relation of the sexes."[53] Similarly, in a speech before the House of Representatives,

J. Randolph Tucker argued, "Introduce polygamy, and we turn back the dial of our destiny—we obliterate the Christian era, and return from the light and glory of to-day to the gloom and barbarism of two thousand years ago!"[54] Thus, nothing less than civilization itself was at stake.

The popular imagination of the United States relied on both the dichotomy between "civilized" and "barbarian" and the myth of American exceptionalism to justify colonialism and American expansion.[55] Mormon polygamy was an especially strong marker of barbarism because of its association with Orientalism and, even more specifically, with popular American conceptions of the harem. Just as the comparison to slavery was explicit, so too was the comparison to the harem.[56] Because the Orient was thought to be the home of the barbarous Other, some assumed that the West must "dominate" and control the Orientals.[57] The commonality of polygamy created a rhetorical connection between the Orient and the land of the Mormons, calling for the need to control and dominate the Mormons as barbarous Others.[58]

In addition to being perceived as a moral threat to civilization, the Mormons posed a physical and economic threat in their potential armed opposition to US regulation of polygamy. The failed 1855 "Mormon War" was widely remembered throughout the long conflict over polygamy, and many Americans remained concerned about the potential cost of life (especially after the Civil War) and the tremendous potential monetary costs of an armed conflict.[59] Just as travel narratives placed Salt Lake City as an exotic location and polygamy as the marker of that location's barbarism, the threat of war built on perceptions of difference. For example, in commenting about Salt Lake City's July 4th celebration, one reporter positioned the celebration ironically and argued, "They are as independent of the United States as Russia is. They hate us and our government with a perfect hatred."[60] In attempting to dissuade Congress from considering Utah statehood, Judge Cradlebaugh argued that the state of Utah would be Brigham Young and the "people of Utah have nothing but ill will towards our Government."[61] The language stressed difference, explicitly marking "us" and "them." Polygamy, then, became the wedge between civilized "us" and barbarous Other, and the potential of war made the Other dangerous.

POLYGAMY AND POLITICS

As opposition to polygamy entered into the public imagination, the issue was addressed in a wide variety of political contexts and came to be implicated in some of the most volatile issues of the day. Polygamy was tackled in congressional debates, presidential speeches, legal decisions, and divisions in the woman's rights movement, and in each of these instances, rather than simply standing on its own, polygamy became a lens through which to understand other significant public issues. Questions of public morality became masked by a variety of other issues as polygamy entered into American politics, and the public regulation of the marriage bed became a significant source of political strife.

Politicians

Polygamy was critical to the formation of the Republican Party as a third party in the 1850s when the party assumed the platform of eliminating the "twin relics of barbarism": polygamy and slavery. While slavery had long been a controversy, the rhetorical framing of polygamy solidified the identity of the party and made slavery seem worse, and there was less political danger in attacking polygamy. Therefore, while slavery was an intrinsic evil to some, polygamy formed the crux of broad unification because it ran counter to common conceptions of American identity. In other words, deviant sexual practice rhetorically functioned as the baseline marker of barbarism, and in the 1850s and 1860s the analogy of polygamy as slavery worked to shift perceptions of slavery from a problematic institution to barbarous and anti-American.

While the analogy between polygamy and slavery constructed a dichotomy between civilized American and barbarous Other, the two issues raised similar legal concerns—namely, the extent of government regulation in the face of local opposition. The *New York Times* reported that Brigham Young drew on the analogy between slavery and polygamy as a defense of polygamy, apparently forgetting, as the *New York Times* argued, "that Utah is not and never was a State of the Union."[62] The *New York Times* concluded that Utah would not and should never become a state until polygamy was eliminated.[63] Indeed, Utah first applied for statehood in 1849 and reapplied seven times until 1896, when Utah was finally admitted as the forty-fifth state in the Union. Utah statehood was granted only after then LDS president Woodruff issued a proclamation eliminating future polygamous marriages. Thus, quite literally, full citizenship became predicated on acceptable sexual practice.[64]

Justin Morrill, a prominent Republican from Vermont, was one of Congress' most vocal opponents of polygamy during the 1850s and 1860s. In an 1857 speech, Morrill represented Mormon women as abused and degraded, using a metaphor that positioned civilized women as being animalized by barbarous Mormon men.[65] His argument about degradation was grounded in an assumption of women's "natural" tendencies for monogamous love. Within this rhetorical framework, polygamy stripped women of what made them civilized, their morality as it was manifest in monogamy, and Morrill concluded that Congress had an obligation to act toward ending polygamy to save women.

Despite apparent support for antipolygamy legislation, Morrill's Antibigamy Act did not pass until 1862. In 1862 the bill passed with an overwhelming majority (with only two opposing votes) and was signed by President Lincoln.[66] The legislation "made bigamy a criminal offense in US territories, invalidated the Utah territorial laws that had sanctioned polygamy and had incorporated the Mormon church, and limited the real estate of a religious organization in the territories to $50,000."[67] The legislation provided the federal government with unprecedented power over private authority.[68] Only five years earlier the Supreme Court decided in *Dred Scott* that the federal government did not have authority to ban slavery in the territories, but with the Morrill legislation the federal government was going further to regulate religious practice and the structure of marriage in the territories. While the legislation was broadly popular, writers in the *New York Times* expressed concern with the policy. They suggested that the law would remain unenforced, which would embolden the Mormons' defiance of the law, or the law would prompt armed resistance and another national conflict, which the country could not afford.[69] Soon the law proved ineffectual because of its lack of enforcement mechanisms.

In 1869 three bills before Congress focused on the issue of the Mormons in Utah: a bill advocating the division of the Utah territory, a bill for the admission of Utah as a state, and a bill proposing women's suffrage in Utah.[70] That year Congress considered "A Bill to discourage polygamy in Utah by granting the right to suffrage to the women of that Territory," and although the federal legislation did not pass, the territorial legislature adopted women's suffrage, making Utah only the second territory (or state) to allow women's suffrage.[71] The purpose of the federal legislation was explicit in both the title and congressional debates—the elimination of polygamy in Utah.[72] If women were oppressed and degraded by the laws of polygamy, they would, presumably, vote to eliminate the practice. The LDS Church, on the other hand, supported suffrage in the hopes that the female vote would increase its political power. When Mormon women ultimately voted with male members of the LDS Church, antipolygamy advocates faced the dilemma of either admitting that their assessment of women's oppression was wrong or labeling Mormon women as so oppressed that they failed to recognize their own oppression. Most antipolygamy advocates chose the latter option. Thus, women's suffrage in Utah came to be understood by many as counterproductive legislation that simply increased the power of polygamous men—the more wives one had, the more votes one had.[73]

The political and economic power of the church was clearly a concern in Congress, as evidenced by the proposed legislation in 1867 that attempted to break up the territory of Utah such that it became too small to attain statehood. Nevertheless, public rhetoric framed the political and economic power of LDS through the lens of polygamy. The *New York Times* stated in reference to the legislation on territorial boundaries, "Polygamy is thus treated like a doomed wild beast, —not, indeed, attacked in his lair, but surrounded with a fatal circle of fire."[74] Polygamy had become the defining characteristic of the Mormon identity, and legislators attempted to eliminate polygamy through a variety of direct and indirect actions. In doing so, Congress rhetorically constructed a framework of a distinctly American morality connected to the symbolic woman. Women were expected to be moral, and that morality was judged primarily through "proper" sexual behavior. Men were obligated to protect women's sexual morality, and a failure to do so was marked as barbaric and anti-American. These moral concerns were deemed so important to the nation that they were used to justify an unprecedented expansion of federal power. In a time when the limits of federal power were hotly debated and became a significant catalyst of national conflict in the Civil War, it is telling that federal regulation of marriage and religious practice elicited so little controversy. The rhetoric suggests that marriage practice was so intimately connected to American identity that federal regulation of polygamy was considered protection of Americans from the threat of a barbarous Other, rather than an invasion of the private marriage bed.

Courts

After the passage of the Poland Act of 1874 the federal government stepped up attempts to prosecute Mormon polygamists, and LDS leaders decided to initiate a test case in an attempt to challenge antipolygamy legislation. George Reynolds, a mild-mannered thirty-two-year-old with only two wives, was selected to initiate the test case.[75] His selection was strategic because he defied the stereotype of the elderly lecher with a large harem of wives, and LDS leaders were confident that they were on the right side of the legal issues. Nevertheless, the legal strategy was extremely risky. Without church cooperation, polygamy was virtually impossible to prove, and, as a result, there were very few polygamy convictions both before and after the Reynolds case. By offering himself for a test case, Reynolds could have provided the end to polygamy prosecutions, but he also risked jail time and the well-being of his wives and children.

Reynolds v. United States was argued before the US Supreme Court in 1878 and featured well-known Democratic lawyer George Washington Biddle, who was hired by the LDS Church, and Republican attorney general Charles Devens, who personally argued for the government. The stakes were high because antipolygamy activism had inflamed passions across the country, and, legally, the Supreme Court was in the midst of negotiating the limits and obligations of federal power following Reconstruction. Thus, *Reynolds* was sure to have implications for the antipolygamy movement but could also change legal precedent in a wide variety of other contexts.

Reynolds' lawyer raised several procedural issues before the Supreme Court, including issues of jury selection and a problem with the subpoena for Reynolds' second wife. However, the weightiest issues challenged the constitutionality of the Morrill Act. Biddle argued that the act violated Article 4, Section 3, giving Congress authority to "make all needful rules and regulations respecting the territory" of the United States. The Morrill Act, Biddle argued, went beyond the power of Congress by regulating local concerns of the marriage bed.

The Supreme Court appeared to adopt uncritically antipolygamy arguments in its decision upholding Reynolds' conviction and dodged most issues of federal power. "Marriage," Chief Justice Waite argued, "while from its very nature a sacred obligation, is nevertheless, in most civilized nations, a civil contract, and usually regulated by law. Upon it society may be said to be built, and out of its fruits spring social relations and social obligations and duties, with which government is necessarily required to deal."[76] Here, the Supreme Court established marriage as a foundation of civilization and, thus, subject to regulation by law. In doing so, however, the Court obfuscated the role of the federal government (as opposed to state and local governments) to make laws regulating marriage. Rather than directly engage the question of jurisdiction, Justice Waite shifted focus to the First Amendment and protection of religion, providing a lengthy historical account of religious freedom in the United States, concluding that "professed doctrines of religious belief" could not be "superior to the law of the land."[77] According to the Court, proper marriage practices provided a limit to individual rights because there was a national interest in preserving a monogamous conception of marriage.

While *Reynolds* had broad public support and reinvigorated the antipolygamy movement, it was controversial among lawyers and some individuals who questioned the power of the federal government to regulate marriage in opposition to local sentiments. One author criticized the decision as harming "many thousands of loyal citizens whose nuptial bonds, personal liberties, domestic rights, legitimacy and title to inherit" would be impacted by the ruling, and the author argued that the decision opened the door to unprecedented federal control over domestic relations.[78] The consensus held that something unique existed about marriage that necessitated critical attention. In the years following *Reynolds*, several voices questioned the power of the federal government to legislate morality, often arguing that conceptions of morality were grounded in community and that the Supreme Court should have considered the norms of the local community in its decision.[79] These statements of fact clearly ran counter to federal law and the Supreme Court decisions, but the controversy also illustrates a failure of stasis because while antipolygamy activists focused on the evils of polygamy, legal opposition questioned congressional jurisdiction. As a result, opposition to antipolygamy legislation never gained public traction because opponents failed to engage the questions of public morality that usurped abstracted legal issues.[80] Antipolygamy forces assumed that the nation itself was at risk, and, thus, they had an obligation to act despite any questions of federal power.

Notwithstanding some pockets of concern, a wave of antipolygamy legislation moved through Congress in the 1880s, including the Edmunds Act and the Edmunds-Tucker Act, which jailed suspected polygamists, established "unlawful cohabitation" as a federal crime, prohibited men from serving on juries if the potential juror believed polygamy to be "right," and disenfranchised men and women for "cohabitation."[81] Between "1884 and 1895 there were more than a thousand convictions of polygamous Mormons for bigamy, polygamy, unlawful cohabitation, adultery, and incest," involving about nine hundred different men.[82] Cohabitation came to be defined so broadly that Mormon attempts at evasion were no longer successful, and many of the LDS leaders went into hiding to escape arrest. Nevertheless, the large number of arrests and convictions unified the LDS community against the law.[83] The aggressive federal campaign against polygamy ended only with LDS president Woodruff's manifesto purportedly ending polygamy in the LDS Church.

Woman Suffrage

Although opposition to polygamy was widespread in the United States, women's movements had a complex relationship with the issue that tended to map into movement divisions. The story of post–Civil War divisions in the woman's suffrage movement is fairly well known. Although there were numerous divisions among suffragists during this period, the formalized split into the National Woman's Suffrage Association (NWSA) and American Woman's Suffrage Association (AWSA) in 1869 is often attributed to disagreement about the insertion of the word "male" into the Constitution with the passage of the Fourteenth Amendment.[84] Nevertheless, the divisions were much more profound.

Congressperson George Julian's proposed bill in 1869 to enfranchise women in Utah for the purposes of suppressing polygamy reflected a commonly held assumption that, given the opportunity, women would eliminate polygamy. Although the bill did not pass, the Mormon-dominated territorial legislature passed suffrage for women in 1870, and, in this case, Utah reflected the norms of several western territories (including Wyoming, Idaho, and Colorado) that adopted suffrage for women in the nineteenth century.[85] In the specific case of Utah, LDS leaders supported woman suffrage as they began to see Mormon women as an important ally to the church position on polygamy, and the territorial governor supported suffrage in the hope that Mormon women would vote to eliminate polygamy.[86]

Prior to the passage of suffrage, the relationship of women's movements to polygamy and the LDS Church was largely antagonistic. Anna Dickenson's vehement opposition to polygamy was well known, and her speech "Whited Sepulchres" was published in Stanton and Anthony's *The Revolution*. Further, Dickenson had close ties to many women speakers and activists, and she was a close friend of Susan B. Anthony's.[87] However, Utah's suffrage law made the relationships more complex. In 1871 Stanton and Anthony visited Salt Lake City during their tour of the western territories. They spoke several times at locations throughout the city, including the Tabernacle, and Stanton considered the high point of the trip to be a five-hour meeting with Mormon women in the Tabernacle.[88]

On one hand, Stanton and Anthony's support for Utah woman suffrage is not surprising given that their commitment to suffrage had led them to other controversial associations (such as with George Train and Victoria Woodhull). Although woman suffrage organizations clearly opposed polygamy, Stanton and Anthony sustained a broad-based critique of patriarchy in marriage and organized religion, and in this context, polygamy was just as problematic as other marriages and religious institutions.[89] On the other hand, many Mormon men and women were deeply skeptical of Stanton and Anthony's radicalism. For the most part, these Mormon women had expressed no desire to challenge polygamist family structures.

Stanton and Anthony's NWSA branch of the woman's movement typically addressed the disconnect between their support for suffrage and opposition to polygamy by simply ignoring the issue of polygamy. Instead, many NWSA activists upheld Utah as an exemplar of woman's suffrage activism. In their seminal The History of Woman Suffrage, Anthony and Harper praised Emmeline Wells as a leader of women's rights in Utah, and they chronicled the struggle to keep suffrage rights for women and to reinstate those rights once they were abolished.[90] Anthony and Harper even applauded Wells' journal the *Woman's Exponent* as a leading journal advocating for women. Emmeline Wells began as editor of the *Woman's Exponent* in 1877 and continued as such until 1914.[91] *The History of Woman Suffrage*, however, simply excluded mention that Wells was not only a plural wife but also a strong advocate of polygamy. Indeed, the *Woman's Exponent* supported polygamy and the Mormon family structure more frequently and earnestly than suffrage. The erasure of critical details in the history of women in Utah rhetorically functioned to make Utah consistent with the authors' larger narrative of rights for woman in the United States. In short, Utah was represented as another state where women struggled to break barriers and where, due to tremendous work, they ultimately succeeded.[92]

AWSA, headed by Lucy Stone, was fairly consistent in its opposition to polygamy. The *Woman's Journal*, an AWSA journal, published sensationalist stories from antipolygamy activists in Utah.[93] Not only did AWSA shun Mormon women, but also the leaders argued that Stanton and Anthony's relationship with the Mormons discredited the woman suffrage movement as a whole. Thus, AWSA developed connections with the Ladies' Anti-polygamy Society (later called the Woman's National Anti-polygamy Society), and although their stance on polygamy was clear, the Ladies' Anti-polygamy Society members were divided in their opinion of suffrage. While many of the leaders of the organization supported suffrage and the connections with AWSA, other women affiliated with the antipolygamy group supported eliminating suffrage for women in Utah in the hope of eliminating polygamy.[94]

The relationships between women's organizations and polygamy became even more complicated as the Woman's Christian Temperance Union (WCTU) and home protection initiatives gained prominence within national women's movements. The WCTU was an immensely powerful organization, and its platform for woman rights was grounded in traditional values of womanhood such that the organization had broad-based support. Despite rhetorical similarities between home protection advocates and Mormon women (privileging of the home, children, sobriety, and morality), the WCTU strongly opposed Mormon polygamy as immoral and destructive to the home, and, as a result, connections between Mormon women and members of women's movements became even more tenuous into the 1880s.[95]

The broad rhetorical salience of the polygamy issue in the nineteenth century illustrates the home as a core site of public morality. The issue inflamed public passions when slavery could not. It pushed some suffrage advocates to question suffrage and intensified movement divisions. Polygamy even provided the grounds for broadly supported expansions of federal power in the wake of the Civil War that divided the country over, in part, the same issue. Polygamy opposition became an issue that unified nearly the entire country at a time of a great division, and the symbolic woman functioned as the common rhetorical trope across this debate. The morality of the home synecdochically represented the morality and, thus, sustainability of the nation as a whole. To be a true American, then, citizens became obligated to protect the traditional patriarchal structure of family, and the tenuous line between individual liberty and dangerous licentiousness came to be rhetorically grounded in the seemingly private space of the home and proper performance of its residents.

PURE, PIOUS, AND POLYGAMOUS

Mormon men actively defended polygamy from the beginning of the controversy, but, with very few exceptions, the arguments from Mormon men became quickly dismissed because these men, many non-Mormons reasoned, profited from the power of the church and the corruption of women.[96] This is precisely why Mormon women needed to speak in defense of polygamy, but in several respects they were in an almost insurmountable double bind.[97] First, the role of women in public culture in the nineteenth-century United States limited the types of ways that women could acceptably enter into the public sphere. Thus, while Mormon women were the only credible source to counter claims of oppression, they had to be careful about the ways in which they defended marriage practices because violations of norms of womanhood would simply function as proof of their degradation and corruption. Second, as Mormon women began to defend polygamy, opponents of polygamy responded with a false consciousness argument stating that Mormon women were simply too degraded to recognize the harm of polygamy. As a result, Mormon women's defense of polygamy simply came to be turned around and used as evidence of oppression. Clearly, Mormon women faced a difficult rhetorical challenge.

In January of 1854, shortly after the public announcement of polygamy, Belinda Marden Pratt wrote a letter to her sister in New Hampshire responding to her sister's concerns over the LDS Church. Belinda Marden Pratt was born in 1820 and was the youngest of fourteen children. After her conversion to the LDS Church in 1843, her first marriage ended and her relationship with her family became strained, especially her relationship with Lydia, the sister with whom she had been especially close.[98] In 1844 Belinda Pratt became the plural wife of Parley P. Pratt. At the time of the letter, Pratt's husband had seven other living wives and a total of twenty-five children (four of whom were born to Belinda Pratt).

The letter was published as a pamphlet titled "Defense of Polygamy by a Lady of Utah" and came to represent one of the earliest examples of Mormon women speaking in defense of polygamy. In a letter Parley Pratt expressed approval of his wife's pamphlet, stating, "Your letter is of world-wide notoriety. It has appeared in a number of Newspapers, and finally in the Millennial Star. It convinces or shuts the mouths of all. . . . The Governors Br. here read it, and remarks that the whole foundation of society was wrong, and needed revolutionizing."[99] The pamphlet was reprinted in newspapers and books across the country and reached a tremendously wide audience.[100]

The form of the letter was rhetorically important. Even though this came to be a public document in the sense that the letter was published and circulated, a letter was ostensibly a private form of communication. It provided an illusion that the audience was peeking in and observing a private conversation between two sisters. Thus, Pratt did not seem to violate norms of womanhood by speaking or writing publicly on the issue, helping to sustain her womanly credibility for her audience.[101]

Pratt primarily defined her identity as religious and womanly. After exchanging pleasantries, she began the letter by asking, "Are we not all bound to leave this world, with all we possess therein, and reap the reward of our doings *here* in a never ending hereafter?"[102] She followed with an extensive argument about why polygamy was the truth as dictated by God. Pratt referred to Abraham, Isaac, Jacob, and King David, and concluded, "To sum up the whole then, I find that polygamists were the friends of God."[103] In some ways this religious justification was not unusual—it had been repeated by many Mormon men and regularly preached to LDS adherents. Nevertheless, Pratt's use of rhetorical questions functioned as an expression of commonality. The rhetorical questions invited the audience into a dialogue and led them to the conclusions that Pratt was suggesting. Pratt emphasized the Old and New Testaments (especially the Old) and did not preach from the *Book of Mormon*. These stylistic choices clearly fit within the constraints of women's speech—sharing instead of preaching, and a relationship of commonality with her audience instead of superiority.[104] At the same time, however, Pratt implied that the Mormons were closer to God. She said, "All those who do not become members of it [the polygamic family] . . . are strangers and aliens to the convent of promise."[105] True piety, then, was a choice, and Pratt rhetorically presented herself as an embodiment of piety. She was represented as more pious and, therefore, more womanly than her sister, who represented the Gentile (non-Mormon) woman stubbornly refusing to abide by the word of God.

In addition to drawing on God's law, Pratt also utilized what she called "nature's law" in her defense of polygamy by arguing that procreation was the natural purpose of marriage. Pratt's understanding of marriage was consistent with cultural assumptions of womanhood, but this strategic framing of marriage also allowed Pratt to claim, "Polygamy then . . . tends directly to the chastity of women, and to the sound health and morals in the constitutions of their offspring."[106] Pratt's representation of natural law defined marriage as a coupling for procreation and ascribed the value of procreation as a priority, which implicitly constituted the identity of women in relation to their procreative role. If the audience accepted this framing, then polygamy made sense because it enabled greater procreation and the fulfillment of women's "natural" roles. Further, the rhetoric of women's procreative role as "natural" functioned to remove choice and create a sense of inevitability. Thus, Pratt represented rejection of polygamy as a failure of women's natural roles.

While challenges to polygamy conceptualized the practice as oppressive to women and contrary to women's natural characters, Pratt appropriated cultural assumptions of women's identity and positioned polygamy as a fulfillment of women's role. Pratt closed the letter by stating, "Dear sister, do not let your prejudices and traditions keep you from believing the Bible; nor the pride, shame, or love of the world keep you from your seat in the kingdom of heaven, among the royal family of polygamists."[107] Instead of Pratt's sister praying for Belinda Pratt's redemption, Belinda Pratt ended by praying for her sister's redemption. The "dear sister" represented all Gentile women, while Pratt represented both the Mormon woman and the proper woman. Pratt's appropriation of true womanhood characterized the identity of Mormon women as culturally idealized women rather than oppressed.

Pratt's letter was only the beginning of Mormon women's public defense of polygamy. In March of 1886, about two thousand Mormon women held a mass meeting at the Salt Lake Theater to protest the Edmunds-Tucker Act. Following the meeting, the women published a nearly one-hundred-page pamphlet, titled " 'Mormon' Women's Protest: An Appeal for Freedom, Justice and Equal Rights," that included a copy of their memorial to Congress, speeches, statements by women, and poems.[108] While certainly dramatic, the 1886 meeting was not an isolated event. Similar meetings had occurred in Salt Lake City and Provo, Utah, and women published their defenses of polygamy in LDS periodicals such as the *Woman's Exponent* and *Juvenile Instructor*.[109] Newspapers across the country reported these meetings, and the *New York Times* called an 1870 meeting "novel . . . presenting the strange spectacle of Anglo-Saxon women contending for the divinity, purity and propriety of plural marriages."[110] These defenses of polygamy painted a complex picture of Mormon women's identities that drew on seemingly contradictory tropes: proper womanhood, rugged pioneer, American citizen, and transcendent beyond simply American. In the Mormon women's rhetoric, seemingly contradictory identities merged to form the emblematic American identity rooted in symbolic womanhood.

Much like Belinda Marden Pratt's earlier letter, "'Mormon' Women's Protest" maintained purity and proper womanhood as a dominant trope. Throughout the 1886 meeting the women rhetorically reinforced their identity as mothers and as women whose sensitivity and decency required protection. The memorial sent to Congress stated, "Womanhood is outraged by the compulsion used in the courts of Utah to force mothers on the pain of imprisonment to disclose their personal condition . . . in relation to anticipated maternity."[111] The memorial framed speaking of pregnancy or sex as a violation of proper womanhood, and the women enacted proper womanhood through their refusal to speak in court. Another woman at the meeting argued that the attack on polygamous families was evidence of a "semi-barbarous state."[112] Thus, the Mormon women not only upheld themselves as models of true womanhood but also marked the men who attempted to enforce antipolygamy legislation as the threat to proper womanhood, shifting the label of barbarism from the Mormons to US government officials. Further, while public speech may ordinarily be unwomanly, Eliza Snow argued, "There is a point at which silence is no longer a virtue. In my humble opinion we have arrived at this point."[113] Thus, the Mormons framed themselves as having no choice but to speak, but they did so only within the constraints of proper womanhood by speaking humbly and virtuously.

Not only did Mormon women evoke conceptions of proper womanhood to create a new set of associations over Mormon women's identity, but also the repeated tropes of home and family in women's speech served this purpose. Dr. Romania Pratt, for example, heavily relied on the repeated tropes of "home circle" and "sanctity of home" to constitute a pure and domestic identity for the Mormon woman.[114] In a similar mass meeting in 1878 Mrs. Margaret T. Smoot argued,

> We are not a degraded community; we are not in abject slavery. We have our privileges and rights—just as many as I want, and as many as I know how to use. Let me repeat—we are not "degraded," neither are our children. We have the happiest of homes. I would be willing to compare my husband's family with anybody's family, to see what defect could be found in them.[115]

In short, Pratt, Smoot, and many other women from the LDS Church responded to the dilemma of their supposed oppression through building a set of associations that constituted their identities in accordance with the cultural expectations of proper womanhood. This strategy relied on both preexisting cultural ideals and a set of rhetorical associations that allowed the Mormon women to fit themselves within those ideals.

At the same time, however, LDS women rhetorically constituted their identity as rugged pioneer. The pioneer identity may seem antithetical to the proper woman because the pioneer was strong, rugged, and independent—everything the supposedly proper woman was not. Nevertheless, the pioneer identity was intimately connected to Mormon origin narratives. The Saints moved west, outside of US territory, to escape what they labeled as religious persecution after the murder of Joseph Smith. They stopped in the Salt Lake Valley because it was desolate and uninhabited, and they built Salt Lake City and surrounding communities as havens for their religious practice. This origin narrative was vital to the Mormon identity because it marked the Mormons as special people who overcame tremendous adversity, much like the Biblical exodus of the Jews. The LDS narrative of moving to a new home in search of religious freedom also paralleled the American origin narrative of pilgrims attempting to find religious freedom in the Americas, and the narrative placed the Mormons as the protagonists in the cultural myths.[116]

Despite the violent conditions forcing the Mormons' move west, the LDS women represented themselves as triumphing over adversity through the combination of pioneer spirit and womanly virtue. Eliza Snow explained that the Saints "came here when this land and soil belonged to Mexico, and who, through our faith, prayers and indefatigable labors, have assisted in reclaiming it—making it habitable and beautiful."[117] Thus, while the identity of the rugged pioneer may seem to differentiate the Mormons from "civilized" Americans, that identity represented the epitome of what it meant to be an American. Rather than challenging the Mormon women's ability to be proper "civilized" women, Snow rhetorically framed the Mormon woman as a pioneer who civilized or domesticated the rugged wilderness—a proper woman in the face of barbarity.

Just as the pioneer trope created differentiation, Mormon women utilized several other subtle markers of differentiation in their defense of polygamy. These markers functioned to represent Mormonism as a transcendent identity that was placed as primary before the identity of American. For example, in an 1886 mass meeting, Dr. Romania Pratt noted, "A mountain of evil . . . has been . . . heaped upon our people."[118] For Pratt, "*our* people" were not American citizens; they were the members of the LDS Church. This characterization placed the primary identity category as Mormon, and the Mormons were set in opposition to Americans. Indeed, she continued to argue that legislators' time would be better spent "making laws for the purifying of their own environments." Thus, not only were "*their* own environments" set in opposition to the environments of the Mormons, but also Pratt suggested that the Saints were more pure and moral than most Americans, especially corrupt and immoral politicians.

Further, Mormon women often represented Salt Lake City as an ethereal world apart. The *Woman's Exponent* painted a vivid picture of Zion as sacred and "a place of safety and refuge for the oppressed."[119] The author continued: "The Latter-day Saints came here that they might have religious freedom, and . . . the local political arrangements were the best that could be, for a people settling in a new country. But the time came when the prosperity and peace . . . was interrupted, and a series of trials and difficulties have arisen."[120] The physical location of Salt Lake City, surrounded by mountains in a new country (Mexico at the time), was used to represent the otherworldly quality of its inhabitants as a people who were separate from the immorality in most of America and closer to God. Zion rhetorically functioned as the shining city on the hill that was the embodiment of America's often failed potential.

Despite such differentiating moves, Mormon women at these mass meetings also appealed to their rights as Americans. The memorial that was sent to Congress after the 1886 mass meeting began, "Whereas, The rights and liberties of women are placed in jeopardy by the present cruel and inhuman proceedings in the Utah courts, and in the contemplated measure in Congress to deprive the women voters in Utah of the elective franchise. . . ."[121] Not only did the women portray the right to vote as core to women's identities as full citizens, but also the very act of congregating in mass meetings as a mode of social protest enacted women's roles as citizens. Mrs. Smith illustrated this enactment of citizenship when she ended her speech at the 1870 mass meeting by saying, "I say to you, my sisters, you are American citizens—let us stand by the truth if we die for it."[122] Further, suffrage was represented as not only a right but also a duty of women. An appeal in the *Woman's Exponent* stated, "It is the sacred duty of every woman who has the right of suffrage to go to the polls on election day and deposit her ballot. . . . It is not only the public duty, but it is an individual responsibility and one that no one can perform for his friend or neighbor, but must be done in person."[123] In the *Woman's Exponent*, Emmeline Wells praised the women involved in the 1886 mass meeting, stating, "It is the duty of every citizen of the United States to stand boldly forth in defense of freedom, justice and the rights of conscience."[124] This rhetoric of "rights" and "duty" makes sense only in the context of Mormon women's citizenship.

The women also explicitly adopted the American origin narrative as their own. Mrs. Wilmarth East referred to the Constitution as the document "for which our forefathers fought and bled and died."[125] Here the Saints claimed the US Constitution as their constitution. Just as those of other Americans had, their forefathers died for its creation and defense. Similarly, in her *Woman's Exponent* article, Emmeline Wells vividly recounted the sacrifice of the country's founders as one of the reasons that rights and liberties must be protected. However, for much of this depiction Wells did not reveal the identities of the "forefathers" she described, and the narrative mirrors Mormon origin narratives so closely that the parallel between the Saints and the American founders becomes striking. She noted,

> Our honored forefathers fought for the freedom of this goodly land, and our noble ancestors, the Pilgrim band, left home, kindred and the graves of their dead, and their native country, to find a place of refuge in which to worship God according to the dictates of their own consciences, enduring the perils of the mighty deep then unexplored, and of the wilderness, where savage Indians and beasts of prey had roamed unmolested from time immemorial. And when oppressed and tyrannized over by unjust men and taxed without representation by the nation that had refused to them the right to worship God in the way that seemed to them the best—they resisted it even to the imperiling of their lives in that great contest of which we are all so justly proud—the war of the Revolution.[126]

The florid language told a confused but typical narrative of the nation's founding, but prior to the last clause, where Wells introduced her referent as the Revolutionary War, she could easily have been talking about the LDS movement west out of the then borders of the United States to avoid religious persecution. Because the movement west was a customary element of the Mormon origin narrative, Wells' rhetorical structure of holding the referent to the end implicitly drew a connection between the plight of the Saints and the founding of the United States, suggesting that the Mormon story was a true American story.

These identities appear to be disparate—how could a Mormon woman be an American but also something beyond American, a true woman and a rugged pioneer? LDS women rhetorically constructed the Mormon identity as part of the mythic American identity. Mormon women framed themselves as more American than Gentile Americans, discovering a public rhetoric that challenged antipolygamy forces while embracing traditional norms of femininity. Mormon women's rhetoric drew on the frontier myth that was widely utilized by women in the west.[127] Yet Mormon women illustrate that western women's rhetoric may have been even more complex, unifying traditional eastern tropes of womanhood, national ideals of citizenship, and masculine pioneer myths. Despite its ultimate failure, the Mormon women's defense of polygamy exemplified the ways in which the rhetoric of marriage became implicated in identity and citizenship.

ELIMINATING POLYGAMY AND BECOMING AMERICAN

By the end of the nineteenth century, polygamists were disenfranchised, imprisoned, and fined. The 1888 Republican Party platform was explicit in both the party opposition to polygamy and the denial of Utah statehood until polygamy was eliminated.[128] With pressure against polygamy mounting and the church at risk of losing its property, in 1890 LDS president Woodruff announced that the LDS Church would abide by laws prohibiting polygamy.[129] In January of 1896, President Cleveland issued a proclamation admitting Utah to the Union as the forty-fifth state.[130] Thus, full citizenship of the people of Utah was predicated on the elimination of polygamy.

In addition to the literal connections between statehood and polygamy, the debate over polygamy made explicit the rhetorical connections between the symbolic woman and American identity. Thus, while polygamy appeared in some instantiations to be a controversy about the limits of federal power, freedom of religion, and private family concerns, the controversy was also about the true American identity. For many, the polygamous Mormons embodied all that was anti-American. Mormon women were thought to be abused and defiled, rather than revered as wives and mothers. Polygamy became equated in the public imaginary with slavery, the Oriental harem, and the barbarous Other. These were the very people that "real" Americans needed to eliminate.

For the most part, however, members of the LDS Church recognized what was at stake in the controversy. Just as marriage was never private for antipolygamy activists, Mormons viewed marriage as central to their religious expression; polygamy became a public instantiation of religious belief. In their defense of polygamy, the Mormon women attempted to embrace the identity of American, portraying themselves as true pioneers, true women, true followers of God, and the true embodiment of constitutional ideals. Nonetheless, the LDS Church eventually capitulated, and when it became clear that traditional marriage had become a litmus test for full American citizenship, the church (at least publicly) abandoned the practice of polygamy.

Even in failure, the Mormon rhetoric of polygamy illustrates the malleability of morality claims in public controversy. Nearly every participant in the polygamy controversy wanted to protect the symbolic woman and the home, and thus, the attempts to determine public morality reified those cultural expectations while subtly filtering those expectations through seemingly unrelated public issues such as federalism, slavery, and westward expansion. The public regulation of sexual practice, then, became intimately connected to meanings of "American" in the public imagination.

[4]

Free Love, Licentiousness, and Civic Identity

Love and marriage seem to go together. The association between these two concepts was common by the nineteenth century, and the rights and obligations of marriage were thought to provide a rational balance to the passion of romantic love.[1] Yet nineteenth-century free love advocates challenged the association between love and marriage, and for these advocates, love, passion, and sex emerged as markers of good citizenship.

Specific instantiations of free love changed over time. Prior to the Civil War, free love was primarily communal, and passion and sex constituted an important part of civic identity. After the Civil War, however, free love advocacy shifted to become more individualistic. For many of these free lovers, marriage represented state control and repressed the individual, so opposition to marriage was a form of a public resistance. Despite diversity even within general categories of free love, popular responses to free love rarely considered differences and frequently reduced free love to a symbol of licentiousness and social chaos. The long controversy over free love functioned as a lens for Americans to negotiate passionate and restrained models of citizenship. As a result, nineteenth-century free love was about more than sex; it was about the meanings and limits of "proper" American citizenship and public identity.

FREE LOVE AND THE POPULAR IMAGINATION

The rhetoric of opposition to free love was grounded in a set of dichotomies, all of which grew from the perceived divide between civilized and barbarian. In the popular imagination, free love functioned as a symbol of barbarity and chaos that existed within the contested space of what it meant to be an American. In part, this perception was grounded in an American context that privileged the value of self-control, and one place from which the value of self-control emerged was the Second Great Awakening.[2] By the nineteenth century, reform and revivalist cultures had spread across the United State's, and upstate New York, for example, came to be known as the burned-over district, using a metaphor of fire to understand the frequent and strong force of religious revivals.[3] Some of the most prominent religious leaders, such as Charles Finney, perhaps the best-known revival preacher of the time, taught that sin was a choice, and such a conception of sin demanded constant work toward piety.[4] Once Americans understood salvation and sin as choices, personal and social perfection became the ultimate goal. Religious leaders framed overcoming sin as an exercise in self-control, which came to be applied in many areas of life, including sex.[5]

In a culture that privileged self-restraint, Americans frequently represented sexual passion as an archaic emotion. Indeed, as early as 1820, cultural expectations demanded women's purity and passionlessness.[6] The cultural norm of women's purity extended to women's bodies and minds, and public rhetoric tended to represent purity through the lens of women's supposed piety. The conflation between women's purity and piety represented a larger cultural connection between religion and self-control that persisted throughout the rest of the century.[7] The Women's Christian Temperance Union (WCTU), founded in 1874, is a good example of the ways in which women's identities were both constrained and enabled by cultural norms of piety and purity. The WCTU was active in promoting the cause of social purity, a rhetorical extension of women's purity into the public sphere, and by 1890 the WCTU had about 150,000 dues-paying members.[8] The WCTU drew on calls for "home protection" and women's "mother-heart" to mobilize women's public advocacy in the name of protecting the traditional home.[9] In a context that framed sexual passion as physically, morally, and socially dangerous, intellectual love, Platonic love, and maternal love functioned as signs of cultural advancement and were more fitting with norms of proper womanhood.[10] Thus, ways of understanding love (self-restraint verses unrestrained passion) came to function as a litmus test for civilization.

Because free love challenged basic social expectations, popular responses to free love were almost universally negative and grounded in fear that free love was not simply about private behavior in the bedroom but about the state of the nation as a whole. For example, in what appeared to begin as a review of *Mary Lyndon*, a book written by Mary Sargeant Gove Nichols, a prominent author and lecturer, the *New York Times* provided an extensive critique of free love, filling almost the entire second page of the paper. *Mary Lyndon* was dangerous, the *New York Times* author claimed, because it fit within a larger "system" that threatened to destroy marriage.[11] This article revealed a slippage between free love, passion, destruction of marriage, and social collapse that was common in free love opposition. In some ways, the article read as typical fear mongering, but it was also indicative of a public rhetoric that posited a dichotomous view of passion and self-control, with self-control being what was thought to hold a civilized country together. Individual sexual practice functioned synecdochically to represent the possibility that society could practice control and thus continue to advance.

The *New York Times*, however, was not alone in its assessment. An editor of a small journal wrote in response to free lover Juliet Severance, "In plain terms it seems to us like an attempt to make of this grand and beautiful country a national brothel, constituting the legal heads of all departments of justice as keepers and defenders of the same."[12] The *Chicago Tribune* framed American free love as "an experiment of ignorance and fanaticism" and "a bitter experiment of error and wretchedness."[13] Arguments such as this were common and functioned to frame free love as moral licentiousness that ran the risk of pushing the entire country into depravity.

Perhaps nothing illustrated the larger cultural fear of free love more than frequent newspaper stories of "runaway wives." Newspapers were inundated with accounts of otherwise innocent wives that ran away for no apparent reason, left with a lover, and/or ran off to a free love community or brothel. The common theme among these stories was that unless runaway wives were "rescued" by generous husbands they would be trapped in a life of licentiousness. A *Chicago Tribune* account of one rescued wife noted that her story "should be a lesson to young married women and girls who cherish silly romantic notions."[14] The newspaper accounts rarely considered whether the wife wanted to be "rescued," and, instead, the runaway spouse was commonly portrayed as an innocent girl corrupted by the lure of free love. One 1874 pamphlet even framed free love literature as dangerous, assuming that the very act of reading free love literature had in the past and could continue to lure innocent young girls into lives of prostitution.[15] Similarly, the author recounted several instances where "freedomite men" assaulted young girls.[16] These anecdotes portrayed free love as a lure and a corrupting influence on the purity of women and the happiness of families. Notably, by framing adult women as innocent girls, critics of free love infantilized women and positioned them as incapable of reasoned choice.

"Runaway wives" were especially troubling because these wives were supposedly good women who represented the best of the country. In a world like the nineteenth-century United States, where women's primary cultural value was moral influence, free love was represented as not only corrupting individual women but also destroying the moral center of the nation. "Runaway wives" also illustrated a fear of contagion. If a good woman could be corrupted, then it stood to reason that anyone could be at risk. Free love was represented as the dark side of freedom, where freedom (licenses) without restraint was thought to lead to licentiousness. For critics of free love, individual licentiousness was threatening the moral center of the nation as a whole.

As free love represented a symbol of social chaos, it functioned as a lens for understanding some of the most heated controversies of the time. In this sense, the term "free love" did not necessarily coincide with a specific group or practice. Rather, "free love" functioned as a symbol (or shorthand) for attaching value to other issues. Democrats, for example, used free love to amplify the harm of abolition.[17] The influential Southern journal *DeBow's Review* argued that free love was a systematic effort by leaders of the Republican Party, utilizing the repetition of the word "free" to create the appearance of logical association ("free love, free lands, and free negroes").[18] The author slipped between free love, communism, abolition, woman's rights, divorce, and polygamy, not only creating a rhetorical association but also equating the level of harm among these issues. The journal portrayed each social and political issue as part of a system that threatened to dismantle a way of life. The North, then, became the epitome of all that the South had to fear, and free love was the symbol for that fear. Yet the author was ambiguous in the specific meanings of free love. For example, Horace Greeley, editor of the *New York Tribune*, was specifically named as an instigator. Greeley was certainly well known as opposing slavery, but he did not support expanded divorce laws, much less free love.[19] The *DeBow's* author continued by defining free love as divorce, followed by free love as polygamy; and by labeling Utah as "its interesting colony" ("it" referring to the North), the author implicitly framed the North as creating and condoning Utah polygamy. Further, the author labeled Stephen Pearl Andrews as an "abolitionist philosopher" in an attempt to further radicalize abolition. While Andrews began his career as an abolitionist, as did many free lovers, by 1860 he had become most well known as an anarchist and free lover.[20] By labeling Andrews' primary identity as abolitionist, the author framed free love and abolition as one and the same. Rather than "runaway wives" being evidence of abuse and inequities within marriage, Andrews' statistic that there were "ten runaway wives to one runaway negro" was used as evidence of the collapse of the family in the North due to free love. The broad associations in *DeBow's Review* were not particularly unusual. Free love commonly existed in the public imaginary as synonymous with licentiousness and social chaos, with the breakdown in self-control and marital order leading to a general social breakdown.[21] By associating free love with divorce, slavery, abolition, dress reform, or woman's suffrage, rhetors were attempting to appropriate the values and fear that free love represented.

Beyond social condemnation and the occasional prosecution for adultery, there were few ways to regulate the perceived threat of free love. Some level of public regulation of free love became possible when Anthony Comstock began a campaign against vice and obscenity backed by federal obscenity statutes that were known as the Comstock laws. In 1872 with the support of the Young Men's Christian Association (YMCA), Anthony Comstock founded the New York Society for the Suppression of Vice (NYSSV).[22] In 1883 Comstock continued his campaign against vice with the publication of *Traps for the*

Young, which went through several editions.[23] This book, Comstock explained, was "a plea for the moral purity of children," who should be kept pure by having their "appetites and passions controlled."[24] The dangers were vast, but Comstock made particular note of free love literature, which, he argued, "curses self-respect, moral purity, and holy living," causing "sure ruin and death."[25] Passion was represented as beginning a slippery slope to individual ruin, but Comstock also extended the harm of free love beyond the individual to American society as a whole, appealing to themes of social evolutionism in insisting that free love would make Americans like the Turks, who, for many Americans, were the epitome of the unchristian and uncivilized.[26] To remedy these harms, Comstock advocated federal legislation that regulated the distribution of obscenity through the mail for the purported purpose of protecting children.[27] Thus, Comstock appropriated many of the existing themes associated with free love opposition, but he was explicit in his articulation of the harm and had the backing of legislation. The 1874 arrests of Victoria Woodhull and Tennessee Claflin under the Comstock laws were highly publicized, and these arrests marked the beginning of an extensive campaign against free love advocates. Although the prosecution of Woodhull failed, Comstock was eventually successful in prosecuting several free love advocates, including publisher Moses Harman.[28]

A variety of social and institutional forces regulated women's behavior and limited the expansion of the free love movement in the nineteenth-century United States. Expectations of self-control and purity were in stark contrast with the public perception of free love as unrestricted lust and licentiousness. The fears of unrestrained passion in free love came to be rhetorically associated with many of the other social reform movements of the time, including abolition, woman's rights, and divorce, because each of these movements presented a challenge to the social order and norms of civic identity. Perhaps not surprisingly, popular responses to free love failed to recognize the dramatic differences in the theories and practices of free love. Both communal and individualistic advocates of free love grappled with issues of passion, rationality, religion, and self-restraint, and in doing so, these groups aligned their sexual practice to public expression of civic identity. Yet free lovers varied dramatically in their understanding of free love, practice of free love, and ideological assumptions behind the practice.

FREE LOVE AND CONSTITUTING COMMUNITY

Lust, passion, and sex do not seem to be markers of good citizenship. Yet in the late eighteenth through nineteenth centuries there were over one hundred utopian communities in the United States, many of which were grounded in a rhetorical association between sex and civic identity.[29] Utopian communities provided the opportunity for people to unify around common values while rejecting certain social norms. In the context of many nineteenth-century utopian communities, the privileging of personal agency in the Second Great Awakening prompted some to organize through a rhetoric of personal and social perfection that called individuals to find ways of becoming more perfect and closer to God. Further, American spiritualism, which grew rapidly prior to the Civil War, enabled what was often understood as empirical proof and a scientific basis for spiritual connections.[30]

The Oneida and Berlin Heights communities were only two of many, but they were particularly rhetorically significant. Both were used in the popular press as representations of free love communities. They were relatively long lasting, and both communities utilized rhetorical themes that were common among free love communities. Although the rhetorics of both groups posited free love as indispensable to civic identity, they did so in very different ways.

The Oneida Community

Based in the belief of the possibility for human perfection, John Humphrey Noyes' Oneida Community became perhaps the single most successful utopian community in American history. The community greeted over 45,000 visitors between 1862 and 1867 alone and grew in the number of members from 87 in 1849 to 215 in 1867.[31] While most utopian communities failed after only a couple of years, Oneida lasted until 1879, when Noyes succumbed to external pressure and advised members to end their unique experiment with marriage. The end of Oneida marriage practices led to the end of socialism within the community in 1880, instead creating a joint-stock company, and the eventual dissolution of the community itself.[32]

John Noyes was born to a respectable New England family in 1811.[33] While studying law in 1831 Noyes was converted by the revival preacher Charles Finney and changed his career path from law to the ministry.[34] After studying at Yale, Noyes began to preach a doctrine of perfection so radical that he was denied ordination.[35] Other perfectionists, Robert Owen, Charles Fourier, the Shakers, and other utopian communities influenced Noyes, and he began a small utopian community in his home of Putney, Vermont, in 1841.[36] By 1846 the community had adopted a system of "complex marriage," where every member was married to every other member, which so horrified Putney residents that in 1848 Noyes and his followers fled to Oneida, an isolated area in upstate New York.[37]

What was particularly unique with the Oneida perfectionists was that they explicitly connected their religious, familial, and civic identities, grounding sex and family, often thought to be private, as a core marker of civic identity. In doing so, they formed what they called an "association." That is, the Oneida Community recognized themselves as a group of people who voluntarily came together under particular rules, expectations, and beliefs. The label of "association" marked the Oneida Community as a type of public.[38] The Oneida Association's "First Annual Report" rationalized the bases for the association, establishing the community on both a rhetoric of passion and scientific rationality that held sex as central to the group's public identity.

Passion was a defining characteristic of the Oneida identity, a characteristic that was expected of both men and women. However, the rhetorical framing of passion attempted to reassess the cultural value, positioning passion as essential, moral, and potentially consistent with self-restraint. For example, the First Annual Report of the Oneida Association stated, " 'We are required to love one another fervently' (1 Peter 1:22), or, as the original might be rendered, burningly. The fashion of the world forbids a man and woman who are otherwise appropriated, to love one another burningly—to flow into each other's hearts. But if they obey Christ they must do this."[39] The author was not referring to a simply Platonic love; rather, sexual passion was framed as an expression of piety and a way to become closer to God. Here, not only women were passionate but also men, and this passion was a virtue rather than a vice. Although Oneida women were expected to be pious, sexual passion certainly defied larger cultural expectations of purity, which was commonly understood as the only appropriate sex being for the purposes of procreation.

Indeed, rather than exalting procreation, the Oneida Community framed procreation as a limit to individual development and, thus, becoming closer to God. For men, procreation was thought to be a disease-causing drain, and childbirth and child care were thought to "heavily tax the life of women."[40] While these concerns were expressed as scientific and pragmatic, the Oneida Community also expressed a religious concern. The community's First Annual Report posited frequent procreation as part of God's response to the fall, and, thus, the ideal for humanity living in the original state would have been infrequent procreation.[41] As a result, sexual passion became understood as a way to become closer to God, but procreation was limited by Noyes' system of "male continence"—that is, the prevention of male ejaculation. This type of limitation was thought to eliminate the selfishness of sexual passion, enabling a godly expression of passion in sex without the risk of conception. The community, then, limited procreation to instances that were deemed scientifically beneficial.[42] Rather than arguing from the cultural dichotomy between passion and self-restraint, the Oneida Community implicitly challenged that dichotomy by positing certain expressions of sexual passion as an exercise in morality and rational self-restraint.

Sexual passion was also considered a sign of developmental advancement. The First Annual Report explained that the use of sexual organs for amative purposes was what placed people "above the brutes."[43] Male continence, according to Noyes, was the ultimate exercise in self-restraint, further advancing human civilization.[44] Thus, while the community embraced the trope of developmental advancement, they challenged understandings of sexual purity as a marker of that advancement and associated individual spiritual growth with social and biological evolution. Similarly, in the Oneida Community's journal one author stated, "Communism requires a high order of civilization and education, such as is rarely produced by ordinary society in its present state. It demands trained and civilized passions; it demands spiritual and bodily purity; it demands the subordination of one to another as the preliminary to complex social and business organization."[45] From this, it is clear that Oneida self-identified as highly advanced, and passion and purity were markers of that advancement. Yet understandings of passion and purity deviated from conventional understandings of the time when passion was commonly held as dichotomous from self-control, as was purity from nonprocreative sex.

The privileging of sexual passion over procreation led to dramatic challenges to marriage in the Oneida Community. Members challenged traditional marriage and replaced it with what they labeled as "communal marriage." The First Annual Report framed marriage as an artificial construction and not ordained by God.[46] The exclusive union of one man and one woman and "possessive feelings" within that union were thought to subvert the union with God.[47] Instead, communal marriage created a marital union between all members of the community. As a result, members understood the Oneida Community as characterized by both traditionally public markers of associations (decision-making processes, social and political gathering, and a common identity) and what was typically hidden (marriage and sexual relationships). The identity of the community and its members became understood through the lens of marriage and sex.

Given their dramatic reformulation of marriage, it is not surprising that the Oneida Community attempted to reform traditional gendered divisions. Changes in sexual and marital practice reverberated through just about every aspect of life. When women were no longer publicly understood through their identity via coverture, the division of labor within separate spheres ideology was necessarily challenged. The First Annual Report explained, "When the partition between the sexes is taken away, and man ceases to make woman a propagative drudge, when love takes the place of shame, . . . men and women will mingle in all their employments, . . . and then labor will be attractive."[48] Such a reformulation makes sense given the context of Oneida's challenges to marriage. In the context of coverture, marriage provided the social and economic rationale for separate spheres of the sexes, marking women as invisible within the public. Communal marriage, however, made marriage and sex an expression of publicness, necessarily a concern for both men and women. Despite the Oneida Community stance on gender equity, the "principal" work of women tended to fit squarely within traditional labor divisions.[49]

In dissociating sexuality from procreation, the Oneida Community also challenged connections between motherhood and civic identity. Rather than exalting motherhood, the Oneida Perfectionists framed motherhood as a burden. The community responded to the perceived burden by removing children from their mothers and raising those children communally. The report explained that the "only" problem arising from this arrangement was the initial emotionalism of the mothers.[50] On one hand women's civic identities were not defined primarily through child rearing. On the other hand, however, maternal passion was seen as a detriment and trivialized as "melo-dramatic." Thus, only some types of passion (in sex and toward God) were deemed acceptable, and the unacceptable passion was typically associated with women. Indeed, women who showed too much attachment to their children were described as "sickly." The Oneida Community placed a scientific distance between themselves and traditionally womanly emotions while exalting a new type of sexual emotional passion that had an appearance of gender neutrality.

The Oneida Perfectionists created an association between civic, religious, and sexual identities, all of which became manifest in enactments of marriage. Indeed, the problems of conventional marriage were deemed the root of many of the core problems of the country. One Oneida member argued,

> At the present time the great destroyers of the manhood and the womanhood of the nation are false love and sexual abuse. We have found in Communism a cure for both these evils, and the cure has come through the application of these discoveries—by subjecting the affections to the truth—by making sexual intercourse safe and beneficent. If society can be brought to the adoption of them, it will enter on the true preparation for Communism and will advance at railroad speed toward the kingdom of heaven.[51]

Notably the Oneida conceptions of communism and marriage reform were rooted in Christianity. Notions of Christian perfectionism were inseparable from the Oneida civic and social identity. Thus, even though the Oneida Community initially used the term "free love" and critics commonly equated them with free love communities, members of the Oneida community were careful to draw distinctions between themselves and other notable free love communities (such as Berlin Heights) that, as an Oneida member implied, engaged in "whoredom" as opposed to the "marriage" of Oneida members.[52]

Berlin Heights

While Oneida was rhetorically significant in the free love controversy, in practice it was exceptional in both its longevity and its notoriety. The free love community at Berlin Heights, Ohio, was both rhetorically significant and more ideologically typical of mid-nineteenth-century utopian communities. Ohio in the 1850s was a "seedbed for reform activism," and after the economic panic of 1857 many Americans became open to radicalism and utopian socialism.[53] There was no shortage of short-lived utopian experiments in Ohio and in other areas of what is now labeled as the Midwest, but few received as much national attention as Berlin Heights.

When Francis Barry, a young itinerate lecturer, arrived in Berlin Heights in the mid-1850s, the town had already housed a water cure establishment and was easily accessible from the railroad.[54] Barry identified Berlin Heights as an ideal location for a free love community, and he imagined a community that took a flexible stance toward communal living and the ability to retain personal property. By June of 1857, Barry had announced the creation of a free love community that included a farm (that came to be known as "Free Love Farm"), a centrally located meeting place, and other property.[55] Berlin Heights became controversial as a refuge for "runaway wives" because communal living gave women independence to live without their husbands, and Berlin Heights, unlike some other free love communities, accepted married women.[56] Some newspapers reported fears of women being lured to Berlin Heights for the water cure, only to discover upon arrival the true nature of the free love community.[57]

The living and economic structure of the free love community was flexible. Some members opted to live communally on the farm itself, while others set up unconventional households of unrelated men and women.[58] Francis and Cordelia Barry lived as a married couple even though they claimed not to be legally married, insisting that Cordelia Barry's father had filed a marriage certificate without their knowledge or consent. While the opportunity for communal living was an important part of the Berlin Heights Community, free love formed the basis for the community's civic identity.

Joseph Treat, one of the leaders of the Berlin Heights Community, wrote of the necessity of community, "[We] shall UNITE to achieve the means and ends of life, and share the resulting fruit in common: and so we shall sow the whole land with Phalanxes, Associations, Unities."[59] On the surface free love does not appear to entail communism nor communism to entail free love, but Treat's statement is telling of the rhetorical and ideological connections. Treat advanced a moral and pragmatic argument that posited love as a core to mutually beneficent unity. The naturalistic metaphor of sowing seeds suggested that free love was socially productive, not destructive.

Instead of embracing passion, the Berlin Heights Community rhetorically associated their civic performance with scientific rationality. For example, in what was described as "another free-love manifesto" Cordelia (Cora) Barry identified free love as a "natural right."[60] She framed the regulation of sexual passion in marriage as the root of the slavery of women. By conceiving of free love as a natural right, Barry constituted sex as a core element of civic identity, and the free love community, then, created the condition to protect those individual rights. By appropriating the language of natural rights, Barry embodied a detached rationality with which Americans were familiar and valued.

An author writing in the *Social Revolutionist*, Francis Barry's journal, drew on a different aspect of scientific rationality by arguing, "The lower animals are content with routine and monotony; and so are the lower tribes of men. A higher development gives the divergent and comprehensive activities of the upper brain, and variety and change become indispensable conditions of individual growth and happiness."[61] This sentiment directly challenged assumptions of Platonists and those who argued that Platonic love, a focus on the mind rather than the body, was indicative of developmental advancement. Here, the development of the brain was framed as consistent with bodily passion. J. H. Cook drew on a similar relationship between the mental and physical, arguing, "The natural action of Love excites to action the contiguous and cooperative organs, rendering lovers more modest, refined, ideal, imaginative, spiritual, friendly and polite."[62] For Cook, love was the core of human advancement, and the scientific tone framed that knowledge as simple fact, assuming away the controversial nature of the statement.

Dr. Vivian Grey, another writer in the *Social Revolutionist*, extended the scientific argument to dissociate love from lust. She argued that lust was simple "sexual gratification," and without love, marriage was only lust.[63] Yet when marriage was the only acceptable outlet for lust, Grey asserted, people faced an impossible choice. Continuing the scientific tone, she wrote, "LUST, which has led them on to private and illicit sexual abuse, impels them to marriage for freer gratification, as an antidote for Spermatarrhea and Hysteria."[64] She insisted that it was the often unwanted and uncontrolled lust that characterized marriage and destroyed women's bodies and souls.[65] Thus, she framed cultural norms that demanded marriage at the expense of women as the true examples of licentiousness. Love, on the other hand, demanded both passion and self-restraint, and real love was represented as necessary for both individual advancement and broader social development. For Berlin Heights, the dichotomy between passion and self-restraint remained, but members of the community worked to reframe the placement of free love within that dichotomy.

Nevertheless, the non–free love residents of Berlin Heights tolerated the free love community for only a short period of time. By the end of 1857 the Berlin Heights free lovers had become deeply controversial among Berlin Heights residents and a national audience. One anonymous letter writer to the *Sandusky Register* explicitly listed names of "the most prominent of those who have given aid and comfort to this enemy of good morals and good citizenship."[66] The act of naming individuals functioned as a form of public shaming and came to be widely reported. The free lovers were not only represented as morally deviant but also understood as civically deviant; understandings of good citizenship were intimately tied to understandings of proper moral behavior. Further, despite Cordelia Barry's insistence on individual freedom, residents of Berlin Heights viewed free love as a threat to community, and one reporter described the threat as a "moral Free Love leprosy," illustrating the fear of contagion and unrestrained spread.[67]

Much of the Berlin Heights controversy derived from supposed runaway wives and occasionally runaway husbands coming to Berlin Heights. A widely reprinted letter from Anne Hunter, the wife of one of the Berlin Heights founders, illustrated the "wickedness" and pain of abandoned families resulting from free love.[68] However, relations between free lovers and residents of Berlin Heights reached a low point with Dr. Harlow Lewis' charges of adultery. Harlow Lewis' wife, Mary Lewis, was reported to have absconded to Berlin Heights from New York with a free lover named E. S. Tyler. Harlow discovered his wife in Berlin Heights and initiated a widely reported trial against several of the free lovers on charges of adultery.[69] The trial was resolved in many people's minds when it was reported that Mary Lewis returned home with her husband, and the other free lovers were in jail or run out of town.[70] Following the trial in 1857, newspapers around the country reported a seemingly comical incident of Francis Barry being accosted by a group of women who held him by his facial hair while burning Barry's journal, the *Social Revolutionist*.[71] After the burning of the *Social Revolutionist*, free love advocates reassembled in Berlin Heights, but by 1860 many of the prominent leaders of the community had slowly left. In 1863 and 1864 some of the remaining members of the Berlin Heights Community traveled to New York in an attempt to join the Oneida Community. While some joined Oneida, others returned to Berlin Heights, and the Berlin Heights free love community continued in some form for several years before slowly dwindling.[72] For Americans at the end of the 1850s and into the 1860s, Berlin Heights became emblematic of the threat of free love—both the threat of unrestrained licentiousness and the power of community.

The Oneida and Berlin Heights experiments with free love framed sex as central to civic performance. In doing so, community members were negotiating space in the cultural dichotomy between rationality and passion. Because this dichotomy mapped onto a second dichotomy between civilized and barbarian, the free love controversy became a lens to understand the proper civic performance of a civilized community. While Oneida challenged the distinction between scientific rationality and passion, Berlin Heights appropriated the dichotomy and attempted to shift their place in that dichotomy as an embodiment of rationality rather than passion. The failure of these communities suggests that their rhetorical moves were ultimately unsuccessful.

FREE LOVE, INDIVIDUALISM, AND THE POWER OF THE STATE

The strong individualism and lack of Christian ethic in the Berlin Heights free love community were emblematic of shifts occurring in free love advocacy in the second half of the nineteenth century. While

Oneida persisted as an organized community until around 1880, after the Civil War free love advocates no longer tended to organize into communities. Instead of creating enclaves and building community identity around free love, late nineteenth-century free lovers tended to utilize a rhetoric combining a strong individualism and social advocacy. Some spiritualists persisted in their advocacy of free love, as did many former members of utopian communities. However, by the end of the nineteenth century perhaps the most vocal advocates of free love called themselves anarchists and utilized free love to undermine the power of the state.

American anarchism developed out of many of the earlier American social reform movements including abolitionism, Noyes' Perfectionism, and labor reform. Although there was diversity among anarchists, many placed considerable emphasis on economic issues and robust individualism.[73] For many anarchists, free love fit within a larger critique of the state and power of the church. One author described free love as consisting of free love in name only (those who abhor state control of marriage but practice monogamy), free love theorists, and varietists.[74] For many advocates, free love did not promote sexual promiscuity. Rather, it advocated sexual activity based in love instead of obligation through marriage, and the absence of that total commitment and love was a form of "self-pollution."[75] In this context, the only real form of love was rhetorically framed as free love.[76]

For many anarchists, the freedom from governmental and religious restraint became embodied in love and sexual activity. The idealized citizen, then, was not defined through communal relations but the capacity for individual development, and the potential of the individual synecdochically represented the potential for society as a whole. Much like the collectivist free love advocates, individualist free lovers couched their positions in tropes of passion and scientific rationality. The trope of passion was represented as existing in extremes—the agony of bad marriage and the ecstasy of true love/free love. Free love journals often included visceral portrayals of pain and abuse within bad marriages. *Lucifer, the Light-Bearer*, the longest living sex radical paper (1883–1907) with what was likely the widest circulation, frequently included vivid representations of bad marriages that were designed to illicit strong emotion.[77] For example, Theresa Hughes wrote in *Lucifer*,

> The bonds she [a young girl who married at sixteen] thought so pleasing at first soon become galling chains. She was a slave in every sense of the word, mentally and sexually, never was she free from his brutal outrages, morning, noon and night, up almost to the very hour her baby was born, and before she was again strong enough to move about.[78]

Stories of sex abuse were common as were stories of women being "kicked, choked, pinched and bit" for attempting to refuse sexual acts.[79] *Lucifer* editor Moses Harmon was jailed under the Comstock laws for publishing one particularly explicit account of sexual abuse within marriage. In an essay after his arrest, Harmon argued that the shock of vivid portrayals of sex abuse was necessary to awaken people to action.[80] In another *Lucifer* essay, "Diana" argued that women were "demanding that the veil shall be torn aside, and that they shall be freed from the domination of tyrannical lust."[81] On the surface it may seem paradoxical that advocates of free love would focus on the problems and abuses of sex. However, free love advocates called for freedom *from* sex as much as freedom *for* sex. The angry passion that arose from vivid accounts of abuse within marriage framed immorality as residing within marriage, rather than free love, and attempted to incite action to challenge cultural norms of marriage. In the free love accounts of marriage, traditional marriage necessitated women's role as passive victim, while free love created the possibility for a new civic identity of women as agents—an identity that necessarily challenged the power of the state and symbolic womanhood.

In conceiving of women's roles in relation to the state, some late nineteenth-century female free love advocates appropriated the identity of mother, a common way to understand nineteenth-century woman's civic identity that was grounded in constraining and enabling social expectations and obligations. Victoria Woodhull and Voltairine de Cleyre function as representative examples of rhetors who used maternal rhetoric. Both were nationally prominent free love advocates, and both utilized motherhood as a persona and argumentative trope. However, they used motherhood in a way that radically subverted traditional conceptions of motherhood and the power of the state to regulate sex (and, thus, potential motherhood).

Victoria Woodhull

Victoria Woodhull's life had all the makings of the most sensational of soap operas. Woodhull was one of ten children, and her father was, by most accounts, a criminal and scam artist.[82] In the midst of the rise of spiritualism in the mid-nineteenth century, Woodhull's father "discovered" and cultivated the spiritual and healing powers of Woodhull and her sister, Tennessee Claflin, and he moved the girls around the country to perform and "heal," an activity that was often associated with promiscuity.[83] The girls quickly became the main breadwinners for the large family. At the age of fourteen or fifteen, Victoria Woodhull met and married Canning Woodhull, whom she believed was a respected physician, but she soon discovered that her husband was a drunk.[84]

By her mid-twenties Woodhull had two children (her oldest was developmentally disabled), a husband who drank and squandered the family's money, and a growing spiritualist practice that Woodhull used to support her family.[85] During this period of her life, Woodhull met her second husband, Colonel James Harvey Blood, whom many credit with introducing her to the radical movements of the time.[86] With Blood, Woodhull and her extended family moved to New York in 1868, and shortly after the move, Woodhull and her sister, Tennessee Claflin, began working for millionaire Cornelius Vanderbilt.[87] With the support of Vanderbilt, Woodhull and Claflin opened New York's first female stockbrokerage firm, started the publication *Woodhull and Claflin's Weekly*, and gradually became well connected in both New York and national politics.[88] In 1871 Woodhull delivered her memorial to Congress, becoming the first woman to speak before the House Judiciary Committee, and she ran for president of the United States in 1872.[89] During this same period Woodhull became entrenched in scandal after exposing Henry Ward Beecher's affair with one of his parishioners, and she was jailed for violating federal obscenity laws in publicizing the details of the affair.[90] Although she was briefly embraced by suffrage activists, those activists eventually shunned Woodhull because of her controversial public persona, a persona that derived from her dress, association with radicals such as Stephen Pearl Andrews, and advocacy for free love.[91] Thus, by the time Woodhull went on a speaking tour, delivering her oration "Tried as by Fire; Or, the True and the False, Socially" in 1874, she was well known as a controversial and scandalous public figure.[92]

Despite being a controversial public figure, Woodhull embodied the identity of mother throughout her speech. For example, she began by attempting to establish herself as pure and innocent, a difficult feat considering Woodhull's reputation as a promiscuous free lover. She insisted that the "nasty" things said about her were not upsetting. Rather, she expressed "pity [toward] those who write them, and feel that they have need of a loving mother or a darling sister, to snatch them from a degradation in which they can see only vulgarity or vileness, where there is really, nothing except purity and holiness."[93] Here, Woodhull answered the attacks on her character, attacks that not only were the audience aware of but also likely provided the motivation for their attendance at her lecture. However, instead of directly arguing with those who attacked her, Woodhull assumed a type of public speech that seemed to affirm her persona as mother by expressing pity, an emotion that placed her above the pettiness of the attacks. She also supported a claim of her own "purity and holiness" indirectly through the condemnation of her attackers' "vulgarity and vileness." Throughout the speech, Woodhull explicitly advocated purity, as she defined it, and positioned herself as embodying that purity.

While Woodhull's appeal to purity clearly fit within traditional conceptions of maternalism, she framed purity in a radical way by dissociating purity from chastity. Indeed, according to Woodhull, both the pure and the impure can lack chastity. She argued, "Millions of poor, heart-broken, suffering wives are compelled to minister to the lechery of insatiable husbands, when every instinct of body and sentiment of soul revolts in loathing and disgust."[94] By framing the seemingly pure wife as someone who "ministers" to the "lechery" of her husband, Woodhull used the metaphor of the prostitute to understand the role of the wife within marriage. While marriage was framed as licensed rape, Woodhull accused mothers of prostituting their daughters "as though they were so many stud of horses, to be hawked to the highest bidder."[95] Rather than marriage being a marker of purity, Woodhull insisted that to be truly pure, women must "conquer their sexual liberty."[96] In other words, women needed to have control over their sexuality and knowledge of their bodies.

Woodhull utilized her own persona to embody her conception of purity, and she did this by framing herself both as pure and as someone who once mistakenly conflated marriage and purity. Toward the end of her speech Woodhull stepped out of a position that placed herself as more holy and pure than the audience to plead with the audience from her own experience as a misguided mother. She said,

> Go home with me and see desolation and devastation in another form. . . . My boy, now nineteen years of age, who should have been my pride and my joy, has never been blessed by the dawning of reasoning. I was married at fourteen, ignorant of every thing that related to my maternal functions. For this ignorance, and because I knew no better than to surrender my maternal functions to a drunken man, I am cursed with this living death. Do you think my mother's heart does not yearn for the love of my boy? Do you think I do not realize the awful condition to which I have consigned him? Do you think I would not willingly give my life to make him what he has a right to be? . . . Do you think with this sorrow seated on my soul I can ever sit quietly down and permit women to go on ignorantly repeating my crime? . . . Do you think I can ever hesitate to warn the young maidens against my fate, or to advise them never to surrender the control of their maternal functions to any man! Ah! if you do, you do not know the agony that rests here.[97]

The story promoted the audience's identification with Woodhull, which was especially important since Woodhull spent a considerable amount of her speech accusing her audience of prostituting themselves and their daughters. By telling her story, Woodhull exposed her own imperfection and opened space for the audience to sympathize and connect through their commonality as mothers. Woodhull's story also functioned as a specific example of the consequences of impure motherhood, consequences that extended beyond the woman to irrevocably scar the child.[98] The argument was powerful because it drew on social evolutionary theories that were often used against free lovers—namely, the assumption that the moral state of the parents and conditions of conception determined the developmental advancement of the child. Woodhull framed herself as being called to speak as a mother, with a concern for not only her own children but all children.

The need to protect children was central to the value of the mother. For Woodhull, the common ignorance of mothers was not itself framed as an evil. Rather, the evil was in the implications of ignorance on innocent children, a value that clearly fit within traditional understandings of motherhood. Woodhull claimed that the continuing death of half of children under five years old was a type of "murder" by their mothers as a result of ignorance about sex. Such ignorance, Woodhull explained, was "popular barbarity."[99] Much like Woodhull's treatment of purity, the protection of children functioned as a traditional maternalist appeal, but radicalism resided in the meaning of that protection—the need for sexual education and freedom. For example, Woodhull pleaded, "Oh! let me plead with mothers in the name of future generations to rescue your divinely ordered maternity from the horrid debauch in which it is plunged."[100] Here, Woodhull's radical framing of purity was connected to her radical framing of nurturing and protecting children. The inability to protect one's sexuality, Woodhull argued, corrupted future generations and doomed the children that were products of that impure sexuality.

In short, despite being a radical free lover, Woodhull couched her rhetoric in the reformist language of maternalism. Her arguments drew on the values of purity of women, protection of children, and nurturing future generations. However, unlike traditional rhetorical uses of motherhood, Woodhull's rhetoric framed the meanings of those values in a distinctly radical way that created a stark incongruity between what she advocated and the way in which she advocated, using a rhetoric of radical maternalism.

Voltairine de Cleyre

At the end of the nineteenth century and into the beginning of the twentieth, Voltairine de Cleyre became a prominent voice of American anarchists, publishing "hundreds of works—poems, sketches, essays, lectures, pamphlets, translations, and short stories—from the 1880s until her death in 1912 at the age of forty-five."[101] De Cleyre was born to a family with radical roots. Her mother was an abolitionist from the burned-over district of upstate New York, and her father was a freethinker from France.[102] Most of de Cleyre's life was spent in poverty, generating sympathy for and awareness of the conditions of poverty. De Cleyre was also sent to a convent for education for over three years of her later childhood, and despite excelling academically she called that experience scarring and traumatic.[103] De Cleyre, like many radical activists of her time, attributed her final push into anarchism to the Haymarket affair.[104] In May of 1886 Chicago police attempted to break up a protest meeting at Haymarket Square. Near the end of the meeting someone threw a bomb and police began firing on the crowd. Eight anarchists were arrested and tried for the resulting deaths even though they were demonstrably innocent of throwing the bomb. All eight were found guilty, and seven of the anarchists were sentenced to death. The clear unfairness of the trial and the brutality of the sentence led many to label the men as martyrs for the anarchist cause and radicalized many like Voltairine de Cleyre.

In many respects de Cleyre lived the life of an anarchist.[105] She eschewed marriage out of fear of becoming domesticated and lived a life of poverty while publishing her writings in anarchist journals. De Cleyre even resisted social expectations of motherhood, leaving her only child, Harry, to be raised by others while she followed her intellectual calling and economically supported her mother.[106] Moreover, after being shot by a former student she refused to identify her attacker because she would not condone any violence, even brutality in the name of justice.[107]

In 1890 de Cleyre delivered her speech "Sex Slavery" after Moses Harman was jailed for violating the Comstock laws when he published material describing the brutality of marital rape in his journal *Lucifer, the Light-Bearer*.[108] Frequent arrests of Harman and other publishers threatened to quell the free love movement, but those arrests also became rallying points for activists like de Cleyre who were able to bring public attention to free speech and free love issues.

While Woodhull primarily used a metaphor of prostitution to describe the practice of marriage, de Cleyre's controlling metaphor was slavery, and in drawing on this metaphor, de Cleyre appealed to many of the maternalist themes of the abolitionist movement a half century earlier. De Cleyre noted about Harman,

> He held every married woman what she is, a bonded slave, who takes her master's name, her master's bread, her master's commands, and serves her master's passions; who passes through the ordeal of pregnancy and the throes of travail at his dictation—not at her desire; who can control no property, not even her own body, without his consent, and from whose straining arms the children she bears may be torn at his pleasure, or willed away while they are yet unborn.[109]

De Cleyre's comparison between slavery and marriage was particularly powerful because it framed the evils of slavery and, thus, marriage as violations of expectations of motherhood. De Cleyre drew on common themes in abolitionist literature relating to the protection of slave mothers. For example, the evils of slavery were frequently supported by sexual exploitation of female slaves, who could exercise little control over their procreation.[110] De Cleyre's portrayal of the wife as subservient to her "master's [husband's] passions" drew on these same tropes, highlighting that motherhood was often a forced condition because the law left women in marriage with little control over their procreation.

Despite the fear and violence of forced motherhood, one of the greatest evils of slavery was often thought to be the separation of mothers and children, and abolitionist rhetors frequently used vivid imagery of children being ripped from their mothers' arms.[111] De Cleyre represented this evil of slavery as being an evil of marriage and, thus, all woman were potentially in the same condition as slave women once were—unable to secure individual liberty or protect their children. De Cleyre suggested that the maternalist values of care and nurturing, then, could be upheld only outside of the institution of marriage.

The inability to leave marriage also supported de Cleyre's slavery metaphor and disrupted the image of the home as a tranquil sanctuary. She continued to explain that in addition to losing identity and freedom within marriage, women had very little ability to escape from the slavery of marriage and a husband could "follow her [his wife] wherever she goes, come into her house, eat her food, force her into the cell, *kill* her by virtue of his sexual authority!"[112] Divorce was possible only if "he is indiscreet enough to abuse her in some less brutal but unlicensed manner."[113] Through the association with slavery, de Cleyre attempted to dissociate marriage and morality, replacing the tranquil image of the home with the violent imagery of slavery. If the audience wanted to protect the mother they must challenge marriage, placing the value of marriage in conflict with the value of maternalism.

While Woodhull claimed the language of maternalism and used dissociation to radicalize maternalist language, de Cleyre appeared to reject some of the language of maternalism through dissociating appearance and reality.[114] De Cleyre argued, "What an *obscene* thing 'virtue' is!"[115] Drawing on social evolutionism, she identified children born in the name of virtue as "puny" and "sickly." This false virtue, de Cleyre insinuated, harmed both women and children in all of the ways that truly mattered, discounting the label of "illegitimate" as an insignificant label. In other words, while the value of virtue may appear to be consistent with maternalism, de Cleyre framed the good mother as the one who protected her child *despite* calls for "virtue."

Just as the language of virtue was problematic, de Cleyre framed the language of purity and morality as flawed. She continued:

> These are the effects of your purity standard, your marriage law. . . . Half your children dying under five years of age, your girls insane, your married women walking corpses, your men so bad that they themselves often admit *Prostitution holds against PURITY a bond of indebtedness.* This is the beautiful effect of your god, Marriage, before which Natural Desire must abase and belie itself.[116]

In a shaming and accusing tone, de Cleyre framed the ability to protect and care for children as antithetical to traditional manifestations of the value of purity. According to de Cleyre this hypocrisy was endemic to both men and women. Just as men employed prostitutes yet demanded the purity of women, women "sneer[ed]" at "the streetwalker" while caring for the very men who "victimized" the prostitute.[117] Through identifying the disconnect between the purported values of maternalism and the actions of those claiming to uphold those values, de Cleyre reimagined the connection between the value and the act, framing her critique of marriage as more moral and in line with the true values and motivations of maternalism. In short, de Cleyre rhetorically constructed a world where only free love could fit within her radically reshaped understanding of maternalism.

Nineteenth-century radical women faced a tremendous challenge. Not only were their ideas unconventional and disruptive, but also the rhetorical strategies that many women used to justify basic public engagement were antithetical to the ideas they were attempting to advocate. In particular, Woodhull and de Cleyre were attempting to challenge the institution of marriage, an institution that was closely connected to women's identities as mothers. Thus, an appeal to traditional maternal values would appear to be ineffective and counterproductive. Nevertheless, both of these women found ways to subvert maternalism while utilizing it as a rhetorical strategy by placing the values of motherhood as antithetical to the institution of marriage.

PASSION, RESTRAINT, AND CIVIC IDENTITY

While free love was described in the popular press as simple licentiousness, unbridled sex, and destructive to civil society, the public controversy over free love functioned as an extended negotiation over American civic identity. Free love was understood as dangerous because it threatened to challenge core markers of American identity. As "good" Americans were called to exercise self-restraint and privilege rationality to achieve spiritual, social, and biological evolution, free love advocates introduced sexual passion as an enactment of good citizenship. Indeed, at different moments in time, free love advocates experimented with voluntary associations, radical individualism, meanings and practices of true motherhood, and the structure of family—all of which were different ways to understand the relationship between the individual and society.

Although many of the norms and practices of free love (such as condemnation of spousal abuse, marriage for love, sex out of wedlock, and availability of contraception) are commonly accepted in the twenty-first-century United States, the nineteenth-century popular imagination of free love never moved beyond a symbol of social chaos. Free love functions as a powerful example of the ways in which seemingly private sexual acts can be reductively used as a symbol of public morality and the state of the nation as a whole. The free love controversy suggests that Americans enact civic identity in sexual practice, and debates about proper sex are ways of negotiating American values and ideologies.

[5]

Miscegenation and the Future of Civilization

Just weeks before issuing the Emancipation Proclamation, President Abraham Lincoln delivered a message to Congress that declared, "In *giving* freedom to the *slave*, we *assure* freedom to the *free*—honorable alike in what we give, and what we preserve. We shall nobly save, or meanly lose, the last best hope of earth."[1] Indeed, the Civil War was momentous. If the South won, the nation would be torn apart. Yet some people in both the North and South feared the consequences of a Northern victory. Slavery created a type of order to the world where, in the words of Justice Taney in the *Dred Scott* decision, an entire class of persons were not Americans and were inherently different because their presence in the United States was for the purpose of slavery.[2] This reasoning rhetorically constituted an enslaved body that marked everyone of African descent as Other, whether physically enslaved or free. Thus, the existence of slavery in the United States institutionalized a clear demarcation between the supposedly true Americans and the barbarous Other.[3] A Northern victory, however, threatened to destabilize those lines, making Lincoln's "last best hope" a frightening proposition for some.

Without slavery as an institutionalized marker of difference, post–Civil War Americans rhetorically constituted a racialized body that created a seemingly impenetrable boundary between the Other and the national body. Marriage was a critical site for constituting the racialized body, and the topic of marriage often crept into seemingly unrelated racial issues. The US Supreme Court, for example, referred to marriage laws several times in its consideration of Dred Scott's status as property. Similarly, the US Supreme Court decision in *Plessy v. Ferguson* in 1896 justified separate rail accommodations based on race, in part, by referring to seemingly just laws that prohibited interracial marriage.[4] Marriage and race were inseparable concepts, in part because both were culturally understood as intrinsic to national identity. Within this framework, symbolic womanhood was vital to the creation and meaning making of the racialized national body. Public rhetoric inscribed nation onto bodies, and the controversy over interracial marriage was perhaps one of the most significant in publicly constituting the appropriate racialized/gendered national body and, thus, ultimately reifying racial divisions in the post–Civil War United States.

Prior to the Civil War, the institution of slavery created structural limitations to the controversy over interracial marriage. As Justice Taney in the *Dred Scott* decision illustrated, property could not legally marry, and the institution of slavery even shaped the public identities of free men and women of African descent. Therefore, the institution of slavery created both a structural and an attitudinal barrier to the controversy over interracial marriage. Although some states did pass laws prohibiting interracial marriage and there were moments of controversy prior to the Civil War, the fundamental social and legal changes brought by the Civil War reignited the controversy over interracial marriage, and the issue continued to develop throughout the century as Americans negotiated the intersections between gender, marriage, and African American identity.

MISCEGENATION AND THE ELECTION OF 1864

In the midst of a bloody civil war and months before a highly contested presidential election, an anonymous pamphlet titled *Miscegenation: The Theory of the Blending of the Races, Applied to the American White Man and Negro* began to circulate. The pamphlet, although it claimed to be written and endorsed by Republicans, was a hoax that was designed to hurt Lincoln's chances of reelection, and it functioned satirically by exaggerating and, thereby, amplifying radical abolitionist attempts at social equality. The pamphlet claimed to have coined the term "miscegenation" and argued that the mixing of races was the solution to racial problems in the United States. The ensuing debate solidified divisions within the country and positioned race as central to the controversy over marriage and marriage as central to the controversy over race. *Miscegenation* thus fueled a national debate over racial identity, marriage, and the future of the nation at a critical moment of uncertainty.

The 1864 presidential election was in the middle of a violent, expensive, and controversial civil war, and Lincoln's reelection was far from certain. Indeed, no president had been reelected to a second term since 1832, and there was uncertainty that Lincoln would even receive the Republican nomination in the election.[5] Although the war had started turning to the North's favor by Election Day, the first years of the war were marred with disappointing Northern defeats, and the eventual Northern victories came with tremendous loss of life on both sides. The war was massively expensive, and some blamed the Lincoln administration for unprecedented debt.[6] Draft riots occurred across the country, illustrating discontent with the war. Public anger over the war led to Republicans losing a significant number of important seats in the mid-term elections of 1862, many losses in states that were big wins for Lincoln in 1860.[7]

Some of the most vigorous opposition to Lincoln came from a group commonly called "Copperhead" Democrats, who opposed Lincoln, wanted peace with the South, and were especially angered by Lincoln's Emancipation Proclamation, which was viewed by these Democrats as a shift in the purpose of the war from preserving the nation to the abolition of slavery.[8] Yet Lincoln also faced opposition within his own party, especially from radical, abolitionist Republicans who were disappointed by Lincoln's limited response to slavery.[9]

In this context *Miscegenation* was presented to Americans as a voice from within the Republican Party that praised Lincoln's presidency and called for further racial equality. In an attempt to seek endorsements, the pamphlet was mailed to prominent abolitionists and Republicans such as Lucretia Mott, Horace Greeley, and Wendell Phillips. Yet a firestorm ignited during the congressional debate on the Freedom Bureau Bill when Representative Samuel Sullivan Cox of Ohio, a vocal Democrat, began a long attack on the pamphlet and read excerpts from letters of endorsement written by abolitionists and Republicans.[10] However, *Miscegenation* was a hoax penned by staff of the Democratic newspaper the *New York World*, David Goodman Croly and George Wakeman, in an effort to influence the 1864 election.[11]

It may, perhaps, seem odd that Croly and Wakeman would choose marriage as a site of vulnerability for Lincoln. Lincoln had been explicit in the past that he did not favor amalgamation of the races, claiming that he wanted to "leave her [the black woman] alone."[12] Further, marriage was commonly celebrated as a social ideal in the nineteenth century, as illustrated by cultural resistance to divorce and free love. However, explicit racism in the laws of marriage was uniquely American, having no English precedent and developing over the century in response to a changing nation.[13] Emancipation created the potential for new social conditions, augmenting concerns over interracial marriage.

Miscegenation drew on racial fears through satire. The pamphlet functioned as a parody of the form and common tropes of abolitionists, but it did so in a way that took negative (or at least culturally contested) ideas and lauded them as unambiguously positive. The hyperrealism of the parody enabled a type of double meaning. The audience that did not recognize the hoax (which appeared to be a vast majority of commentators on the pamphlet) was invited to attack *Miscegenation* as a true voice of the Republican Party as the pamphlet appeared to confirm and amplify previously existing concerns. At the same time, the audience that recognized the satire was led to attack and judge Republicans as dangerous and deluded, highlighting an apparent incongruity with cultural norms.[14] Both readings of the pamphlet relied on a fear that legal equality would lead to social equality, and social equality would ultimately lead to black men assuming white men's roles as familial and political patriarchs.

Miscegenation utilized a tone that was detached and logical, constantly appealing to expert opinion evidence and an apparent emphasis on reason. The authors never broke character in appearing to favor miscegenation, but in doing so, they strategically deployed common racial fears that created alarm about not only miscegenation but also political and social equality. The pamphlet began with definitions.[15] The authors declared, "The word is spoken at last. It is Miscegenation—the blending of the various races of men—the practical recognition of the brotherhood of all the children of a common father."[16] According to the authors, the word "miscegenation" derives from the "Latin *Miscere,* to mix, and *Genus*, race," but "melaleukation" would be a more precise word because it is "derived from two Greek words, viz,: *Melas* . . . black; and *Leukos* . . . white."[17] "Amalgamation," the authors insisted, is a poor word because it actually refers to the mixing of metal and "was, in fact, only borrowed for an emergency."[18] Rather than changing the controversy in any substantive way, the apparent precision of language in the beginning of the pamphlet is rhetorically significant because it modeled a tone of logical reason and scientific precision, a rhetorical form that enabled the satire.

The rhetorical forms of rationality and logical precision were present in both the style of the pamphlet—coining new words because they were more accurate—and the forms of reasoning. The authors drew on religion, democracy, and science to insist that the future of the nation was dependent on adopting the practice of racial mixing. In particular, they insisted that the elimination of racial difference was an inevitability that would lead to the advancement of civilization. History proves, the authors insisted, "wherever, through conquest, colonization, or commerce, different nationalities are blended, a superior human product invariably results."[19] Such evolutionary rhetoric would have been familiar to the audience but more so in the context of opposition to miscegenation. Scientists frequently utilized a rhetoric popularized by Darwinian and Lamarckian theories of evolution and argued that humans of African descent had smaller brains and bestial sexual passions, marking them as simply less advanced than Europeans and European Americans.[20] The satiric rhetoric, in appearing to support miscegenation with evolution, drew on existing racist tropes, reifying racial fears.

Miscegenation also disrupted the American progress narrative. Americans heavily relied on the narrative of American exceptionalism, which functioned as a way of seeing both the past and the future through the lens of preordained greatness.[21] *Miscegenation* disrupted this narrative by insisting that progress was not linear, and Americans were not exceptional in their greatness. The authors argued, "We see races emerge from barbarism, flourish for a hundred or two hundred years, then become degenerate, and relapse into a condition worse than their former barbarism."[22] From this point of view, the white race was either in or near a state of regression. The authors' description of corporality of the white race was presented as evidence of its decline. Anglo-Americans, the authors insisted, were "dry and shriveled," unhealthy, and unattractive.[23] White men, the pamphlet explained, were gaunt, bald, and weak.[24] The authors described the ideal woman as "ripe and complete," with a "warm and dark" complexion.[25] Such a claim defied social convention that associated female beauty with whiteness and delicacy. If white readers were going to see themselves in this text, they would be pushed to identify with what was represented as the unattractive and regressive white race.[26]

Through these pronouncements of inevitable regression, the authors told the audience that not only were Americans not as good as they may have assumed but also they, as human beings, were unattractive and more degenerate than black men and women, who for most of the audience were the epitome of brutishness. "We," the authors insisted, "must become a yellow-skinned, black-haired people—in fine, we must become miscegens, if we would attain the fullest results of civilization."[27] In using the constitutive pronoun "we," the authors positioned the audience within the flawed category of white Americans and proposed not just a change in behavior but also a change in identity, calling on the audience to "become miscegens." While the rhetoric of "we" and "them" is often used to create unity through division from an often racialized Other, *Miscegenation* rhetorically constructed a "we" that unified the audience around racial identity while appearing to advocate for the demise of that very identity category. The argument drew on existing tropes that inscribed nation onto the body. In sustaining the logic that good bodies make good citizens, who, in turn, make a good nation, readers were indirectly pushed to reject the premise of African superiority while accepting a logic that privileged the connections between body and nation. It was this logic that demanded a public interest in controlling raced and gendered bodies for the good of the nation as a whole.

Miscegenation drew on the cultural conflation of sex and marriage in appealing to fears grounded in the double myth of the black male rapist and white female virgin. The authors argued that "black loves blond" and vice versa. "Our police courts," the authors continued, "give painful evidence that the passion of the colored race for the white is often so uncontrollable as to overcome the terror of law."[28] Such a claim built on the myth that black men commonly raped white women, a myth frequently present in Copperhead newspapers and often used to justify lynching and other forms of racial violence.[29] Under the pretense of claiming that miscegenation was inevitable and natural, the authors of *Miscegenation* indirectly drew on this fear by describing black men as incapable of restraining or controlling their lust, particularly for white women. The subtext of *Miscegenation* was that white women were always at risk, particularly after Emancipation because those passions would no longer be restrained through the institution of slavery. The power of this fear appeal drew upon cultural myths while seeming to be unaware of those myths. Marking the black man as irrational and driven by hypersexual lust simply reified the cultural assumption of barbarity. Similarly, by framing the white woman as at risk of losing her virtue, the pamphlet called white men to perform their culturally appropriate masculine role in saving white women from that risk.

Miscegenation also drew on a cultural fear that white women, if given the opportunity, would prefer black men to white men. Southern women, *Miscegenation* claimed, had a "strange magnetism of association with a tropical race." The pamphlet continued to argue that Southern women had "frenzy of love" for the "negro," and this love was represented as evidence of the inevitability and naturalness of miscegenation.[30] Here, the fear of uncontrolled passion was reversed. Not only were women at risk of losing their purity, but also the pamphlet asserted that women's passion could lead to black men taking white men's supposed place in the family. As men represented the head of the family government, to risk removing white men from that role represented a dramatic shift in power. While sexual relationships certainly existed between black men and white women during slavery, the condition of slavery forced a rigid social structure. However, Emancipation and the Civil War destabilized formal structures that created a clear binary between the races. Black men's performance of similar social, familial, and economic roles to white men challenged racialized divisions and power structures.

The threatening performance of white masculinity by black men was manifest in sexual relationships with white women, but also manifest in landownership. *Miscegenation* represented Lincoln's emancipation of Southern slaves as the first step in an inevitable move toward social, political, and economic equality. The authors asserted that Republicans would reward "loyal negros" by giving them lands confiscated from "rebel whites."[31] The pamphlet extended this fear further by suggesting that the prevalence of miscegenation in the South meant that many freed slaves were related to their owners and, thus, entitled to inherit. Property ownership represented a form of performing white masculinity. Taken together, property ownership and sex and marriage to white women represented the ultimate expression of "passing" or mimesis.[32] If black men could perform white masculinity, they could, presumably, take what "belonged" to white men.

Perhaps not surprisingly, a vast majority of responses to *Miscegenation* were negative, perhaps none more so than those in the Southern and Democratic presses. Even before the publication of the pamphlet, amalgamation, as it was then known, was represented as a social evil and violation of nature. In typical fashion one paper declared, "The negro, when not in contact with the white man, is still a savage."[33] The statement not only asserted intrinsic difference but also utilized the rhetoric of the civilized/barbarian to ascribe value. Under the guise of scientific rationality, commentators framed racial difference as a difference in species, which positioned racial boundaries as necessarily insurmountable and simple scientific fact. For example, one commentator stated, "The law of nature against the propagation of hybrids vindicates its supremacy by a visible deterioration from both races, before reaching the octoroon, when propagation entirely ceases."[34] The assumed scientific and natural difference provided the grounds for religious judgment, and proclamations such as "The mulatto is a blasphemy" built off the assumption of difference to assert value in the eyes of God.[35] The languages of both science and religion drew on what appeared to be intrinsic and natural difference. To disrupt the seemingly natural division between the races was to disrupt God's plan.

Especially once *Miscegenation* was published, Democratic and Southern publications worked to equate Republicans, in general, and Lincoln, in particular, with miscegenation. Some papers labeled miscegenation as the "pet doctrine" of the Republican Party, spread rumors of clandestine interracial marriages, and made claims about the "mysterious 'yearnings' of Northern bellies."[36] These claims would have been more easily dismissed without the logic that constructed a slippery slope from abolition to miscegenation. Under this logic, abolition would lead to legal equality, which would lead to voting, which would lead to social equality, which would inevitably lead to miscegenation. Each of these steps was framed as inevitable with the abolition of slavery and the hidden agenda of the Lincoln administration. One paper described the Republican platform, "Abolition Platform—War, Conscription, Taxation, Confiscation, Miscegenation, and no peace until slavery is abolished, the final result of which is Disunion and certain irrevocable ruin."[37] The simple listing created the impression of logical association, and, thus, the visible presence of war and conscription in the United States was framed as evidence of inevitable miscegenation.

The evolution of the debate signaled not simply a concern for racial mixing but also a concern over the ownership of women. Sex, especially the rape of slave women, was not represented to be as harmful as the intimacy and connection entailed in marriage. The Democratic indictment of the supposed Republican scheme of miscegenation focused on the protection of white women. A satirical poem that was reprinted in several papers exclaimed, "Mother, fond mother you know 'tis your duty! / Give up your darlings to some negro beauty; / Give your fair daughters like angels that are / Beautiful, lovely, for black men to share."[38] References to white women were imbued with the rhetoric of possession—"giving" white women to black men. Much like in the pamphlet *Miscegenation*, the result of racial mixing was labeled as a "darkening" of the race, implying that women's bodies represented the purity of the race.[39] To give a woman was to give the future of the race.

Rather than defending miscegenation, Republicans argued that the practice occurred almost exclusively at the hands of white Southern men, thereby inverting the myths of the black male rapist and highlighting the structure of Southern power that enabled white men to fulfill their bestial lust with black women who were hardly their wives. Republicans claimed to "want to put an end to the vile practice [of miscegenation] by releasing the female black [*sic*] from the lustful clutches of the master."[40] Most "mulattos," several commentators explained, "belonged" to the slave-holding states. Indeed, in the 1860 census 69,969 people classified as mixed race lived in free states, while 518,383 lived in slave states.[41] In highlighting this discrepancy, Republican commentators were not challenging that miscegenation was an evil; rather, they were accusing Southerners and Democrats of "bleaching" the enslaved people.[42] Republicans, one newspaper asserted, "want to have the blacks let alone and the only way to prevent an amalgamation with them is to give freedom to them. When once free, the male blacks will take care of the female blacks and prevent miscegenation."[43] Under the guise of protecting black women, the Republican response naturalized racial division and assumed that after Emancipation the black family would replicate the supposedly ideal structure of the white family.

On both sides of the debate, the woman synecdochically represented the purity of the race, extending the cultural assumption that women represented the moral purity of the nation to a pseudo-scientific racial purity. Thus, when Southerners and Democrats referred to white women in interracial sexual relationships, the white race was "darkening" or being tainted. However, when Republicans referred to the rape of black slave women by white men, the black race was being "bleached." At a time when whiteness represented purity, cleanliness, and good, many Americans may have been inclined to view "bleaching" as positive or, at least, less threatening than "darkening" the white race, an especially disturbing assumption considering that this "bleaching" was often occurring through the rape of slave women. Thus, the rhetoric of the miscegenation debate positioned women as a symbol of the race. Women's symbolic position along with language of possession (both sexual possession of women and the legal possession entailed in marriage) rhetorically constituted the threat of a dramatic power shift if black men were to have access to white women. Both sides of the debate fed into this racial fear. Women's bodies represented a contested space where sexual "possession" of women represented the ownership of culture.

Miscegenation not only claimed to have introduced a new word into the American vocabulary, but also participated in a larger controversy that highlighted marriage as a primary locale of racial conflict. In 1864 a vast majority of Americans seemed willing to accept racial difference as an incontrovertible fact, and difference necessarily entailed value judgment. Marriage symbolized the ultimate expression of racial challenge because marriage was about race and the future of civilization. Of course, Lincoln was reelected in 1864, the Civil War ended, and the Union was restored. However, *Miscegenation* contributed to both a language and a fear of race and marriage in the United States. Following the Civil War, states across the country responded to that fear by passing legislation that prohibited interracial marriages, and many of those laws remained in effect until the 1967 US Supreme Court decision in *Loving v. Virginia*.[44]

FREDERICK DOUGLASS AND THE LIMITS OF RACE

In January of 1884, the country was scandalized by a marriage between a black man and a white woman. Although this was certainly not the first interracial union in the country, it elicited such controversy because the groom was Frederick Douglass. By 1884 Douglass had been a public figure for over forty years. In his widely read biography, *Narrative of the Life of Frederick Douglass: An American Slave*, Douglass told readers that his father was likely his enslaved mother's owner, although he was unsure about the identity of his father and he met his mother only a few times before her death. Douglass was best known for his abolitionist work, but after the abolition of slavery he continued to be a prominent public figure, labeled by newspapers as "a representative colored man of the country," a "seething caldron of indignation," a "leader" of his race, and "old man eloquent."[45] Douglass' age was reported in papers as anywhere from sixty-five to seventy-three, and his new wife, Helen Pitts, was reported to be anywhere from a near teen to forty-six years old.[46] Pitts was described by the newspapers as "handsome and sprightly," a woman suffragist, and "worthy."[47] Francis Grimké, the interracial nephew of Angelina and Sarah Grimké, conducted the marriage in secret, and news of the marriage came as a surprise to the couple's friends and family.[48] The Douglasses' marriage not only reignited controversy over interracial marriage but also challenged public meanings and the significance of race in the United States.

At the time of Douglass' marriage, interracial marriage remained deeply controversial. In 1661 Maryland was the first colony to adopt an official ban on interracial marriage, and such bans were in effect in most states at some point over the course of the nineteenth century.[49] Even when it was not explicitly prohibited, many nineteenth-century writers assumed that interracial marriage was not a significant problem because "no white with any self-respect will consort with any person of color."[50] In 1883 the US Supreme Court decided that bans on interracial marriage did not violate civil rights because the law applied to both races (black and white) equally. Both were permitted to marry someone of their own race, and both were prohibited from marrying outside of their race.[51] The rhetoric of interracial marriage laws and court decisions reified race as natural, immutable, and unambiguous.

Many of the responses to Douglass' marriage built off the same assumptions as the Supreme Court—race as natural, immutable, and unambiguous. In some of these instances, Douglass was represented as embodying the perceived threat of the Other. Despite his appearance of sophistication and similarity to many white Americans, some objectors to Douglass' marriage reduced him to a symbol of the black race. In these instances Douglass often existed unnamed, as if to name him justified his public importance. Just days after Douglass' marriage but without explicitly naming Douglass, Representative Risden Tyler Bennett (D-N.C.) introduced a bill in Congress to prohibit interracial marriage in Washington, D.C.[52] Despite some newspapers' claims, Douglass' marriage was legal.[53] Although interracial marriage was prohibited in Maryland, a state that Douglass could see from the front porch of the home he shared with his new wife, and the laws of Washington, D.C. were based on Maryland state law, the district came to be known as a safe place for interracial marriage, and it appears that interracial marriage laws were quietly nullified probably in the late 1860s.[54] Bennett's attempt to outlaw interracial marriage in D.C. never made much progress, but his response is indicative of a continuing opposition to interracial marriage.

Even those who appeared sympathetic or respectful to Douglass rarely considered his marriage to be prudent. Some noted that it "will prove a bad example to other colored men" whose uncontrollable passions and deficient reasoning often led to "horrible criminal brutality."[55] In these cases, Douglass was framed as an exception to his race. Rather than Douglass functioning as proof that "colored men" could be rational and dignified, the counterexample of Douglass was simply dismissed as an exception. The reasoning behind this objection privileged rationality above the passionate, and within this hierarchy of values, white was associated with rational and black with passionate. This hierarchy allowed the reader to feign respect for Douglass while feeding the same biases that were used to justify racial violence under the guise of protecting white women.

Other commentators used Douglass as a starting point to extend their assumptions of intrinsic racial difference. No one seemed to believe that Douglass would be having children with his new wife; rather, the marriage was framed as one of love or comfort in old age.[56] Nonetheless, Douglass appeared to provide an entryway for claims that interracial relationships violate "nature," producing children that were less intelligent, less attractive, and unable to procreate.[57] For these critics Douglass functioned as a symbol for a larger perceived problem. Interracial marriage was a threat, even a marriage without procreation, because it signaled what was represented as a dangerous level of intimacy and social equality.

Other commentators praised Douglass and his marriage for elevating his race and challenging racial divisions. For example, the *Independent* praised Douglass and suggested that "miscegenation" was "one of the best things that could happen for the race in America."[58] Some African American papers agreed with the assessment of the *Independent*. One writer in the *Cleveland Gazette*, an African American weekly newspaper, praised the Douglass marriage as an end to "barbaric racial lines." "It means progress!" the author continued. "It means a wiping out of the lines of racial distinctions, caste and prejudice! It means amalgamation—*natural*, not *forced!*"[59] Even in praise, Douglass functioned as a synecdoche for the African American race, and his marriage became read as an accomplishment for his race.[60]

The spirited defense of Douglass by Jane Grey Swisshelm, pioneering female journalist, illustrates that even praise of Douglass' marriage had the tendency to reify problematic racial divisions. Swisshelm began in a fairly typical fashion by inverting the civilized/barbarian dichotomy, arguing that the "barbarism of slavery" created unjust prejudice.[61] According to Swisshelm, the racist was the barbarian, not the African American. However, as she continued in her defense she argued that Douglass' marriage was acceptable because in his "mental and moral qualities . . . Douglass is ninety-nine-hundredths white."[62] In other words, Swisshelm attributed the best aspects of Douglass to his whiteness, sustaining assumptions of inherent racial difference. Further, in answering the objection that interracial marriages would increase black men's violence against white women, Swisshelm did not challenge the myth. Instead, she asked, "Is a man more likely to assault a woman he may hope to marry than one who is removed from him by legal barriers?"[63] In what appears to be a defense of interracial marriage, Swisshelm sustained the myth of black male violence and suggested that black men would become less violent if they were allowed to marry white women. The praise of Douglass' marriage, such as that from Swisshelm, was often as problematic in sustaining assumptions of naturalized racial difference as the objections to his marriage.

The praise of Douglass' marriage, however, was fairly limited, and some of the most fervent objections came from the black press, where Douglass was represented as a traitor to his race. Many of these newspapers proclaimed Douglass' marriage to be the greatest mistake of his life because it signaled a disloyalty to his people.[64] This objection occurred in several overlapping stages. The first stage was to establish race as an immutable identity category. Occasionally writers explicitly interwove racial lines and identity categories. For example, one writer demanded, "Stand by your colors!"[65] More often, however, subtle rhetorical markers conveyed statements of racial unity and naturalized racial identity categories. Authors would make an argument such as "The public, particularly *his* race, has a right to be interested in his every move."[66] Similarly, "GOD FORBID that any man from our ranks should lead us or our race, in whom there is not race pride enough to own he is a Negro."[67] In these examples pronouns such as "his" and "our" rhetorically demarcated lines of belonging and group identity; one is either inside or outside of the racial identity category. Further, statements of fact (such as "he is a Negro") reified the seeming immutability of the identity category. Within this framework, one does not choose to join the group or leave the group. Rather, the rhetoric from the African American press constructed racial identity as a natural and unchangeable fact.

If race functioned as a naturalized identity category, then perhaps it makes sense for critics of Douglass' marriage to demand a celebration of that racial category. Statements such as "race pride" and "We did not make our color, let us not be ashamed of it" not only suggested an affinity in racial identity but also demanded a positive value attached to that identity.[68] One writer asked, "Could we, without losing our self-respect, recognize a man as our leader, when he thinks himself above us, and does not even think enough of the race to marry one of its number?"[69] Further, some critics in the black press appropriated the language of racial purity that was commonly deployed by white critics of miscegenation.[70] Once race became rhetorically framed as a positive identity category, then it followed for its members to want to preserve the racial identity. In this frame, Douglass' marriage signaled a trend that threatened to "bleach" or eliminate the African American race.[71]

Finally, women's bodies functioned as a symbol for what was considered beautiful and valuable within the racial identity category. Several papers noted that African American women were insulted that Douglass chose a white wife.[72] As long as racial identity was primary, the race of one's wife functioned as a metric for more general racial affinity. Thus, Douglass did not need to say anything negative about the African American race because his choice to possess the body of a white woman was read as a rejection of his race. Some writers responded by celebrating the beauty and refinement of "their" women and, thus, their race. One commentator described the choice of wife like the choice of clothing from a store, stating, "We do not have to go to the white race to find wives; we have every desirable color and trait we want within our own race, from the luscious blonde to the plume blue-black, varying of shades to suit all demands, etc."[73] Another writer asserted, "Now that our sisters and daughters are growing to greater loveliness and comeliness than ever; now that all the womanly graces are theirs, with the added luster of culture, let us treat as idle words the advice of the *Independent* to prefer white ladies."[74] Both descriptions of African American women functioned as ways of valuing racial identity by rhetorically positioning women's bodies as symbolic of the race as a whole. However, "womanly graces" and the "luster of culture" were both ways of appropriating upper-class white values of womanhood as a metric for female value.

Douglass made one widely reprinted public statement responding to the criticism of his marriage, and in this short statement Douglass challenged the very grounds of the controversy. He stated, "I have advocated the cause of the colored people . . . not because I am a negro, but because I am a man."[75] By asserting his primary identity as a "man," Douglass shifted his identity from one that derived from race to one that, although gendered, prompted identification across racial division and destabilized race as a naturalized construct. Douglass continued:

> All this excitement, then, is caused by a marriage of a woman a few shades lighter than myself. If I had married a black woman there would have been nothing said about it. Yet the disparity in our complexions would have been the same. I am not an African, as may be seen from my features and hair, and it is equally easy to discern that I am not Caucasian.[76]

Douglass rhetorically appropriated his interracial body and read his corporality as a challenge to inherent racial division. Rather than race functioning dichotomously as black or white identity, Douglass articulated race as a visual spectrum manifest in different "shades." Douglass specifically identified what he is *not*, challenging relationships between visual appearance and identity category. He continued, saying, "You may say that Frederick Douglass considers himself a member of the one race which exists."[77] Thus, Douglass challenged not only race as a naturalized identity category but also the very concept of racial division, utilizing a rhetoric that asserted the lack of different races as a simple incontrovertible fact.

In a nation starkly divided by racial lines, Douglass rhetorically embodied a liminal space as black, white, and neither black nor white. In a later speech, Douglass claimed that he occupied a "middle position."[78] This movement within and among racial boundaries was not only rhetorically expedient for Douglass but also allowed his body to symbolize the permeability and instability of racial categories. Douglass' critique of "race pride" further emphasized the limits of public conceptions of race. Douglass argued in a later speech that "to be a man is better than to be a race."[79] He underscored his criticism of "race pride" in other speeches as well, arguing that people do not choose or create their color, so it doesn't make sense to be proud of one's race.[80] Thus, the public meanings of race, according to Douglass, were rhetorically constructed. Taken together, Douglass' rhetoric framed race as a concept distinct from skin color or physical appearance, and Douglass' body functioned as evidence of this distinction.

Douglass' comments after his marriage were perhaps the most clear in constituting race itself as a social concept with permeable boundaries, and Douglass had long advocated for monogenesis, the theory that all humans derived from the same creation.[81] However, in many speeches both before and after his marriage to Helen Pitts, Douglass also seemed to essentialize race as a stable identity category.

Douglass would occasionally refer to "our people" when speaking to an audience of African Americans, seeming to place himself in the identity category that he appeared to disavow following his marriage.[82] He also identified seemingly essential characteristics of race. For example, "Speaking for him [the negro], I can commend him up on every ground. He is loyal and patriotic; service is the badge of all his tribe."[83] Douglass also said that "blacks . . . can work," which framed an inherent value to the race.[84] Even as Douglass insisted that racial division was an artificial human creation, he occasionally appeared to fall into rhetorical patterns that drew on seemingly essential racial difference.[85]

Douglass' inconsistency in meanings and significance of race is indicative of a larger cultural conflict over the racialized body. In the decades following Emancipation, the racialized body took on many of the cultural meanings of the enslaved body as a natural and immutable group identity. For this system to work, race needed to be dichotomous (white and nonwhite) and unambiguous. Thus, race came to mark status and ascribe value. The black press and activists such as Douglass challenged white assumptions of status and value, often through calling for "race pride" or appropriating white norms of culture, refinement, and beauty. Nevertheless, very few people, with the occasional exception of Douglass, challenged race itself as a cultural construct.

One of the few people who challenged cultural conceptions of race in a way similar to Douglass was American author Charles Chesnutt. Chesnutt was widely read, and his fiction was praised as "interesting and touching"[86] and belonging "to the list of the most dramatic and powerful studies of American life."[87] In his 1899 book, *The Wife of His Youth and Other Stories of the Color Line*, Chesnutt wrote of the "Blue Vein Society," a group of upper-class, light-skinned black Americans; a mixed-race child who was adopted and raised as white; a white daughter who unknowingly killed her black half brother; and other stories that challenged dichotomous and unambiguous notions of race. In these stories Chesnutt destabilized the metaphor of the "color line." Yet most reviews praised the stories as touching descriptions of "relations between whites and blacks," not appearing to recognize that Chesnutt challenged the very notions of white and black.[88] One review was a notable exception, describing Chesnutt's writing as "studies of that middle world," explicitly acknowledging the author's destabilization of race, but according to the review "the paler shades dwell as hopelessly, with relation to ourselves, as the blackest negro."[89] Thus, even in acknowledging the instability of race, the reviewer reinscribed seemingly stable racial divisions that posited "us" versus "them," even when the "them" was not as different in appearance as one may expect. In Chesnutt's 1889 essay, "What Is a White Man?," he was more explicit, stating "the line which separates must in many instances have been practically obliterated."[90] He continued to list the "manifest absurdity" of legal racial classifications across the country.

Yet the fiction of the "color line" retained cultural importance, and attempts at crossing (or passing) that line were often met with violence. Lynching is perhaps the most predominant example of this violence. Although Ida B. Wells called it an "old thread-bare lie," public rhetoric associated lynching with the rape of white women by black men.[91] The protection of white women was a myth that helped sustain racial violence against black men who threatened white men's cultural, economic, political, or social position—black men who passed the color line in some way, real or imagined. This myth seemed to permit white men to act in their cultural role of protecting vulnerable and sexually pure white women. The myth was represented as plausible because of representations of people of African descent as brutish Other, and that intrinsic difference was the basis for the same cultural logic that was used for prohibiting interracial relationships; those relationships threatened women's moral purity and the assumed purity of the race.

As with race, marriage marked status and ascribed value through the possession of women's bodies. Many in both the black and white presses read Frederick Douglass' marriage to a white woman as a sign of what Douglass valued (whiteness) and an attempt to shift class (become whiter). Douglass' resistance to cultural understandings of his body as black came to be framed as a disavowal of his race and a potential threat if other black men were to follow Douglass' lead. Douglass' marriage could have been an opportunity to question the very concept of race—a questioning that could ultimately promote racial equality. Yet a significant proportion of responses to Douglass' marriage simply reified the logic of the Supreme Court that prohibited interracial marriage and sustained separate but equal for decades to come.

MARRIAGE, RACE, AND THE NATION

The debates over marriage illustrate that, despite Lincoln's hope, Emancipation did not assure freedom. The lines that marked the enslaved body as less than American became reinscribed after the war in constituting the racialized body. The logic of the racialized body created a cultural and political justification for separation—separation in schools, transportation, dining, and most importantly separation in marriage. Indeed, one of the most persistent justifications for segregation in a variety of different contexts was the fear that social mixing could result in miscegenation.

Following Emancipation, laws prohibiting interracial marriage proliferated. Some of these laws were explicit in applying to Chinese or Native Americans, and many attempted to define words such as "negro" or "mulatto," inscribing a rhetorical certainty on ambiguous racial lines. Each of these specifications met the needs of a given community to constitute the racialized body and, thereby, define who was part of the national body and who was Other. Marriage ascribes group identity, and the regulation of marriage is one way of controlling who belongs within and outside of that group identity. Thus, prohibition of interracial marriage was a way of drawing lines, separating those who belong from the Other. Even the language of amalgamation or miscegenation began with an assumption of racial difference, differences that were rhetorically constituted as natural and immutable.

With marriage controversies, racial identity resided in women's bodies, and racialized bodies were always gendered bodies. While to possess a woman was rhetorically framed as the possession of a race, the performance of white masculinity was carefully guarded, and perceived transgressions were often met with fear and violence. Part of this performance was the possession of white womanhood, and, thus, for a nonwhite man to attempt to be in a marital or sexual relationship with a white woman was crossing invisible yet rhetorically real boundaries. Laws and cultural norms prohibiting interracial marriage functioned to sustain racial and gender boundaries in the national body, boundaries that, in many ways, continue today.

CONCLUSION

State of the (Marital) Union

When a "foremost" American commentator on "political and theological science" warns that the future of the civilization is at risk, many people listen.[1] Elisha Mulford argued in 1870 that if certain social conditions prevailed, the nation and its moral foundation would be under threat of collapse, much like the Roman Republic. Yet this imminent risk did not derive from the state of the military, lack of reverence for the flag, or rates of democratic participation. Rather, Mulford perceived that the moral ground and, thus, the future stability of the nation were rooted in the sanctity of family and marriage. Mulford was not alone in his concern about marriage and its supposed connection to the future of the nation. Indeed, this seemingly private relationship has long been a public national obsession, an obsession manifest in the popular press, literature, the courts, and legislation. This book has unpacked the American fixation with marriage, showing that public handwringing over the "state of marriage" is but the most obvious manifestation of a complex field of argument and interpretation that figures the connections between marriage as an expression of individual love and marriage as a moral foundation of the nation. Indeed, debates about marriage are not simply about private, intimate relationships; these controversies are ways of negotiating the meanings and values of the nation.

Considerations of national identity in the United States address "one of the most persistent questions in US history"—"What does it mean to be an American?"[2] Put another way, how do diverse people with often competing interests unite around a common mythic identity of "citizen"? We can attempt to answer this question by looking at the rhetoric of presidents and other public officials, and scholarship of presidential rhetoric has often grappled with contradictions in the US commitment to equality while sustaining a long history of exclusion.[3] In a similar vein the language of law constitutes community, and, as a result, careful analysis of legal decision making can reveal values, norms, and expectations of the nation.[4] Even iconic national documents and their re-appropriations participate in constituting the myth of nation.[5]

The "official" voice of the nation, be it from a president, a judge, or another official representative, is necessarily exclusive. As nation is mythologized and "American" defined, rhetorical borders are constituted, and these borders maintain divisions between an "us" and a "them." However, these distinctions and their borders have been challenged. Counterpublics and a plurality of publics provide one model for understanding unification around resistance to dominant understandings of the public and, thus, dominant understandings of national identity.[6] Vernacular voices, not simply the voices of the empowered, also participate in constituting public identity,[7] and meanings and anxieties in national identity emerge through narratives written by public figures.[8] A wide variety of rhetorics constitute and challenge citizenship, including the choice of clothing, the choice of where to shop, participating in protests, and casting a vote.[9] As an imagined community, the United States sustains a myth of what it means to be an American through public discourse, constitutive claims, narratives, and silences.[10]

Myths of Americanness, although perhaps changing, maintain ideological commitment to inclusivity and diversity despite persistent exclusions and division. President Theodore Roosevelt, for example, constructed a mythic American identity around tropes of strength and character, and this myth of national identity helped sustain a complex relationship between the nation and the Other, which at times has included Native Americans, immigrants, and African Americans.[11] Although understandings of citizenship have shifted over time, perhaps with distinct eras, the abstract conception of citizenship is part of what enables a sense of national unity in the face of actual diversity.[12] White masculinity, for example, was a marker of civic unity that persisted through the early years of the nation and through much of the nineteenth century. Masculinity, however, had specific meanings and entailed characteristics such as disembodied reason and strength, characteristics that humans could never fully realize but used as a metric to judge themselves and others.[13] Public expectations of masculine citizenship in the United States drew on both liberal and civic republican traditions, but despite lofty ideals, these expectations were (and in many ways continue to be) plagued with contradictions and exclusions.[14]

Public rhetorics, from the institutional and official to the vernacular and the vulgar, are present in the public controversies over marriage, and all of them have to grapple with the central tension in the US tradition of understanding marriage: public versus private. The myth that marriage is or should be part of a private sphere persists, and home has long represented the private sphere as a site of refuge from public life. Yet conceptions of public and private are complex and shifting; indeed, feminist and queer theories have challenged the division between public and private as a dichotomy that sustains silence and hierarchy.[15] This book extends the critique of public and private not only to challenge the dichotomy but also to insist that the rhetoric of the private sphere in relation to marriage and womanhood has functioned to maintain social hierarchies. Characterizations of women's roles through the lens of absence sustain a blindness to the ways in which women's bodies have long been the grounds on which nation was negotiated. Such blindness sustains and naturalizes hierarchy.

This book builds a case that marriage has been a lens through which the normative identities of citizens were debated throughout a significant part of American history because that which is often conceived to be a private identity (husband or wife) both enables and constrains the status and enactments of citizenship. The individual functions as a mirror for the nation at large, reflecting or (sometimes) challenging constructions of US identity.[16] In this sense, "private" identity, as it is commonly understood, is never really private; instead, individual identity is always understood through its public context, and the meanings associated with identities enable visibility (or invisibility) within the public sphere. Public understandings of individual identity then make possible cultural practices of defining national identity. For example, marriage debates reveal that the status of women in the nineteenth century was always a public status, even though it was a status that sustained women's public invisibility, and that invisibility was important in characterizing women as "good citizens." Although the myth of the political public sphere is grounded in a model of citizen as voter and the home as a space removed (and perhaps safe) from the public sphere, this book proves that the rhetoric of marriage and symbolic womanhood was an important aspect of a myth of national identity.

The supposed division between public and private is grounded, in part, in the liberal tradition that reaches back to John Locke but was "widely institutionalized in politics and law by the nineteenth century." In this frame, people "possessed publicly relevant rights by virtue of being private persons," rather than public status ("fief owner, copyholder, husband, lord of the manor").[17] Yet even as men came to be understood in many respects through their contractual rather than status relations, marriage, especially for women, remained a marker of status that was absolutely central to public identity. Legally, marriage was thought to exist in a unique space: originating as contract but grounded in status.[18] Thus, there is a persistent tension between the culture of individualism in the nineteenth century and the importance of status in public discourse and policy of marriage. It is, in part, this tension that makes marriage an important site of inquiry in understanding public identity.

After the American Revolution, the nation experienced what has been labeled as a culture of republicanism that challenged unchecked governmental power and reinforced a sense of mutual obligation. According to some, this spirit of republicanism extended to the family, creating what has been labeled as the "Republican Family."[19] By the end of the eighteenth century and into the nineteenth, public notions of marriage and family were changing, creating a type of cultural anxiety, where authority entailed in marriage became limited by duties, affection, and other familial emotions. Yet labeling the American family as a "Republican Family" risks obfuscating a complicated relationship between family and the state. Theoretically, this conception of family would protect individuals from arbitrary authority while enabling members of the family to contribute toward the betterment of civil society. Through the nineteenth century, such a conception of family was true only within very constrained understandings of proper manhood and womanhood. The closer one came to the mythic ideals of manhood and womanhood, the more an individual was considered to be positively participating in civic society, but too much deviation was considered harmful and required regulation from authority outside of the family. As this book illustrates, the concept of marriage was not stable in the nineteenth-century United States, nor were the relationships between marriage and republican or liberal principles.

No other public institution is quite like marriage, and the legal idiosyncrasies of marriage, especially in the nineteenth century, made for a complex rhetorical geography. Like a business contract, marriage was a partnership that typically entailed obligations and benefits for those involved. However, marriage was much more than a simple contract because it transformed the legal and social identities of its participants, making the law of contract inadequate to govern the complexities of marriage. There was, for example, a fundamental legal and social difference between the unmarried (*femme sole*) and married (*femme covert*) woman. A woman did not simply join another family but, for legal and public purposes, became a different person within marriage, signaled by the change in her name. A married woman in the nineteenth century had different property rights, different social status, and different legal protections, indicative of a shift in status not typically associated with contract law. Indeed, marriage was (and continues to be) a legal, cultural, and political institution unlike any other. Although not transparently about citizenship or national identity, this book builds a case that the public concept of marriage provides a bridge between seemingly public and private identities and, thus, between spheres that are often treated as separate. While a study of marriage controversies certainly does not replace attention to voting, protesting, or presidential rhetoric, it contributes an important part to the larger picture, especially in attempts to understand the role of women in American public culture.

In the nineteenth century, women's bodies functioned as sites of constituting culture and public morality. Within this context, womanhood, as an abstracted myth, functioned symbolically in marriage debates to represent the state of the nation as a whole. One important recurring theme was a container metaphor that posited women as the containers of the "future of the race" and purveyors of public morality. "Race" in the nineteenth century included, often indiscriminately, biology, culture, norms, ideals, values, and ethnicity. This book traces the symbolic appropriation of womanhood through nineteenth-century marriage debates to illustrate the significance of the appropriation and the complexity and contradictions. In particular, actual women intersect with the symbolic woman in ways that reify, modify, and challenge the myth. As women's public identities were intimately connected to their status in marriage, public debates about marriage provide a critical site to interrogate the symbolic function of womanhood and public morality in the culture of the nineteenth-century United States.

Although debates about marriage foreground issues of home, masculinity, and femininity, nineteenth-century marriage controversies were also about regulating a line between civilized and barbarian nations. The public negotiation of "civilization," ranking and comparing various nations and people, has a long history.[20] When tallying up the lists of things about which "they" are barbarians, marriage customs will be prominent, just as they will when this rhetoric is turned inward and anxieties surface about whether "we" are sufficiently civilized or sinking into barbarity. Concepts of civilized and barbarian can be used rhetorically to draw a line between self and Other, and these rhetorical borders contribute to the mythic national identity, seeming to justify inclusions and exclusions from that identity.

Throughout the nineteenth century, scientific and religious rhetorics were influential in creating both a discourse and rationale for the line drawing between the seemingly civilized and barbarian. Early in the century, people such as Jean-Baptiste Lamarck and phrenologists debated the roles of environment and inheritance on human development.[21] By the second half of the nineteenth century, Darwin's theory of evolution was tremendously influential in the United States.[22] Even before Darwin's *The Descent of Man*, several theorists attempted to extend evolutionary concepts into the social realm. Herbert Spencer was probably the most prolific of the social evolutionary thinkers, establishing "evolutionary science as the 'master discourse defining sexuality, knowledge, and power in the second half of the nineteenth century,'" through the concept of "survival of the fittest."[23] Francis Galton is often given credit for founding the eugenics movement that came to be influential toward the end of the century, and this concept maintained that society could be improved with the procreation of its most "fit" members.[24] That determination of fitness was always imbued with cultural expectations of gender, race, and class. Public discourse of evolutionism was intertwined with religion, nature, and, at times, American exceptionalism.[25]

Similarly, throughout much of US history, a rhetoric of religion has been strongly influential, and religious and scientific rhetorics often functioned as mutually reinforcing. The United States has long been viewed as a Christian nation. Tocqueville, for example, commented that religion was intermingled with national customs, and conceptions of American exceptionalism were commonly framed through a Christian rhetoric.[26] Yet Americans have also contested the meaning and practices associated with being a Christian nation, and marriage controversies are one of the locations of this contestation.

Although perhaps not transparently about "civilized" American identity or "fit" citizens, debates about marriage have an enduring public importance, in part because they participate in constituting the perceived line between civilized self and barbarous Other. Because these concepts are rhetorical, ways of understanding "civilized" and "barbarian" evolve and shift over time. Marriage controversy provides a lens through which to trace these evolving rhetorical borders, explicitly considering the roles of gender, race, ethnicity, and class. Different times within the decade and different specific marriage controversies reveal diverse ways in which the lines are drawn, as well as challenges and contradictions. A broad analysis of marriage in the nineteenth century contributes a fuller account of American public identity as it is defined in opposition to an Other.

LEGACY OF NINETEENTH-CENTURY MARRIAGE CONTROVERSIES

The rhetorical logic of nineteenth-century marriage controversies became manifest in a variety of areas, and one perhaps unexpected area was naturalization laws. In January of 1913 Ethel Mackenzie attempted to register to vote. Mackenzie had been a supporter of women's suffrage, and when California amended its state constitution in October of 1911, Mackenzie expected that she would be able to exercise her newfound right. Mackenzie was surprised to find that she was prohibited from voting, not because of her status as a woman but because she was no longer a US citizen. Without her knowledge or consent, Ethel Mackenzie was expatriated, even though she was born in the United States and had never left the country. She lost her US citizenship because of her marriage to a British citizen.[27]

Ethel Mackenzie was not alone in discovering that her status as citizen was dependent on her husband's citizenship. In 1855 the United States adopted legislation that automatically conferred US citizenship on most women who married a US citizen or were married to a man who subsequently attained naturalization.[28] The rhetorical logic of the 1855 immigration legislation was that marital unity meant that if a husband was good enough for citizenship, so too would be his wife. This legislation built off the logic of the family government and its legal counterpart of coverture in positing the husband as the public voice of his family, so the naturalization of the head of the family government was considered a *de facto* naturalization of the rest of the family.[29] The public rationale framed US citizenship as universally desirable, and the only question was whether an individual was worthy of US citizenship.

In 1907 the United States passed legislation that explicitly divested women who were US citizens of their citizenship if they married a foreigner. The US Supreme Court upheld this legislation in a case involving Ethel Mackenzie, arguing that there is both a national and an international interest to marital unity. Marriage, the court argued, was a voluntary act, and long-standing legal and cultural norms that merged the public identities of husband and wife appeared to make expatriation the natural extension of such a marriage.[30] Although the Mackenzie case brought some public scrutiny, the 1907 legislation was not very controversial at the time. Indeed, the status of women was treated as an afterthought in the congressional debate, and the sponsor of the bill noted that the section on women simply clarified and codified existing practice.[31]

However, immigration laws as they related to marriage cannot be understood simply through coverture and the family government. There were entire groups of women who were denied US citizenship, and occasionally even denied entry into the United States, even after their marriage to US citizens. Chinese women are examples of this disparity. In 1884 Ah Moy attempted to enter the United States with her new husband, a laborer who was legally residing in the United States. The courts, without ever mentioning her by name (the closest the judges came to actually referring to her was as the "child-wife"), denied her entry into the United States, arguing, "The fiction of the law as to the unity of the two spouses does not apply under the restriction act."[32] In 1901 Tsoi Sim was detained as illegally residing in the United States and ordered by a California district court to be deported to China, even though she was married to a US citizen of Chinese descent. The 1855 Citizenship Act was not thought to apply to Tsoi Sim because she was Chinese, and although her deportation was reversed by the California Appeals Court, Sim would not become a US citizen through her marriage to a citizen.[33] Courts appeared to deny the seemingly natural rights of coverture, instead appealing to a combination of ethnic and gender performance to constitute these women as Other and, thus, unworthy of entering the United States, much less American citizenship.

The aversion to Chinese women occurred at several different intersecting levels. Many Chinese women attempting to enter the United States were reported to be prostitutes and, thus, immoral.[34] The public rhetoric often framed Chinese women as deviant, particularly sexually deviant. Regardless of their reason for entry, Chinese women in the United States also posed a unique threat in that their children, if born in the United States, would be US citizens, irrevocably increasing the presence of the racialized Other in the United States. Rather than viewing values of coverture and limits to citizenship as conflicting, the public rhetoric about Chinese wives posited the family government, class, ethnicity, race, and gender as inseparable concepts; one could not be properly understood without reference to the others. Women's bodies functioned as symbolic containers of American values and culture, and, as with the controversy over interracial marriage, many Americans claimed an interest in regulating marriage as a means of regulating women's bodies and, thus, the future of the nation.

Even as women's suffrage became national law, marriage was a frequent part of the public controversy, especially the notion that voting wives would disrupt family unity.[35] In responding to this fear, suffrage activists often reframed citizenship within common feminine frames, suggesting that women could retain their traditional roles within marriage while also assuming their roles as citizens.[36] The nation, the public rhetoric suggested, depended on women's performance of traditional roles as purveyors of public morality.

Indeed, the nineteenth-century rhetoric of marriage was so powerful that some of the most basic conceptions of the family government were not meaningfully changed until the 1970s.[37] It was not until this time, for example, that "marital rape" and "domestic violence" began to enter into the public lexicon, a particularly significant linguistic change because the act of naming constitutes meaning and shapes possibilities for understanding. Although Moses Harman was jailed in the nineteenth century for his vivid descriptions of marital rape, the rhetorical logic of the time kept this violence largely hidden. Despite there currently being a vocabulary for domestic violence in the United States, violence against women continues to be a pertinent issue.

Throughout the twenty-first century, marriage equality, especially as it pertains to same-sex marriage, has been an enduring controversy. The rhetorical contours of the current controversy are strikingly similar to those of the nineteenth century. Marriage matters because it functions as a metric of public morality. As Theodore Roosevelt said, the "average family . . . represent[s] the kind of citizenship fit for the foundation of a great nation."[38] In the 2013 decision of *United States v. Windsor* the US Supreme Court repeated values such as "pride," "recognition," and "dignity" as those emerging from marriage.[39] Within this framework marriage appears to function as a type of individual affirmation. Yet that affirming role exists within the context of monogamy and the nuclear family, a connection that is most evident in the Court's reference to the children of same-sex parents. These associations posit self-worth as emerging from proper performance of social roles, even while broadening who has access to those proper social roles. The twenty-first-century controversy is about not simply individual families but also the ways in which those individuals reflect the nation as a whole. As with the nineteenth century, social change is destabilizing, and marriage controversies are about more than changes in public policy—they reach the core of the nation's public morality and, thus, national identity.

Marriage controversies are about drawing lines, rhetorically constituting the moral geography of the nation and, thus, the nation itself. While electing a president or establishing voting laws may seem to be a more direct way of defining a nation and constituting a people, marriage has been an enduring part of this process. Marriage matters because it prescribes and regulates "proper" American behavior, it defines and sustains divisions between American and Other, and it establishes the moral framework on which the nation is supposedly built. Marriage becomes controversial when these boundaries and norms threaten to be disrupted, and the controversy itself is where meaning and identity become inscribed. As Americans continue a fixation on marriage and the connections between seemingly private relationships and public identities, citizens must also continue to interrogate the ways that the public rhetoric of marriage inscribes American public identity.

Notes

Introduction

1 Address by President Roosevelt before the National Congress of Mothers, March 2, 1905, MS Am 1541 (315), 5, Theodore Roosevelt Collection, Houghton Library, Harvard University.

2 See Lauren Berlant, *The Queen of America Goes to Washington City: Essays on Sex and Citizenship* (Durham, N.C.: Duke University Press, 1997), 2–3, 56; idem, *The Female Complaint: The Unfinished Business of Sentimentality in American Culture* (Durham, N.C.: Duke University Press, 2008). Berlant (in *The Queen of America*) ascribes what she labels as a shift from the "political public sphere" to the "intimate public sphere" to the Reagan Republicanism of the 1980s. She argues that the Republican Right during the Reagan years privatized citizenship through its false and nostalgic conception of the "American Dream" and "American way of life," making seemingly private actions markers of citizenship. What Berlant labels as a privatization of citizenship, in turn, ascribes a normative vision of American identity, and increases the stakes in regulating American identity because the private citizen becomes a mirror for the nation itself. This study suggests that intimate and seemingly private actions have long been used as a mirror for the state of the nation. Marriage is one important location where this process has been happening since at least the nineteenth century, and, perhaps, this sense of "privatized citizenship" is an endemic part of American public identity.

3 Benedict Anderson, *Imagined Communities*, rev. ed. (New York: Verso, 1991); Leroy G. Dorsey, *We Are All Americans, Pure and Simple: Theodore Roosevelt and the Myth of Americanism* (Tuscaloosa: University of Alabama Press, 2007); Mary E. Stuckey, "One Nation (Pretty Darn) Divisible: National Identity in the 2004 Conventions," *Rhetoric and Public Affairs* 8, no. 4 (2005).

4 Vanessa B. Beasley, *You, the People: American National Identity in Presidential Rhetoric* (College Station: Texas A&M University Press, 2004); Mary E. Stuckey, *Defining Americans: The Presidency and National Identity* (Lawrence: University Press of Kansas, 2004); Dorsey, *We Are All Americans*; Stuckey, "One Nation"; Garry Wills, *Inventing America: Jefferson's Declaration of Independence* (New York: Vintage Books, 1979).

5 Jeninne Lee-St. John, "To Love, Honor and Save Money," *Time*, June 2, 2008; Ashley R. Harris, "Brides Go on a Budget in This Lousy Economy," *Newsweek*, June 23, 2008.

6 This book builds off of Nancy Cott's book that argues, "Public preservation of marriage on this model [monogamy and consent] has had tremendous consequences for men's and women's citizenship as well as for their private lives" (3). While Cott paints a picture of marriage in fairly broad strokes, my study provides snapshots of specific marriage controversies within the nineteenth-century United States. Similarly, Stephanie Coontz's sweeping history of marriage has been extremely influential. The breadth of this previous research is very important in understanding marriage in its broad historical trajectory, as well as recurring themes in the United States, but, at the same time, the specificity of my study enables a different type of depth through analysis of important case studies. In particular, I approach marriage using a rhetorical methodology, which can enable a greater sensitivity to discursive constructions of marriage. In other words, while Cott, Coontz, and others have done important work on the lived reality of marriage, by unpacking how "marriage" is used discursively in public culture, I will establish that the public meaning of marriage helps constitute who counts as a "real" American. Nancy Cott, *Public Vows: A History of Marriage and the Nation* (Cambridge, Mass.: Harvard University Press, 2000); Stephanie Coontz, *Marriage, A History: From Obedience to Intimacy, or How Love Conquered Marriage* (New York: Viking, 2005). Similarly, Elizabeth Freeman's analysis of the wedding as a metonymic ritual uses cultural texts such as literature and film to uncover the relationships between cultural fictions of the wedding and gender in American culture. I am concerned with some of the same questions that Freeman addresses, but by focusing on key moments of public controversy, I am able to analyze moments of reinforcement and resistance to gendered (and raced) conceptions of citizenship. Rather than challenging Freeman's research, this book contributes to a larger conversation about the importance of marriage and the complex interrelationships of politics, law, institutions, and culture. Elizabeth Freeman, *The Wedding Complex: Forms of Belonging in Modern American Culture* (Durham, N.C.: Duke University Press, 2002).

7 Catherine E. Beecher, *A Treatise on Domestic Economy, for the Use of Young Ladies at Home and at School*, rev. ed. (New York: Harper & Brothers, 1854), 37.

8 Linda Kerber, *No Constitutional Right to Be Ladies: Women and the Obligations of Citizenship* (New York: Hill & Wang, 1998), 11.

9 Barbara Welter, "The Cult of True Womanhood: 1820–1860," *American Quarterly* 18, no. 2 (1966).

10 Patricia Bizzell, "Chastity Warrants for Women Public Speakers in Nineteenth-Century American Fiction," *Rhetoric Society Quarterly* 40, no. 4 (2010); Joanne E. Passet, *Sex Radicals and the Quest for Women's Equality* (Urbana: University of Illinois Press, 2003).

11 Bonnie J. Dow and Mari Boor Tonn, "Feminine Style and Political Judgment in the Rhetoric of Ann Richards," *Quarterly Journal of Speech* 79, no. 3 (1993); Mari Boor Tonn, "Militant Motherhood: Labor's Mary Harris 'Mother' Jones," *Quarterly Journal of Speech* 82, no. 1 (1996); Elizabeth Clapp, *Mother of All Children: Women Reformers and the Rise of the Juvenile Courts in Progressive Era America* (University Park: Pennsylvania State University Press, 1998); Jennifer A. Peeples and Kevin M. DeLuca, "The Truth of the Matter: Motherhood, Community and Environmental Justice," *Women's Studies in Communication* 29, no. 1 (2006); Seth Koven and Sonya Michel, "Introduction: Mother Worlds," in *Mothers of a New World: Materialist Politics and the Origins of Welfare States*, ed. Seth Koven and Sonya Michel (New York: Routledge, 1993); Leslie J. Harris, "Motherhood, Race, and Gender: The Rhetoric of Women's Antislavery Activism in the *Liberty Bell* Giftbooks," *Women's Studies in Communication* 32, no. 3 (2009); Linda Gordon, "Putting Children First: Women, Maternalism, and Welfare in the Early Twentieth Century," in *U.S. History as Women's History*, ed. Linda K. Kerber, Alice Kessler-Harris, and Kathryn Kish Sklar (Chapel Hill: University of North Carolina Press, 1995); Molly Ladd-Taylor, *Mother-Work: Women, Child Welfare, and the State, 1890–1930* (Urbana: University of Illinois Press, 1994).

12 Linda K. Kerber, *Women of the Republic: Intellect and Ideology in Revolutionary America* (Chapel Hill: University of North Carolina Press, 1980); address by President Roosevelt before the National Congress of Mothers.

13 Mary Ryan, *Women in Public: Between Banners and Ballots, 1825–1880* (Baltimore: Johns Hopkins University Press, 1990); Stephen H. Browne, *Angelina Grimké: Rhetoric, Identity, and the Radical Imagination* (East Lansing: Michigan State University Press, 2000); Karlyn Kohrs Campbell, "Gender and Genre: Loci of Invention and Contradiction in the Earliest Speeches by U.S. Women," *Quarterly Journal of Speech* 81, no. 4 (1995); A. Cheree Carlson, "Creative Casuistry and Feminist Consciousness: The Rhetoric of Moral Reform," *Quarterly Journal of Speech* 78, no. 1 (1992); Nan Johnson, *Gender and Rhetorical Space in American Life, 1866–1910* (Carbondale: Southern Illinois University Press, 2002); Kristy Maddux, "When Patriots Protest: The Anti-suffrage Discursive Transformation of 1917," *Rhetoric and Public Affairs* 7, no. 3 (2004); Angela Ray and Cindy Koenig Richards, "Inventing Citizens, Imagining Gender Justice: The Suffrage Rhetoric of Virginia and Francis Minor," *Quarterly Journal of Speech* 93, no. 4 (2007); Susan Zaeske, *Signatures of Citizenship: Petitioning, Antislavery, and Women's Political Identity* (Chapel Hill: University of North Carolina Press, 2003).

14 Cott, *Public Vows*, 1; Kerber, *No Constitutional Right*. Kerber insists that part of the impetus for limiting women's ability to enter into contract derived from a need to preserve "the husband's [supposed] right to sexual access to the wife's body" (14). The laws of coverture were thought to protect the husband, but also protect the wife from "the stresses of public life, from the need to risk property and reputation in political encounter" (15).

15 William Blackstone, *Commentaries on the Laws of England, in Four Books*, 12th ed., vol. 1 (London: A. Strahan & W. Woodfall, for T. Cadell, 1793–1795), 441.

16 The concept of coverture was consistently invoked in legal treaties and judicial decisions—for example: "Can a Married Woman Maintain an Action of Tort

against Her Husband for a Tort Committed during Coverture?," *Yale Law Journal* 22, no. 3 (1913); "Married Women's Act. Coverture. Statute of Limitations. Bliler v. Boswell, 59 Pac. Rep. 798 (Wyo.). Feme Covert," *Yale Law Journal* 9, no. 6 (1900); Reva Siegel, "She the People: The Nineteenth Amendment, Sex Equality, Federalism, and the Family," *Harvard Law Review* 115 (2002); "In the Supreme Court of Pennsylvania, 1858. Williams and Wife vs. Coward and Wife," *American Law Register* 6, no. 5 (1858). One can also see Richard Chused, *Private Acts in Public Places* (Philadelphia: University of Pennsylvania Press, 1994), 1361, 1410; Reva Siegel, "The Modernization of Marital Status Law: Adjudicating Wives' Rights to Earnings, 1860–1930," in "Symposium: Divorce and Feminist Legal Theory," special issue, *Georgetown Law Journal* 82 (1994): 2131. It is true that by the middle of the nineteenth century in the United States, people were questioning the public status of women and, thus, the meanings and implications of coverture. Married women's property rights are frequently cited as an example of a weakening in coverture. In 1848, for example, the New York Married Women's Property Rights Act passed, and this legislation was part of a larger national trend of married women's property legislation. However, Chused argues that while property rights legislation signaled a weakening in coverture, these acts were not revolutionary. Instead, they were limited in scope and an expected response to economic trends of the era. In fact, the first round of acts was limited to protecting women's property from their husbands' debts. According to Chused, the laws solidified women's separate spheres because women's property was placed in a category of special protections. Additionally, Siegel argues that only property gained entirely outside of the home and not associated with a wife's duties was considered the woman's property. Thus, everything from housework to farm work to piecework remained the husband's legal property under the principles of coverture. In short, 1848 did not signal a revolution in women's status but was a sign of the emerging public debate over women's status. It is precisely this emerging and developing debate that contributed to public controversies over marriage.

17 Leslie J. Harris, "Law as Father: Metaphors of Family in Nineteenth-Century Law," *Communication Studies* 61, no. 5 (2010).

18 Siegel, "She the People."

19 State v. Rhodes, 61 N.C. 453 (1868); Gordon v. Potter, 17 Vt. 348 (1845); Lander, Jr. v. Seaver, 32 Vt. 114 (1859); State v. Jones, 95 N.C. 588 (1886); Foley v. Foley, 61 Ill. App. 577 (1895); Martin v. Robson, 65 Ill. 129 (1872).

20 Dana D. Nelson, *National Manhood: Capitalist Citizenship and the Imagined Fraternity of White Men* (Durham, N.C.: Duke University Press, 1998); Stuckey, *Defining Americans.* Nelson, for example, examines conceptions of citizenship as residing in a mythic sense of white masculinity.

21 Michael Leff, "Things Made by Words: Reflections on Textual Criticism," *Quarterly Journal of Speech* 78, no. 2 (1992): 228.

22 Leff, "Things Made by Words," 229.

23 Kathleen J. Turner, "Introduction: Rhetorical History as Social Construction," in *Doing Rhetorical History: Concepts and Cases*, ed. Kathleen J. Turner (Tuscaloosa: University of Alabama Press, 1998); David Zarefsky, "Four Senses of Rhetorical History," in *Doing Rhetorical History: Concepts and Cases*, ed. Kathleen J. Turner (Tuscaloosa: University of Alabama Press, 1998).

Chapter 1

1 Poor v. Poor, 8 N.H. 307 (1836).

2 Moyler v. Moyler, 11 Ala. 620 (1847).

3 George A. Hickox, *Legal Disabilities of Married Women in Connecticut* (Hartford: Case, Lockwood & Brainard, 1871), 5.

4 *Rhodes*, 456–57.

5 Joel Prentiss Bishop, *Commentaries on the Law of Marriage and Divorce: With the Evidence, Practice, Pleading, and Forms: Also of Separation without Divorce and of the Evidence of Marriage in All Issues*, 5th ed., 2 vols. (Boston: Little, Brown, 1873), 1:624.

6 Walter C. Tiffany, *Handbook on the Law of Persons and Domestic Relations* (St. Paul: West Publishing, 1896), 51.

7 My rhetorical analysis focuses on frequently cited upper court decisions. These upper court decisions are more likely than lower court decisions to have a preserved text available for analysis. Because I am interested in the reasoning of the decisions, it is important to have access to the actual text of the decision and not simply the holding. Upper court decisions are also more likely to be engaged as precedent by other courts.

8 Bishop, *Commentaries on the Law of Marriage and Divorce*, 626.

9 *Poor*, 315–16. Also Close v. Close, 24 N.J. Eq. 338, 339 (1874); Kate Williams, Plaintiff in Error v. Edward L. Williams and Elizabeth M. Williams, Defendants in Error, 1 Colo. App. 281, 285 (1892); George S. Henderson v. Rebecca Henderson, 88 Ill. 248, 250 (1878); William J. Ward v. Marietta E. Ward, 103 Ill. 477, 625 (1882).

10 Betsy Ann Hoshall v. Nicholas Hoshall, 51 Md. 72 (1879); *Williams*, 287; *Ward*, 482.

11 Harriet P. Reed, Appellant v. John Reed, Respondent, 4 Nev. 395, 396 (1868). Also *Ward*, 483.

12 There has been extensive research documenting the significance of definition for public deliberation. This research has established that definition can function as an important topic of debate, but definition can also be stipulated to change the framework of debate and shape the possibilities for public deliberation. See, for example, David Zarefsky, "Strategic Maneuvering through Persuasive Definitions: Implications for Dialectic and Rhetoric," *Argumentation* 20, no. 3 (2006); idem, "Definitions," in *Argument in a Time of Change: Definitions, Frameworks, and Critiques*, ed. James F. Klumpp (Annandale, Va.: National Communication Association, 1997); Martin Medhurst, "The First Amendment vs. Human Rights: A Case Study in Community Sentiment and Argument from Definition," *Western Journal of Speech Communication* 46, no. 1 (1982); Katheryn M. Olson, "The Controversy over President Reagan's Visit to Bitburg: Strategies of Definition and Redefinition," *Quarterly Journal of Speech* 75, no. 2 (1989); Edward Schiappa, *Defining Reality* (Carbondale: Southern Illinois University Press, 2003).

13 *Obiter dicta* in judicial decisions are considered to be comments or examples extraneous to the actual holding of the decision. Rhetoricians and legal scholars have argued for the significance of analyzing *obiter dicta* and the rhetoric of law. See Anthony Amsterdam and Jerome Bruner, *Minding the Law* (Cambridge,

Mass.: Harvard University Press, 2000); Maria Aristodemou, *Law and Literature: Journeys from Her to Eternity* (New York: Oxford University Press, 2000); Haig Bosmajian, *Metaphor and Reason in Judicial Opinions* (Carbondale: Southern Illinois University Press, 1992); Leslie J. Harris, "Law as Father: Metaphors of Family in Nineteenth-Century Law," *Communication Studies* 61, no. 5 (2010); Marouf Hasian, "Critical Legal Rhetorics: The Theory and Practice of Law in a Postmodern World," *Southern Communication Journal* 60, no. 1 (1994); Marouf Hasian, Celeste Michelle Condit, and John Louis Lucaites, "The Rhetorical Boundaries of 'the Law': A Consideration of the Rhetorical Culture of Legal Practice and the Case of the 'Separate but Equal' Doctrine," *Quarterly Journal of Speech* 82, no. 4 (1996); James Boyd White, *Heracles' Bow* (Madison: University of Wisconsin Press, 1985); idem, *The Legal Imagination* (Chicago: University of Chicago Press, 1985).

14 *Moyler*, 626.

15 Farnham v. Farnham, 73 Ill. 497 (quoted in *Ward*, 483).

16 *Moyler*, 12.

17 *Poor*, 308.

18 *Poor*, 310–11.

19 *Poor*, 313, 19.

20 *Poor*, 319–20.

21 State v. Simpson Pettie (80 N.C. 367 [1879]) utilized similar language. The judge said that a husband could chastise his wife but not out of his own "bad passion."

22 David v. David, 27 Ala. 222, 225 (1855).

23 *David*, 227.

24 Louisa Skinner, Appellee, Petitioner v. William H. Skinner, Appellant, Defendant, 5 Wis. 449, 452 (1856).

25 *Skinner*, 453.

26 *Skinner*, 452.

27 The judges upheld the fine of ten dollars (this is equivalent to about $200 in 2013). State v. Richard Oliver, 70 N.C. 60 (1874).

28 Robert L. Griswold, "Law, Sex, Cruelty, and Divorce in Victorian America, 1840–1900," *American Quarterly* 38, no. 5 (1986): 721–45; idem, "Sexual Cruelty and the Case for Divorce in Victorian America," *Signs* 11, no. 3 (1986): 529–41; Reva B. Siegel, "'The Rule of Love': Wife Beating as Prerogative and Privacy," *Yale Law Journal* 105 (1996): 2134; Jonathan L. Hafetz, "'A Man's Home Is His Castle?': Reflections on the Home, the Family, and Privacy during the Late Nineteenth and Early Twentieth Centuries," *William and Mary Journal of Women and the Law* 8 (2002): 189. Griswold ("Law, Sex, Cruelty, and Divorce") argues that around the middle of the nineteenth century there was an expansion in definitions of cruelty that reflects changing attitudes toward women in the Victorian era. My analysis is not inconsistent with Griswold's argument, but my analysis suggests that the intersections of class, race, and the performance of gender roles were important determinates of judicial perceptions of cruelty. Further, Griswold's article in *Signs* that same year appears to suggest that the legal decision making was complicated, inconsistent, and not clearly temporal. Siegel makes a similar argument and describes a movement from a chastisement doctrine to a privacy doctrine. By the end of the century, Siegel argues, judges had shifted from explicitly condoning extreme violence to ignoring much violence in the

name of family privacy. She also argues, "Judges reasoned about the propriety of violence in the marriage relationship with attention to the economic status of the married couple, with the result that the evidence required to prove 'extreme cruelty' varied by class, on the doctrinally explicit assumption that violence was a common part of life among the married poor." Hafetz comes to a similar conclusion, arguing, "When the state took action against marital violence, investigations tended towards the homes of poor and working-class immigrants. When an agent did investigate a middle-class home, he or she usually did so with greater respect for the privacy of the inhabitants." My study builds off of these conclusions. However, rather than focus on temporality, I insist that public representations of the symbolic woman, especially as the concept intersects with race and class, were an essential element to understanding domestic violence. These patterns are evident by moving analysis away from holdings to rhetorical analysis of the *obiter dicta* of the trials. Much of this previous research, for example, has determined that courts prohibited violence against women, especially toward the end of the century. It would, however, be a faulty assumption to conclude from this pattern that courts upheld women's individual rights as equal citizens. Rhetorical analysis of the available reasoning and *obiter dicta* suggests that individual rights were not nearly as important as women's status.

29 This data comes from "Homicide in Chicago 1870–1930," Northwestern University School of Law, last modified 2012, http://homicide.northwestern.edu/. Thank you to Sang-Yeon Kim for analysis of the quantitative data. Walter Nugent, "Demography: Chicago as a Modern World City," in *The Encyclopedia of Chicago*, ed. James R. Grossman, Ann Durkin Keating, and Janice L. Reiff (Chicago: University of Chicago Press, 2004), 233, 235; "Chicago Metropolitan Population," in *The Encyclopedia of Chicago*,, 1011; Robert G. Spinney, *City of Big Shoulders: A History of Chicago* (DeKalb: Northern Illinois University Press, 2000), 123. Chicago provides a useful case study because of the availability of both newspaper records and police records. Police records are available through the Homicide in Chicago database. The rapid growth and immigration profile of Chicago are notable and enable a study of the intersections between immigration and gender violence. According to Nugent, in 1837, when Chicago was first charted as a city, it had about four thousand residents. It was an unremarkable frontier town that grew to be the second largest city in the nation by the end of the century. By 1900 the population had reached nearly 1,700,000, with a huge jump in growth occurring in the 1880s. While some of this growth came from emigration within the United States, Chicago quickly became a destination for immigrants, especially European immigrants. By 1860 half of the city was foreign-born, and by 1890 79 percent of Chicago residents were either foreign-born or children of immigrants. According to Spinney, between 1880 and 1920 2.5 million immigrants came to Chicago, and most came from southern or eastern Europe.

30 In order to identify newspaper articles for rhetorical analysis, I searched for newspaper reports of the spousal murders recorded in the Homicide in Chicago Database that occurred between 1870 and 1899. In order to account for the constituted reality that newspaper readers would have encountered, I also included a selection of representative articles about murders occurring in other cities that were reported in the Chicago papers.

31 "Homicide in Chicago 1870–1930."
32 "Wife-Murder: Jerry Kennedy Kills His Spouse, and Tries to Kill Himself. The Facts in Regard to the Murder of an Innocent and Much-Enduring Woman," *Chicago Daily Tribune*, July 15, 1878.
33 "Wife Murderer No. 3: Albert Dolyse, a Blacksmith, Shoots and Kills in Cold Blood," *Chicago Daily Tribune*, December 2, 1897.
34 Myriam Poauillac, "Near West Side," in *The Encyclopedia of Chicago*, ed. James R. Grossman, Ann Durkin Keating, and Janice L. Reiff (Chicago: University of Chicago Press, 2004); Spinney, *City of Big Shoulders*, 71. Chicago immigrants tended to settle within ethnic communities. By the 1870s Chicago's Near West Side, for example, was a diverse mosaic of ethnic communities established by Irish, German, Czech, Bohemian, Jewish, Russian, Polish, and Italian immigrants. The Near West Side was also described as an overcrowded slum. The connections between immigration and poverty, however, were not unique to this specific area of Chicago. Spinney argues, "Ethnocultural issues were also class issues. . . . In 1848 and 1849, the wealthiest 1 percent of the city's population possessed a staggering 52 percent of the city's wealth, and the richest 10 percent controlled 94 percent of the wealth. Seventy-four percent of the city's head of families—most of whom were immigrants or sons of immigrants—owned no land or commercial wealth and few personal belongings." Jane Addams and Ellen Gates Starr responded to this mixture of poverty and immigration by establishing Hull House on the New West Side in 1889. Hull House became the best-known settlement house in the country with its mix of social services, Americanization, and ethnic diversity.
35 "Attempted Murder: A Divorced Wife Shot and Seriously Injured by Her Former Husband," *Chicago Daily Tribune*, November 30, 1872.
36 "Wife-Murder: A Wretch Shoots His Young Wife for Having Caused His Arrest," *Chicago Daily Tribune*, June 24, 1883.
37 "Wife Murderer No. 3."
38 "Jealousy and Murder: The Tragedy at Columbus, O.," *Chicago Tribune*, September 20, 1872.
39 "The Wife-Murder: Full Particulars of the Death of Mrs. Dr. Grosse. The Most Beastly Case of Wife-Murder on Record," *Chicago Tribune*, August 6, 1871.
40 "The M'namara Murder," *Chicago Daily Tribune*, August 3, 1882.
41 "A Fatal Kick," *Chicago Daily Tribune*, August 1, 1882.
42 "Wife-Murder: Full Particulars of the Death of Mrs. Dr. Grosse."
43 "Fatal Kick."
44 "An Argument for High License," *Chicago Daily Tribune*, May 12, 1883.
45 "Argument for High License."
46 "Flogged to Death," *Chicago Daily Tribune*, February 20, 1883.
47 "Walsh's Fate," *Chicago Daily Tribune*, May 16, 1883.
48 "Beaten to Death," *Chicago Daily Tribune*, December 27, 1885.
49 "The Wife's Temper Considered," *New York Times*, April 17, 1886.
50 "A Mass of Bruises: Inquest on the Wife of Tom Walsh. Details of a Horrible Murder," *Chicago Daily Tribune*, February 21, 1883.
51 "The Hot Coffee Murder: Conclusion of the Trial of Joachim Geist for Scalding His Wife to Death," *Chicago Tribune*, February 28, 1872.

52 "The Condon Murder-Trial: Insanity and Self-Defense," *Chicago Daily Tribune*, September 10, 1875.
53 "Condon Murder-Trial."
54 Hendrik Hartog, "Lawyering, Husbands' Rights, and 'the Unwritten Law' in Nineteenth-Century America," *Journal of American History* 84, no. 1 (1997): 67.
55 Dawn Keetly, "From Anger to Jealousy: Explaining Domestic Homicide in Antebellum America," *Journal of Social History* 42, no. 2 (2008). Keetly argues that the introduction of jealousy as a natural and inevitable emotion, as well as a form of insanity in domestic murder, emerged with the Sickles case (1859).
56 Hartog, "Lawyering, Husbands' Rights," 78, 83.
57 "Wife-Murder: Full Particulars of the Death of Mrs. Dr. Grosse."
58 "Desperate Attempt at Wife-Murder: Henry Jansen Stabs His Better Half Three Times with a Knife," *Chicago Daily Tribune*, November 27, 1886.
59 "The Latest Wife Murder," *Chicago Tribune*, May 22, 1870.
60 "Love and Murder," *Chicago Daily Tribune*, March 17, 1878.
61 "To Drag for Wife's Body," *Chicago Daily Tribune*, May 9, 1897.
62 "Mrs. Luetgert's Fate Still Mystery," *Chicago Daily Tribune*, May 10, 1897.
63 "To Drag for Wife's Body."
64 "A. L. Luetgert, Charged with the Murder of His Wife," *Chicago Daily Tribune*, May 18, 1897.
65 "Luetgert Is at Bar," *Chicago Daily Tribune*, August 24, 1897.
66 "Trial Is on Today," *Chicago Daily Tribune*, August 23, 1897.
67 "Tales of Love," *Chicago Daily Tribune*, September 5, 1897.
68 Throughout the nineteenth century, it was common for activists to use the term "woman" instead of "women" in reference to women's rights or the women's movement. When I refer to a specific movement or organization, I use the term "woman," consistent with nineteenth-century usage. However, when referring to rights or movements more generally, I use the term "women," consistent with contemporary usage. For example, when referring to women's movements in general, I use the plural, but for a specific woman's movement, I use the singular.
69 "Declaration of Sentiments and Resolutions, 1848," in *Man Cannot Speak for Her: Key Texts of the Early Feminists*, ed. Karlyn Kohrs Campbell, vol. 2 (Westport, Conn.: Praeger, 1989), 35.
70 Lucinda B. Chandler, "Justice and Judicial Murder," *Woman's Tribune* 5, no. 42 (1888).
71 An Act to Inflict Corporal Punishment upon Persons Found Guilty of Wife-Beating, Laws of Maryland, special session, ch. 120, p. 172 (passed March 30, 1882). For more on responses to domestic violence, see Elizabeth Pleck, *Domestic Tyranny: The Making of Social Policy against Family Violence from Colonial Times to the Present* (New York: Oxford University Press, 1987).
72 "Maryland Legislature," *Baltimore Sun*, March 16, 1882.
73 "Maryland Legislature," *Baltimore Sun*, March 3, 1882.
74 "Maryland Legislature," *Baltimore Sun*, March 3, 1882.
75 "Maryland Legislature," *Baltimore Sun*, March 16, 1882.
76 "To Whip or Not to Whip. Various Opinions Expressed Regarding the Public Lash. No Sympathy for Wife-Beaters," *Washington Post*, October 7, 1897; "Punishment That Punishes," *Washington Post*, October 29, 1895.

77 "Testimony from the Opposition," *Washington Post*, October 20, 1895; "Efficacy of the Whipping-Post," *Baltimore Sun*, July 13, 1885.
78 "Punishment That Punishes"; "Favors the Whipping Post. Judge Scott's Comment on the Case of Edward H. Johnson," *Washington Post*, July 18, 1899.
79 "To Whip or Not to Whip."
80 "This Is Not the Millennium," *Washington Post*, October 8, 1895; "Give Us the Whipping Post," *Washington Post*, October 2, 1895; "We Say the Whipping Post," *Washington Post*, August 7, 1895.
81 Charles Foote, a black man, was the first man sentenced to whipping as a result of the Maryland law. Henry Meyers was reportedly the first (or one of the first) white men sentenced. The record is unclear on whether Meyers was actually whipped. "Whipping for a White Man. Twenty Lashes and a Year in Jail for Wife-Beating in Baltimore," *Baltimore Sun*, June 16, 1885.
82 "The Whipping-Post. Fifteen Lashes in Sixteen Seconds for Wife-Beater," *Baltimore Sun*, June 20, 1885.
83 "Brutal Wife-Beater. Sentenced to Be Whipped and Imprisoned in Cecil County," *Baltimore Sun*, August 18, 1896.
84 "Brutal Wife-Beater."
85 "To Whip or Not to Whip."
86 "Whipping-Post Advocated. Sons of Delaware Debate Its Merits and Demerits and Decide in Favor of It," *Baltimore Sun*, February 25, 1897.
87 "The Lash as a Corrective," *Washington Post*, May 25, 1894.
88 "Cecil's Whipping Post. The Cat O'nine Tails Borrowed from a Delaware Sheriff," *Baltimore Sun*, August 24, 1896; "State of Maryland. Whipping-Post for a Wife-Beater in Cecil County. John Boots Gets Ten Lashes. He Wanted to Make a Statement in His Own Defense," *Baltimore Sun*, August 25, 1896.
89 "State of Maryland. A Colored Wife-Beater Whipped by the Sheriff in Queen Anne's," *Baltimore Sun*, May 26, 1897.
90 "A Wife-Beater Whipped. Seven Lashes Well Laid On. The Punishment Calmly Endured," *Baltimore Sun*, January 30, 1883.
91 "The Whipping Post. Move in the Virginia Legislature Looking to a Restoration of an Old Law," *Washington Post*, January 4, 1890.
92 "Recommended a Whipping-Post. Sixteen Grand Jurymen Think It Would Decrease Wife-Beating," *Washington Post*, October 1, 1895.
93 "Whipping Post Again. Possibility of Its Restoration in Several of the States. Commodore Gerry Talks," *Washington Post*, March 4, 1895; "The Whipping Post," *Washington Post*, February 26, 1897; "Topics in New York: Restoration of the Whipping Post for Wife Beaters. Statistics from Maryland. Argument from Two Delaware Jurists," *Baltimore Sun*, May 19, 1899. According to the *Baltimore Sun*, whipping was also supported by the medico-legal society in New York.
94 "Topics in New York. Commodore Gerry's Whipping-Post Bill Finds Favor," *Baltimore Sun*, March 8, 1895.
95 "Scrapbook," 1899–1900. Illinois Humane Society Records, University of Illinois–Chicago. Marion S. Lane and Stephen L. Zawistowski, *Heritage of Care: The American Society for the Prevention of Cruelty to Animals* (Westport, Conn.: Praeger, 2008), 28. The American Society for the Prevention of Cruelty to Animals did not initially include the protection of children. The founder of the organization did act to protect abused children, but he was reportedly concerned

about children being cared for by the ASPCA. He apparently supported the creation of separate organizations for the protection of children.

96 "Illinois Humane Society Annual Reports, 1879–1899," 3, Illinois Humane Society Records, University of Illinois–Chicago.

97 "Illinois Humane Society Annual Reports, 1879–1899," 5.

98 "Illinois Humane Society Annual Reports, 1879–1899," 8–9.

99 Linda Gordon, *Heroes of Their Own Lives: The Politics and History of Family Violence, Boston 1880–1960* (New York: Viking, 1988), 252.

100 "Illinois Humane Society Annual Reports, 1879–1899," 5.

101 "Protective Agency for Women and Children Annual Reports," 1887, 14, Chicago History Museum.

102 "Protective Agency for Women and Children Annual Reports," 1887, 17; Henriette Greenbaum Frank and Amalie Hofer Jermone, eds., *Annals of the Chicago Woman's Club: For the First Forty Years of Its Organization 1876–1916* (Chicago: Chicago Woman's Club, 1916), 51, 153. The participating organizations changed every year, and the Protective Agency eventually split from the leadership of the Women's Club, although the two organizations appeared to maintain a cooperative relationship. The Chicago Women's Club changed its name to the Chicago Woman's Club in 1895.

103 "Protective Agency for Women and Children Annual Reports," 1887, 13.

104 "Protective Agency for Women and Children Annual Reports," 1887, 16.

105 "Protective Agency for Women and Children Annual Reports," 1888, 5.

106 "Protective Agency for Women and Children Annual Reports," 1887, 31.

107 "Protective Agency for Women and Children Annual Reports," 1891, 5.

108 "Protective Agency for Women and Children Annual Reports," 1887, 10; 1890, 10; 1888, 10; 1890, 12.

109 "Help Those Women," *Union Signal*, January 24, 1889; "A Day Full of Philanthropies," *Union Signal*, April 19, 1888.

110 George E. Foster, "Shall We License the Dram Shops," *Union Signal*, February 14, 1884; Mary S. Robinson, "The Old, Old Story," *Union Signal*, April 2, 1891.

111 Frances E. Willard, "Tenth Annual Address," in *Minutes of the National Woman's Christian Temperance Union at the Sixteenth Annual Meeting* (Chicago: Woman's Christian Temperance Union, 1889), 95. Frances Willard Memorial Library and Archives, Evanston, Ill.

112 Spinney, *City of Big Shoulders*, 72.

Chapter 2

1 Extensive media coverage of divorce trials and related adultery and child custody trials fueled the public debate about divorce and participated in shaping its intertextual context. The civil trial between Henry Ward Beecher and Theodore Tilton was perhaps the most publicized example. In this trial Tilton sued Beecher, a nationally known religious leader, for alienation of affections, accusing Beecher of having an affair with Theodore Tilton's wife, Elizabeth. Similarly, Daniel McFarland's murder trial, where McFarland was accused of murdering his wife's lover, Albert Richardson, a reporter for the *New York Tribune*, received widespread newspaper coverage. Such extensive public attention to divorce and related trials was part of a deep-seated anxiety over gender and the future of

marriage in the United States, and this anxiety necessitated the emergence of new tropes and identities of womanhood. As Carlson and Ganz argue, the core element of both the Beecher and McFarland trials was a feminization of the male subject of the trial. By expanding the scope of analysis to include media coverage of the seemingly trivial and salacious divorce trials that were regularly covered in newspapers across the country, I argue that the media coverage of these trials not only involved the reformulation of male identity but also was a prolonged negotiation over the newly emerging identity of the divorced woman. Basch argues, "On the one hand, trial reports took some of the shame out of divorce through their open-endedness, their sheer repetitiveness, and their sympathetic representations of accused women; on the other hand, sentimental novelists, who began appropriating divorce as a subject in the late 1840s, worked to put the shame back in." My analysis complicates this distinction between the sentimental novel and the popular trial by reading the popular trial as an extension of the sentimental form. My analysis suggests that popular trials did not remove shame from divorce. Cheree Carlson, "The Role of Character in Public Moral Argument: Henry Ward Beecher and the Brooklyn Scandal," *Quarterly Journal of Speech* 77, no. 1 (1991); Richard Wightman Fox, *Trials of Intimacy: Love and Loss in the Beecher-Tilton Scandal* (Chicago: University of Chicago Press, 1999); Laura Hanft Korobkin, *Criminal Conversations: Sentimentality and Nineteenth-Century Legal Stories of Adultery* (New York: Columbia University Press, 1998); Melissa J. Ganz, "Wicked Women and Veiled Ladies: Gendered Narratives of the McFarland-Richardson Tragedy," *Yale Journal of Law & Feminism* 9 (1996); Norma Basch, *Framing American Divorce: From the Revolutionary Generation to the Victorians* (Berkeley: University of California Press, 1999), 176–77.

2 Hendrik Hartog, "Lecture: Marital Exits and Marital Expectations in Nineteenth Century America," *Georgetown Law Journal* 80 (1991): 121.

3 Glenda Riley, *Divorce: An American Tradition* (New York: Oxford University Press, 1991), 78.

4 Public trials often entered into the public through a prevailing melodramatic form. According to Brooks, melodrama is an entertainment form that began in eighteenth-century France as a theatrical form where words were accompanied by music. By the nineteenth century, however, melodrama had developed into a distinct theatrical form that became ubiquitous. Melodrama had become an integral part of American culture—it extended beyond theater and the domestic novel into all spheres of life, including law and the popular press. Nevertheless, melodrama can be difficult to define. It is possible, however, to identify some central features of the melodramatic form. Mason explains, "Melodrama works on us in layers, each a bit more removed from our immediate experience but supporting the one before it." He identifies three layers: (1) a thrilling event occurs, (2) there is a clear hero and villain, and (3) there is a "struggle between virtue and evil as irreconcilable." Unifying these layers of melodrama is the notion that characters and situations are clearly dichotomous—there is an unambiguous good and bad—and an expectation that virtue will win in the end. The rhetorical action of melodrama is plot-driven in the sense that it creates and meets the audience's expectations that good will persevere. In short, the public identity of the divorced woman was publicly negotiated through media coverage of popular trials, and melodrama was the means through which this identity emerged in

culturally contested space. Peter Brooks, *The Melodramatic Imagination* (New Haven: Yale University Press, 1976), 4, 36; Jeffrey Mason, *Melodrama and the Myth of America* (Bloomington: Indiana University Press, 1993), 15, 17; Bruce A. McConacie, *Melodramatic Formations* (Iowa City: University of Iowa Press, 1992), ix; Thomas Postlewait, "From Melodrama to Realism: The Suspect History of American Drama," in *Melodrama: The Cultural Emergence of a Genre*, ed. Michael Hays and Anastasia Nikolopoulou (New York: St. Martin's Press, 1996), 40; Robert M. Lewis, *From Traveling Show to Vaudeville* (Baltimore: Johns Hopkins University Press, 2003), 156. Sentimentalism is a related but distinct rhetorical form. For more on sentimentalism, see Stephen Hartnett, "Fanny Fern's 1855 *Ruth Hall*, the Cheerful Brutality of Capitalism, and the Irony of Sentimental Rhetoric," *Quarterly Journal of Speech* 88, no. 1 (2002); Edwin Black, *Rhetorical Questions: Studies of Public Discourse* (Chicago: University of Chicago Press, 1992), 133; Korobkin, *Criminal Conversations.*

5 Theodore Dwight Woolsey, *Essay on Divorce and Divorce Legislation, with Special Reference to the United States* (New York: C. Scribner, 1869), 190.

6 Cott, *Public Vows*, 50; Woolsey, *Essay on Divorce*, 206; Ransom H. Tyler, *Commentaries on the Law of Infancy: Including Guardianship and Custody of Infants, and the Law of Coverture, Embracing Dower, Marriage and Divorce, and the Statutory Policy of the Several States in Respect to Husband and Wife* (Albany: W. Gould, 1869). A reporter from the *Woman's Journal* explained, "'Chicago is a very wicked city,' we are often told, and the recent developments in relation to divorce cases is [*sic*] a very considerable straw to show how the wind blow [*sic*], and it is a very nauseating blast." S. W. B., "Divorce Made Easy," *Woman's Journal* 8, no. 12 (1877).

7 The content of Robert DeWitt, ed., *Report of the Beardsley Divorce Case* (New York: Robert M. DeWitt, 1860) is more detailed yet consistent with newspaper coverage of the trial. In several places, *Report of the Beardsley Divorce Case* mentions extensive coverage in the *Brooklyn Eagle*, and the judge apparently allowed jurors access to that coverage during their deliberations. The Beardsley trial was covered in the *New York Tribune* on November 24 (p. 10), November 26 (p. 6), November 28 (p. 7), November 29 (p. 8), and November 30 (p. 4). It was covered in the *New York Times* on November 23 (p. 5), November 26 (p. 5), November 27 (p. 8), and November 28 (p. 8). It is also important to note that the newspapers did not cover these trials simply because there was no other news. Coverage of the Beardsley and Burch (from Illinois) divorce trials shared space in the *New York Tribune* with headlines about the "Secessionist Crisis."

8 Advertised at the end of the *Report of the Beardsley Divorce Case*. DeWitt was exaggerating when he asserted the importance of the Beardsley case. The case had little legal significance, and it was one of many divorce trials that received daily coverage. For example, the Burch divorce trial of Napierville [*sic*], Illinois, received daily coverage in the *New York Tribune* for the several-week duration of the trial. Nevertheless, the *New York Tribune* did state, "Much of the evidence [in the Beardsley trial] is quite unfit for publication" (November 26, 1860, 6). Thus, it may be accurate to say that the Beardsley trial was particularly scandalous.

9 DeWitt, *Report of the Beardsley Divorce Case*, 5.

10 DeWitt, *Report of the Beardsley Divorce Case*, 6.

11 DeWitt, *Report of the Beardsley Divorce Case*, 7.

12 DeWitt, *Report of the Beardsley Divorce Case*, 5.
13 DeWitt, *Report of the Beardsley Divorce Case*, 69.
14 DeWitt, *Report of the Beardsley Divorce Case*, 76.
15 DeWitt, *Report of the Beardsley Divorce Case*, 76.
16 DeWitt, *Report of the Beardsley Divorce Case*, 15.
17 Korobkin, *Criminal Conversations*, 46.
18 DeWitt, *Report of the Beardsley Divorce Case*, 31.
19 Within the context of the melodramatic narrative, Alfred Beardsley's evil character was used to explain away evidence against Mary Elizabeth Beardsley. Shaffer argued that in order to get his hands on more money, Alfred Beardsley conspired with Thomas Mahan to set a trap for Mary Elizabeth Beardsley. He continued to explain that Mahan had actually married Mary Elizabeth Beardsley's friend Mary Elizabeth Greenwood, who was also Alfred Beardsley's lover, and this marriage was part of an elaborate plot to secure a divorce for Alfred Beardsley.
20 DeWitt, *Report of the Beardsley Divorce Case*, 63, 59. Even Greenwood's betrayal of her friend was described within the context of women's natural failings and the expectations of womanhood. Shaffer explained, "It is easy to see why Miss Greenwood should lead that woman into toils which would inure to her benefit; for when a woman's virtue is lost, there is no crime she will not perpetuate in obedience to him who has ruined her."
21 Basch, *Framing American Divorce*, 160, 170. According to Basch, who was writing in reference to a similarly sensational trial, "The final outcome was a hung jury, but the popular 'Shawmut edition' of the trial, published by the *Boston Bee*, was rushed into print even before the verdict was known. The legal fate of Nellie Dalton presumably had less effect on sales than the vivid tableau of her suffering." The actual decision in the Beardsley case was similar in that it did not appear to be as publicly important as the drama of the trial. The decision in the Beardsley divorce was complex. The jury found Mary Elizabeth Beardsley innocent of attempting to procure a second marriage, but they also found that she had committed adultery. However, they found that Alfred Beardsley had committed adultery first, making him the guilty party in the divorce. The decision was mentioned only briefly in DeWitt's account of the divorce and the newspaper coverage. The absence of attention to the actual decision suggests that it was the salacious drama of the trial that was publicly significant, and the trial, not a judge or jury decision, framed the identity of the divorced woman as shamed and punished regardless of her actual guilt or innocence. Basch also argues that the trial reporters turned against Mary Elizabeth Beardsley because of her "duplicity," framing her as inevitably guilty.
22 Geo. A. Jr. Shufeldt, "Marriage and Divorce," *Chicago Tribune*, January 7, 1868, 2.
23 *Chicago Tribune*, January 5, 1868.
24 "The Ticknor Divorce Case," *Chicago Republican*, December 19, 1867, 8.
25 "The Ticknor Divorce Case," *Chicago Republican*, December 19, 1867.
26 "The Ticknor Scandal," *Chicago Republican*, December 20, 1867, 3.
27 "The Ticknor Scandal," *Chicago Republican*, December 20, 1867, 3.
28 Robert Dale Owen, "Divorce," in *Love, Marriage, and Divorce and the Sovereignty of the Individual* (New York: Source Book Press, 1972), 152.
29 Owen, "Divorce," 152.

30 "The Ticknor Scandal," *Chicago Republican*, December 22, 1867, 4; "The Ticknor Scandal," *Chicago Republican*, December 24, 1867, 5.

31 "The Ticknor Scandal," *Chicago Republican*, December 27, 1867, 3.

32 "The Ticknor Scandal," *Chicago Tribune*, January 6, 1868, 4. The *Tribune* noted that the jury voted first on the issue of cruelty, and the vote was eleven to one in favor of Susan Ticknor. The one vote against Susan Ticknor then asked what they were voting on, and once the vote was clarified, they decided unanimously in favor of Susan Ticknor.

33 "The Custody of Children," *Chicago Legal News*, December 26, 1868.

34 In addition to the melodramatic constraint, there was also a legal constraint that in order for a divorce to be granted, one person had to be guilty. There was no concept of a "no fault divorce."

35 E. Ann Kaplan, *Motherhood and Representation: The Mother in Popular Culture and Melodrama* (New York: Routledge, 1992), 78. E. Ann Kaplan explains that one common motif of melodrama during the mid- to late nineteenth century is the theme of the "innocent (often working class) young girl [who] is sexually abused and destroyed by an unscrupulous, lascivious aristocratic male." Kaplan uses the example of *East Lynne* (1861) to illustrate her point.

36 My characterization of "substantial attention" is admittedly subjective and based on my observation that there were several cases that received extensive daily newspaper coverage.

37 "The Quimby Case," *Chicago Tribune*, January 8, 1868; "The Quimby Scandal," *Chicago Republican*, December 20, 1867; "Another Scandal," *Chicago Tribune*, January 12, 1868.

38 Charles Cowley, *Browne's Divorce and Its Consequences* (Lowell, Mass.: Penhallow Printing, [1877?]), 86. Even though this melodrama came out after the trial itself, it fed into the general cultural acceptance of melodrama as the appropriate frame for understanding divorce in America at this time.

39 The Spirit of the Jail, Confidential Secretary, *Chicago Tribune*, January 1, 1868, 4.

40 "Pistoled," *Chicago Times*, June 4, 1873.

41 "Pistoled."

42 "Pistoled."

43 Riley, *Divorce*, 19.

44 Riley, *Divorce*, 78.

45 Cott, *Public Vows*, 50; Woolsey, *Essay on Divorce*, 206; Tyler, *Commentaries on the Law of Infancy*.

46 Riley, *Divorce*, 62.

47 Basch, *Framing American Divorce*, 44.

48 See, e.g., "Notes on Books and Booksellers," *American Literary Gazette and Publishers' Circular* 9, no. 1 (1867); "Book Notices," *American Law Review* 1, no. 4 (1867); "Book Notices," *American Catholic Quarterly Review* 16, no. 62 (1891).

49 Auguste Carlier, *Marriage in the United States*, trans. B. Joy Jeffries, 3rd ed. (Boston: De Vries, Ibarra, 1867), 176.

50 Woolsey, *Essay on Divorce*, 217.

51 Horace Greeley, "Marriage—Divorce," in *Love, Marriage, and Divorce and the Sovereignty of the Individual* (New York: Source Book Press, 1972), 155; Woolsey,

Essay on Divorce, 10–11. Woolsey used the Hebrew definition of marriage as the necessity of a man to "cleave to his wife, and they twaine shall be one flesh."

52 Greeley, "Marriage—Divorce," 155.

53 Karlyn Kohrs Campbell, *Man Cannot Speak for Her*, vol. 1, *A Critical Study of Early Feminist Rhetoric* (Westport, Conn.: Praeger, 1989), 85. Ernestine Potowski Rose, an outspoken atheist, abolitionist, and woman's rights advocate, spoke in support of Stanton's position at the 1860 convention. Wendell Phillips and William Lloyd Garrison, both well-respected abolitionists and supporters of woman's rights, responded with speeches arguing that the question of divorce was irrelevant to the convention and should be stricken from the record. While the motion ultimately failed, the 1860 debate revealed deep divisions in the woman's rights movement. Debates over divorce forced questions of whether the goal of the movement was woman suffrage or the broader civic identity of women, and these debates suggested a political conflict over the point at which individual concerns of women should become public issues. These divisions persisted well beyond 1860 through the split of the woman's movement in 1869 into the American Woman's Suffrage Association (AWSA), headed by Lucy Stone, and the National Woman's Suffrage Association (NWSA), headed by Susan B. Anthony and Elizabeth Cady Stanton.

54 Antoinette Brown Blackwell, "Speech of Rev. Antoinette Brown [Blackwell]," in *Man Cannot Speak for Her*, vol. 2, *Key Texts of the Early Feminists*, ed. Karlyn Kohrs Campbell (Westport, Conn.: Praeger, 1989), 203. Also see Woolsey, who argued that divorce is like an amputation because marriage makes two people into "one flesh." Woolsey, *Essay on Divorce*, 10–11.

55 David Zarefsky, "Definitions," in *Argument in a Time of Change: Definitions, Frameworks, and Critiques*, ed. James F. Klumpp (Annandale, Va.: National Communication Association, 1997), 4.

56 Woolsey, *Essay on Divorce*, 24.

57 Blackwell, "Speech of Rev. Antoinette Brown [Blackwell]," 211. Blackwell explained, "I believe that God has so made man and woman, that it is not good for them to be alone, that they each need a co-worker."

58 Greeley, "Marriage—Divorce," 165; Woolsey, *Essay on Divorce*, 235. For example, Greeley argued, "The Divine end of Marriage is parentage or the perpetuation and increase of the Human Race. To this end, it is indispensable—at least, eminently desirable—that each child should enjoy protection, nurture, sustenance, at the hands of a mother not only, but of a father also." Also, Woolsey said, "Divorce cannot in fact be separated from the ends and uses of marriage which lie within the province of morals, and adultery cannot and never has been regarded as a mere breach of contract. And so the better the laws are, the more they watch over and exact the fulfillment of those obligations to which marriage gives rise by bringing new beings into the world."

59 See *State v. Rhodes*.

60 Ch. Perelman and L. Olbrechts-Tyteca, *The New Rhetoric: A Treatise on Argumentation*, trans. John Wilkinson and Purcell Weaver (Notre Dame: University of Notre Dame Press, 1971), 282.

61 Greeley, "Marriage—Divorce," 156; Woolsey, *Essay on Divorce*, 252. For example, Greeley argued that divorce challenges marriage in the same way as polygamy, free love, and concubinage. Woolsey made a similar analogy to polygamy.

62 Elisha Mulford, *The Nation: The Foundations of Civil Order and Political Life in the United States* (New York: Hurd & Houghton, 1870), 279.

63 William L. O'Neill, "Divorce in the Progressive Era," *American Quarterly* 17, no. 2 (1965): 215. O'Neill explained, "Before 1900 no important American magazine defended the right to divorce except the radical *Arena*. Articles favorable to divorce were very rare in the general press."

64 Carroll D. Wright, *A Report on Marriage and Divorce in the United States, 1867–1886* (Washington, D.C.: Government Printing Office, 1889), 15; *The National Divorce Reform League: An Abstract of Its Annual Reports* (Montpelier: Vermont Watchman and State Journal Press, 1885), 1. Rev. Samuel W. Dike, LL.D., secretary of the National Divorce Reform League, influenced content of the report.

65 Wright, *Report on Marriage*, 10.

66 Wright, *Report on Marriage*, 12. Senator Edmunds, antipolygamy leader, reintroduced the bill in 1886 and pushed for the study and report.

67 Wright, *Report on Marriage*, 15.

68 W. E. Gladstone, Joseph P. Bradley, and Senator Joseph N. Dolph, "The Question of Divorce," *North American Review* 149, no. 397 (1889): 650–51.

69 Jos. R. Long, "Tinkering with the Constitution," *Yale Law Journal* 24, no. 7 (1915): 585; C. LaRue Munson and William D. Crocker, "The Divorce Question in the United States," *Yale Law Journal* 18, no. 6 (1909): 390; O'Neill, "Divorce in the Progressive Era," 204. As O'Neill explains, "Serious attempts to secure uniform marriage and divorce legislation through a constitutional amendment began in 1892 when James Kyle, the Populist Senator from South Dakota, introduced a joint resolution. . . . Senator Kyle's resolution died in committee as did all later resolutions."

70 F. J. Stimson, "National Unification of Law," *Harvard Law Review* 7, no. 2 (1893).

71 "Declaration of Sentiments and Resolutions," 35.

72 Elizabeth Cady Stanton, Susan Brownell Anthony, and Matilda Joslyn Gage, *History of Woman Suffrage*, vol. 1 (New York: Fowler & Wells, 1881), 232.

73 Mary A. Livermore, "Marriage and Divorce," *Woman's Tribune* 7, no. 3 (1890); idem, "Marriage and Divorce," *Woman's Standard* 4, no. 7 (1890); "Mrs. Livermore on Divorce," *Woman's Journal* 21, no. 3 (1890). Livermore also said, "She [the married woman] is expected to work for food, shelter, and clothing, and is thus made a pauperized dependent on her husband."

74 One of the strongest early critiques of marriage came with the marriage of Lucy Stone and Henry Blackwell. This couple married, but they framed their marriage as one occurring under protest to the current laws of marriage. Stone even decided to keep her last name, a symbolic resistance to coverture. Although the protest challenged the norms and laws of marriage, it was based in a definition of marriage that foreshadowed a significant divide in the woman's rights movement. In their protest Stone and Blackwell insisted that marriage should be an "equal and permanent partnership" (Stanton, Anthony, and Gage, *History of Woman Suffrage*, 261). By defining marriage as a "permanent partnership," Stone and Blackwell suggested that the goal of the woman's movement should be attempting to ensure equality in marriage, not ensuring the possibility for divorce. According to DuBois, it was not until the 1860 Woman's Rights Convention in New York that the issue of divorce came to a boiling point. Activists, primarily from AWSA

(American Woman's Suffrage Association), attempted to dissociate suffrage from divorce reform. At the same time, however, other women, many of whom were active in NWSA (National Woman's Suffrage Association, headed by Stanton and Anthony), argued for the expansion of divorce laws to account for the disparity in the laws of marriage. Despite the formal reunification of the woman's movement in 1890, divisions over divorce had become deeply entrenched. In the 1890s Frances Willard and the Woman's Christian Temperance Union (WCTU) became active in working with the National Divorce Reform League for a constitutional amendment that would restrict divorce. Stanton, on the other hand, became increasingly radical toward the end of the century. Despite the complex relationship between woman's rights and divorce, the woman's rights movement came to be publicly associated with expanded divorce. In part, these associations stemmed from attempts to discredit the movement by making it seem to be a threat to family, even though the reality was much more complex. Ellen Carol DuBois, "'The Pivot of the Marriage Relation': Stanton's Analysis of Women's Subordination in Marriage," in *Elizabeth Cady Stanton, Feminist as Thinker: A Reader in Documents and Essays*, ed. Ellen Carol DuBois and Richard Candida Smith (New York: New York University Press, 2007), 83, 88; "Marriage and Divorce," *Woman's Journal* 1, no. 18 (1870); H. B. B., "Woman Suffrage and Divorce," *Woman's Journal* 1, no. 22 (1870); L. S., "Divorce Laws," *Woman's Journal* 12, no. 13 (1881); "Marriage and Divorce," *Woman's Tribune* 12, no. 12 (1895); Alice Stone Blackwell, "The Divorce Question," *Woman's Column* 12, no. 21 (1899); Suzanne M. Marilley, "Frances Willard and the Feminism of Fear," *Feminist Studies* 19, no. 1 (1993): 138; Elizabeth Cady Stanton, "Divorce versus Domestic Warfare (1890)," in *Elizabeth Cady Stanton, Feminist as Thinker: A Reader in Documents and Essays*, ed. Ellen Carol DuBois and Richard Candida Smith (New York: New York University Press, 2007), 260; "Miss Chapman on Divorce," *Woman's Herald* 2, no. 75 (1890).

75 Elizabeth Cady Stanton, "Address of Mrs. E. C. Stanton," in *Man Cannot Speak for Her*, vol. 2, *Key Texts of the Early Feminists*, ed. Karlyn Kohrs Campbell (Westport, Conn.: Praeger, 1989), 192–93; Agonistes, *Doctrine of Divorce* (Albany, 1857), 25, 34–35. Elizabeth Cady Stanton argued in the 1860 woman's rights convention in New York, "If marriage is a human institution, about which man may legislate, it seems but just that he should treat this branch of his legislation with the same common sense that he applies to all others. If it is a mere legal contract, then should it be subject to the restraints and privilege of all other contracts." Also, Agonistes argued, "The connexion is of so deep toned, solemn and vital a character, that the public has more interest in preserving it inviolate, than the parties themselves. It is a triangular arrangement, the adherents to which are a man, a woman, and the state. And though a contract in its inception between the two first of mutual partnership and personal cohabitation, it is governed afterwards by the laws made in the premises by the last. The rights and obligations attending it are derived from the legislation regulating it, rather than from the contract itself—although resting on the consent of the individuals, still the harmony, the decorum, and the very existence of every well organized society makes it necessary that the sovereign power should control its elements, its formation and its dissolution." The author also argued that social changes necessitate

changes in laws and noted, "The 1848 property rights act enabled women to have their own property and gave them a means to desert their husbands at will."

76 Agonistes, *Doctrine of Divorce*, 2, 5. For example, Agonistes declared, "Toleration of all religious creeds is a cardinal principle with us, and yet in construing a contract, we adopt and give preference to a dogma interpolated by one sect, succumbed to by another, denied by the rest, and disputed by many of the most able writers of all denominations." This author also said, "The text they rely upon is exceedingly equivocal, difficult of translation, and teeming with contradictions."

77 Owen, "Divorce," 151, 153; Agonistes, *Doctrine of Divorce*, 22; Stanton, "Address of Mrs. E. C. Stanton," 194. Owen also said, "I regard the marriage relation as the holiest of earthly institutions. It is for that very reason that I seek to preserve its purity, when other expedients fail, be the besom of divorce." Also see Agonistes, who lists the problems with desertion as it existed at the time and argues, "These illustrations sufficiently demonstrate the evils, and the danger of desertion, especially on the part of the female, and the crying need for some remedy." Further, Stanton argued, "Marriage, as it now exists, must seem to all of you a mere human institution. Look through the universe of matter and mind,—all God's arrangements are perfect, harmonious, and complete! . . . Where two beings are drawn together, by the natural laws of likeness and affinity, union and happiness are the result. Such marriages might be Divine."

78 Stanton, "Address of Mrs. E. C. Stanton," 192.

79 Stanton, "Address of Mrs. E. C. Stanton," 192.

80 Stanton, "Address of Mrs. E. C. Stanton," 192; Owen, "Divorce," 150. Another example of inductive reasoning is when Owen noted that the laws of Indiana, which were used as an example of lax divorce laws, had worked for 40 to 50 years and, Owen argued that the people of Indiana were moral.

81 Owen, "Divorce," 151.

82 Edith Lowther Bailey, "The Morality of Divorce," *Woman's Herald* 2, no. 97 (1890).

Chapter 3

1 Some material in this chapter appeared in Leslie J. Harris and Mike Allan, "The Paradox of Authentic Identity: Mormon Women and the Nineteenth-Century Polygamy Controversy," in *Reason and Social Change*, ed. Robert Rowlands, 340–47 (Washington, D.C.: National Communication Association, 2011) and is included with the permission of the National Communication Association.

2 Consistent with the rhetoric of the time, I refer to members of the Latter-Day Saints Church as "Mormons," "LDS Church members," or "Saints" interchangeably. I also refer to polygamy as practiced by the LDS Church members as "polygamy," "plural marriage," or "celestial marriage" interchangeably.

3 Alice Felt Tyler, *Freedom's Ferment: Phases of American Social History from the Colonial Period to the Outbreak of the Civil War* (New York: Harper & Row, 1944), 87–88; Sarah Barringer Gordon, *The Mormon Question: Polygamy and Constitutional Conflict in Nineteenth-Century America* (Chapel Hill: University of North Carolina Press, 2002), 19.

4 Gordon, *Mormon Question*, 21.

5 Gordon, *Mormon Question*, 24–25.

6 Gordon, *Mormon Question*, 8–9.

7 Gordon, *Mormon Question*, 9. The federal government not only denied the application for the State of Deseret's statehood in 1849 but also created the territory of Utah with much smaller boundaries. Utah officially became a territory in 1850.

8 B. Carmon Hardy, *Solemn Covenant: The Mormon Polygamous Passage* (Urbana: University of Illinois Press, 1992), 9; Stan Larson, introduction to *Prisoner for Polygamy: The Memoirs and Letters of Rudger Clawson at the Utah Territorial Penitentiary, 1884–87*, ed. Stan Larson (Urbana: University of Illinois Press, 1993), 2.

9 Hardy, *Solemn Covenant*, 7.

10 Louis J. Kern, *An Ordered Love: Sex Roles and Sexuality in Victorian Utopias—the Shakers, the Mormons, and the Oneida Community* (Chapel Hill: University of North Carolina Press, 1981), 146.

11 Gordon, *Mormon Question*, 27.

12 Hardy, *Solemn Covenant*, 16–17.

13 Hardy, *Solemn Covenant*, 1.

14 David Whittaker, "Early Mormon Polygamy Defenses," *Journal of Mormon History* 11, no. 1 (1984): 44.

15 Orson Pratt, "Discourse," 1869, 1, Schroeder Collection, Wisconsin Historical Society, Madison.

16 Pratt, "Discourse," 2; Jeffrey Nichols, *Prostitution, Polygamy, and Power: Salt Lake City, 1847–1918* (Urbana: University of Illinois Press, 2002), 10.

17 Pratt, "Discourse," 2.

18 Pratt, "Discourse," 7.

19 Pratt, "Discourse," 8; Orson Pratt and J. P. Newman, *The Bible and Polygamy: Does the Bible Sanction Polygamy?* (Salt Lake City, Utah: Deseret News Steam Printing, 1874), 34, Schroeder Collection, Wisconsin Historical Society, Madison. Pratt said, "Much may be said upon this subject: much, too, that ought to crimson the faces of those who call themselves civilized, when they reflect upon the enormities, the great social evils, that exist in their midst. Look upon the great city of New York, the great metropolis of commerce. . . . What exists in the midst of that city? Females by the tens of thousands, females who are debauched by day and by night; females who are in open day parading the streets of that great city! Why, they are monogamists there! It is a portion of the civilization of New York to be very pious over polygamy; yet harlots and mistresses by the thousands by night."

20 Pratt, "Discourse," 1.

21 Gordon, *Mormon Question*, 29, 32; Mrs. T. B. H. (Fanny Warn) Stenhouse, *An Englishwoman in Utah: A Life's Experience in Mormonism* (London: Samson Low, Marston, Searle, & Rivington, 1882); Eric Eliason, "Curious Gentiles and Representational Authority in the City of the Saints," *Religion and American Culture: A Journal of Interpretation* 11, no. 2 (2001): 160; Karen M. Morin and Jeanne Kay Guelke, "Strategies of Representation, Relationship, and Resistance: British Women Travelers and Mormon Plural Wives, ca. 1870–1890," *Annals of the Association of American Geographers* 88, no. 3 (1998). According to Gordon, this literature was immensely popular, and Metta Victor's *Mormon Wives*, for example, sold about forty thousand copies during the 1850s alone. These stories appeared to provide a window into the private lives of polygamous families, claiming to expose the "truth" of polygamy in the United States, and the stories fit within

the emerging tradition of travel writing. Further, claims to truth gave the authors license to write what would otherwise be deemed pornographic and unsuitable for women.

22 Joan Smyth Iversen, *The Antipolygamy Controversy in U.S. Women's Movements, 1880–1925: A Debate on the American Home* (New York: Garland, 1997), 134.

23 Eliason, "Curious Gentiles," 161.

24 Iversen, *Antipolygamy Controversy*, 101.

25 Harriet Beecher Stowe, "Preface," in Mrs. T. B. H. (Fanny Warn) Stenhouse, *Tell It All: The Tyranny of Mormonism or an Englishwoman in Utah,* iii (1875; repr. Sussex: Centaur Press, 1971).

26 Irving Wallace, *The Twenty-Seventh Wife* (New York: Simon & Schuster, 1961), 15.

27 James Burton Pond, *Eccentricities of Genius: Memories of Famous Men and Women of the Platform and Stage* (London: Chatto & Windus, 1901), xxii.

28 Other estimates indicate that Ann Eliza Young may have been Brigham Young's twenty-seventh wife.

29 The records of the divorce are mysteriously missing from the Utah State Archives. The surrounding case numbers are available on microfilm, but the Young divorce is "missing." Archivists at the Utah State Archives and the Church History Museum were unable to locate the records.

30 Ann Eliza Young, *Wife No. 19, or The Story of a Life in Bondage, Being a Complete Expose of Mormonism, and Revealing the Sorrows, Sacrifices and Sufferings of Women in Polygamy* (New York: Arno Press, 1972), 12.

31 Young, *Wife No. 19*, 12.

32 Young, *Wife No. 19*, 159.

33 The Mountain Meadows Massacre was an attack on and murder of members of a wagon train most likely by members of the LDS Church. Blood atonement was a sacrificial offering of one's self to atone for sins.

34 Young, *Wife No. 19*, 155.

35 Young, *Wife No. 19*, 310.

36 Young, *Wife No. 19*, 323.

37 Angela Ray, *The Lyceum and Public Culture in the Nineteenth-Century United States* (East Lansing: Michigan State University Press, 2005), 149–50; "Polygamy in Judgment," *Every Saturday: A Journal of Choice Reading*, October 28, 1871, 410. In the years following the lecture, Salt Lake City came to be described by others as a whited sepulchre.

38 Ray, *Lyceum*, 151.

39 Anna Dickenson, "Whited Sepulchres," in Angela Ray, *The Lyceum and Public Culture in the Nineteenth-Century United States* (East Lansing: Michigan State University Press, 2005), 221.

40 Perelman and Olbrechts-Tyteca, *The New Rhetoric*, esp. ch. 4.

41 Dickenson, "Whited Sepulchres," 231.

42 H. W., "Utah and the Mormons," *Chicago Tribune*, July 16, 1869, 2. A *Chicago Tribune* reporter explained to readers, "It appears that Mormon women, both married and unmarried, are universally opposed to polygamy."

43 Mrs. E. E. Evans, "At Sea with the Mormons, from the Notebook of a Gentile Traveler," *Herald of Health* 17, no. 1 (1871); "Mormon Life," *Oneida Circular* 8, no. 15 (1871).

44 H. W., "Utah and the Mormons," 2.
45 "Utah," *Chicago Tribune*, November 25, 1869, 2.
46 John Cradlebaugh, "Mormon Horrors! Judge Cradlebaugh's Speech in Congress in 1863. Terrible Arraignment of the Blood-Stained Mormon Church. Graphic Account of the Mountain Meadows Massacre. Blood Atonement Openly Preached by Brigham Young and His Apostles. A Reeking, Filthy, Bloody Scar on the Nation. Let No Tool Stand in the Way of Wiping It Out," *Supplement to the Salt Lake Tribune* [1863?], 2, Church History Library, Salt Lake City, Utah.
47 D. C. Haskell, *Mormonism and Polygamy: An Address Delivered by D. C. Haskell, of Kansas, at Central Music Hall, Chicago, June 8th, 1881, before the National Convention of the American Home Missionary Society* (Lawrence, Kans.: Republican Journal Steam Printing, 1881), 25, Schroeder Collection, Wisconsin Historical Society, Madison.
48 G. W. C., "Utah," *Chicago Tribune*, January 18, 1869, 2.
49 "Polygamy in Utah: Lecture by Mrs. C. V. Waite on 'Mormonism,'" *Chicago Tribune*, March 5, 1870, 4.
50 "More about the Mormons," *New York Times*, November 8, 1869, 1.
51 "Shall We Have a New Conflict with the Mormons?," *New York Times*, January 27, 1870, 4.
52 "The Abolition of Polygamy," *Chicago Tribune*, April 14, 1870, 2.
53 "Abolition of Polygamy," 2.
54 J. Randolph Tucker, "Polygamy. Speech of Hon. J. Randolph Tucker, of Virginia. In the House of Representatives" (Washington, D.C.: Franklin Printing House, 1887), 5, Schroeder Collection, Wisconsin Historical Society, Madison.
55 Karrin Vasby Anderson, "'Rhymes with Rich': 'Bitch' as a Tool of Containment in Contemporary American Politics," *Rhetoric and Public Affairs* 2, no. 4 (1999): 601.
56 E.g., Mrs. E. B. Duffey, *The Relations of the Sexes* (New York: Estill, 1876), 78.
57 Edward W. Said, *Orientalism* (New York: Vintage Books, 1979), 36.
58 Martha M. Ertman, "Race Treason: The Untold Story of America's Ban on Polygamy," *Columbia Journal of Gender and Law* 19 (2010). Ertman labels the primary frame for antipolygamy as "race treason," while arguing that antipolygamy activists were "hardly concerned with gender equity." While I agree with Ertman's introduction of race into our understanding of antipolygamy, I argue that both race and gender are important lenses in understanding the connections between marriage and citizenship because proper racial performance is always gendered.
59 "Polygamy in Utah," 4. The *Chicago Tribune* reported that the 1855 invasion cost the country $20 million.
60 Douglas, "Utah," *Chicago Tribune*, July 14, 1869, 2.
61 Cradlebaugh, "Mormon Horrors!," 2.
62 "The 'Twin Relics of Barbarism,'" *New York Times*, July 18, 1869, 4.
63 Also, "The Proposed Admission of Utah," *New York Times*, March 8, 1869, 4.
64 James Buchanan, "State of the Union Address" (1857); idem, "State of the Union Address" (1858); Ulysses S. Grant, "State of the Union Address" (1871); Rutherford B. Hayes, "State of the Union Address" (1879); idem, "State of the Union Address" (1880). In 1857 James Buchanan was perhaps the first president to introduce polygamy as a significant national issue. Even in his first State of the

Union address, Buchanan drew connections between the situation in Utah and slavery. He introduced the Utah conflict only after extensively speaking about conflict over slavery in the Kansas territory and insisting that the laws of slavery in the territory must reflect the will of the people living in the territory in order to avoid civil war. In contrast, however, Buchanan called for military action to quell Brigham Young's power in Utah, despite the will of the people in the territory. He argued, "This is the first rebellion which has existed in our Territories, and humanity itself requires that we should put it down in such a manner that it shall be the last." Despite the significant differences between Kansas and Utah, Utah functioned as an example of the consequences of rebellion, and Buchanan placed the Mormons as "deplorable," "revolting," and more significant than slavery. The "Mormon War" came to be known as a failure and an embarrassment of the Buchanan administration. Still, in his State of the Union one year later, Buchanan congratulated himself on his handling of Utah. Polygamy remained an important part of presidential agendas for much of the nineteenth century. Grant called Mormon polygamy "barbarism," and Hayes (1879) was explicit that despite the importance of statehood for Utah, the territory would not become a state until polygamy was eliminated. Further, in 1880 Hayes called polygamy a threat to "American society and civilization." To remedy this threat he made a fairly extreme proposal: "I recommend that the right to vote, hold office, and sit on juries in the Territory of Utah be confined to those who neither practice nor uphold polygamy." Legislation that disenfranchised Mormons was adopted soon after Hayes' recommendation.

65 Gordon, *Mormon Question*, 63; Justin S. Morrill, *Utah Territory and Its Laws—Polygamy and Its License; Delivered in the House of Representatives, February 23, 1857* (Washington, D.C.: Office of the Congressional Globe, 1857), 10. Gordon called Morrill's 1857 speech one of his most important antipolygamy speeches. Morrill argued, "It is not enough to make woman no longer an equal and man the tyrant; it is not enough to tear the endearing passion of love from the heart, and install in its place the rage of jealousy; it is not enough to usurp the complete sovereignty over woman, and degrade her to the level of a mere animal; but the Mormons, when their appetites become sated, through the intervention or favor of their high-priests, are enabled to indulge their caprice in the luxury and latitude of change and variety. As well might religion be invoked to protect cannibalism or infanticide."

66 "Polygamy and a New Rebellion," *New York Times*, June 19, 1862, 4.

67 Larson, introduction, 3.

68 Gordon, *Mormon Question*, 81.

69 "Polygamy and a New Rebellion," 4.

70 "The Mormon Question," *New York Times*, March 17, 1869, 6.

71 *A Bill to Discourage Polygamy in Utah by Granting the Right to Suffrage to the Women of That Territory*, 1st, H.R. 64. L., 1869, Tom Perry Special Collections, Brigham Young University Library, Provo, Utah.

72 "The Women of Utah," *New York Times*, March 5, 1869, 6.

73 Douglas, "Utah," *Chicago Tribune*, March 3, 1870, 2. For example, Douglas states, "They [Mormon women] are most effectually broken in spirit, subdued, and their interests and those of their lords are one,—peculiarly so in this matter. They can always be depended on to vote as the men tell them to."

74 "The Dismemberment of Utah—a Blow at Brigham Young," *New York Times*, January 18, 1869, 4.
75 Gordon, *Mormon Question*, 114.
76 Reynolds v. United States, 98 U.S. 145, 165 (1878).
77 *Reynolds*, 167; Gordon, *Mormon Question*, 120–21. Gordon describes the *Reynolds* decision as "a sea change in federalism, even applied against a territory, but one that was cloaked in a comforting layer of familiarity."
78 Henry Reed, *Bigamy and Polygamy, Review of the Opinion of the Supreme Court of the United States, Rendered at the October Term, 1878, in the Case of George Reynolds, Plaintiff in Error, vs. The United States, Defendant in Error* (New York, 1897), 11, Wisconsin Historical Society, Madison; A Citizen of Massachusetts, *The Mormon Problem. A Letter to the Massachusetts Members of Congress on Plural Marriage: Its Morality and Lawfulness* (Boston: James Campbell, 1882), 51–52, Schroeder Collection, Wisconsin Historical Society, Madison. Also, a "Citizen of Massachusetts" said, "At the present time, this very year, it is within the legal and constitutional power of the people of each and every State of the Union, to ordain monogamy, polygamy, or either one or both of these modes of social life, as the legal marriage for the people of their respective States. Congress has no constitutional power to legislate for or against such action. Any law that it might enact to punish polygamy in any State would be usurpation on the part of Congress. It would be a robbery of the rights of the people, by the servants of the people."
79 Reed, *Bigamy and Polygamy*, 12.
80 David Zarefsky, "Echoes of the Slavery Controversy in the Current Abortion Debate," in *Argument in Controversy* (Annandale, Va.: National Communication Association, 1991), 92. Zarefsky makes a similar observation of stasis in the antislavery and abortion controversies. In theory, procedural questions (such as federal jurisdiction) should preempt substantive questions (such as whether polygamy is moral). However, this understanding of stasis is complicated when starting premises of the argument are incommensurable (not simply different). In the context of polygamy, the moral question is framed as simply too important to be limited by questions of jurisdiction.
81 "The Edmunds Bill," *Woman's Exponent*, May 1, 1882.
82 Larson, introduction, 6. Some men were convicted on multiple charges.
83 "Thoughts on the Times," *Woman's Exponent*, February 15, 1886, 141.
84 Aileen S. Kraditor, *The Ideas of the Woman Suffrage Movement 1890–1920* (New York: Anchor Books, 1971), 2.
85 Iversen, *Antipolygamy Controversy*, 22; Tiffany Lewis, "Winning Woman Suffrage in the Masculine West: Abigail Scott Duniway's Frontier Myth," *Western Journal of Communication* 75, no. 2 (2011): 127.
86 Rebecca Edwards, "Pioneers at the Polls: Woman Suffrage in the West," in *Votes for Women: The Struggle for Suffrage Revisited*, ed. Jean H. Baker (New York: Oxford University Press, 2002), 93.
87 Iversen, *Antipolygamy Controversy*, 24.
88 Iversen, *Antipolygamy Controversy*, 26.
89 Carol Weisbrod and Pamela Sheingorn, "Reynolds v. United States: Nineteenth-Century Forms of Marriage and the Status of Women," *Connecticut Law Review* 10 (1977–1978): 841.

90 Susan B. Anthony and Ida Husted Harper, *The History of Woman Suffrage*, vol. 4 (Rochester, N.Y.: Susan B. Anthony, 1902), 936–46.

91 Iversen, *Antipolygamy Controversy*, 61. Iversen argues, "It is difficult to overestimate the importance of the *Woman's Exponent* and its role in proving credibility for Mormon women."

92 Myra Bradwell, "Notes to Recent Cases," *Chicago Legal News*, May 4, 1872, 236; Iversen, *Antipolygamy Controversy*, 28, 166; "Belva A. Lockwood, and 'Mormon' Mothers," *Woman's Exponent* 14, no. 19 (1886): 150. Belva Lockwood presented a different picture of the relationship between polygamy and the larger woman's movement. An attorney in Washington, D.C., and member of NWSA, Lockwood gained national prominence after she became the first woman permitted to practice law. Myra Bradwell, whose rejection from the bar based on sex was upheld by the US Supreme Court, described Lockwood as "a finely educated lady, a pleasant, able speaker, possessed of great energy and determination, yet perfectly womanly, and has the ability to make a successful practitioner at the bar." While nearly all female activists created a distinction between their support of Utah woman suffrage and the broader "Mormon question," Lockwood was vocal in her criticism of antipolygamy legislation. According to Iversen, in 1876 she argued before the Senate Committee on Territories and consistently risked ostracizing herself from other female activists through her adamant support for Mormon rights. Lockwood was reported to have said, "I think it [the Edmunds Law] unjust and revolutionary in the extreme. . . . I am a thorough monogamist . . . But I do not recognize the right of our government, after allowing the system thirty-five years existence . . . to now threaten to disfranchise both men and women, and confiscate their property, if they will not renounce the relations of a lifetime which they conscientiously believe to be an essential part of their religious system." This legalistic defense stood in opposition to both the silence of NWSA and the vocal opposition of polygamy by AWSA.

93 Iversen, *Antipolygamy Controversy*, 33.

94 E. B. W., "Petition to Disfranchise Women," *Woman's Exponent* 13, no. 2 (1884): 11.

95 Iversen, *Antipolygamy Controversy*, 110.

96 "Trouble Ahead in Utah," *Chicago Tribune*, June 27, 1862, 2. E.g., the *Chicago Tribune* described Mormon men as "duly grateful to the power which fills their bellies and ministers to their lust. . . . That they are deluded does not make them less dangerous."

97 "Our Little Paper," *Woman's Exponent* 14, no. 24 (1886): 188. The *Woman's Exponent* reported that many Gentiles (non-Mormons) were interested in hearing the perspectives of Mormon women.

98 Whittaker, "Early Mormon Polygamy Defenses," 53–54.

99 Whittaker, "Early Mormon Polygamy Defenses," 57.

100 Whittaker, "Early Mormon Polygamy Defenses," 57.

101 Michael Leff and Ebony A. Utley, "Instrumental and Constitutive Rhetoric in Martin Luther King's 'Letter from Birmingham Jail,'" *Rhetoric and Public Affairs* 7, no. 1 (2004): 37–52; Kristin S. Vonnegut, "Poison or Panacea? Sarah Moore Grimké's Use of the Public Letter," *Communication Studies* 46 (1995).

102 Belinda Marden Pratt, "Defense of Polygamy by a Lady of Utah, in a Letter to

Her Sister in New Hampshire," 1854, 1, Schroeder Collection, Wisconsin Historical Society, Madison.

103 Pratt, "Defense of Polygamy," 3.

104 Campbell, "Gender and Genre."

105 Pratt, "Defense of Polygamy," 4.

106 Pratt, "Defense of Polygamy," 5.

107 Pratt, "Defense of Polygamy," 10–11.

108 "Notes from Washington," *Woman's Exponent* 14, no. 23 (1886): 180. The memorial was delivered to Washington, D.C., by four Mormon women who met with several officials. "In the senate the memorial was allowed to lie on the table, and appeared in full in The Record of April 7." The memorial was also delivered to the president, and the women spoke to the president about the issue.

109 Other mass meetings of Mormon women were reported in newspapers: "Utah Women in Favor of Polygamy," *Chicago Tribune*, October 31, 1871, 4; "The Women of Utah," *Chicago Tribune*, November 14, 1871, 1; A. J., "Mass Meeting," *Woman's Exponent* 7, no. 14 (1878): 109.

110 "The Mormon Question," *New York Times*, February 8, 1870, 1.

111 *"Mormon" Women's Protest. An Appeal for Freedom, Justice and Equal Rights. The Ladies of the Church of Jesus Christ of Latter-Day Saints Protest against the Tyranny and Indecency of Federal Officials in Utah, and against Their Own Disfranchisement without Cause. Full Account of Proceedings at the Great Mass Meeting, Held in the Theater, Salt Lake City Utah,* 1886, 17, Schroeder Collection, Wisconsin Historical Society, Madison.

112 *"Mormon" Women's Protest*, 24; selected speeches from the pamphlet were reprinted in "The Ladies' Mass Meeting; 'Mormon' Women Meet, Speak, and Resolve," *Woman's Exponent,* March 15, 1886, 158.

113 "Proceedings in Mass Meeting of the Ladies of Salt Lake City to Protest against the Passage of Cullom's Bill, January 14, 1870," 1870, 4, Church History Library, Salt Lake City, Utah; "More Severe Measures," *Woman's Exponent*, October 1, 1889, 68. Snow continued:

> Were we the stupid, degraded, heart-broken beings that we have been represented, silence might better become us; but as women of God, women filling high and responsible positions, performing sacred duties, women who stand not as dictators but as counselors to their husbands, and who, in the purest, noblest sense of refined womanhood, being truly their helpmates, we not only speak because we have the right, but justice and humanity demand that we should. ("Proceedings," 5)

Further, the *Woman's Exponent* framed the women jailed for violating polygamy laws primarily as mothers, transferring the meaning of the laws from prosecution of polygamists to the persecution of mothers. The editor explained:

> Annie Gallifant the first woman sent to the Penitentiary under the Edmund's law, and whose babe was born immediately after; then Belle Harris seared from one little child took her babe with her to prison, Nellie White who was in a very delicate condition, was also kept there awaiting the pleasure of the court to dismiss the Grand Jury which they held over as long as possible, Mrs. Argyle who was there until it caused the death of her babe; —these are cases well known to the public.

The names of women were listed to personalize and create identification, and the women were described only through their status as mother. The article did not indicate the details of why the women were imprisoned, suggesting that the women and their babies were imprisoned because of the women's status as mothers. In a way, this suggestion was not inaccurate because the physical presence of maternity functioned as evidence for unlawful cohabitation, but the *Woman's Exponent* used maternal language to frame the law as an attack on motherhood.

114 "Ladies' Mass Meeting," 158.

115 *"Mormon" Women on Plural Marriage. Fifteen Hundred "Mormon" Ladies Convene in the Salt Lake Theatre, to Protest against the Misrepresentations of the Ladies Engaged in the Anti-polygamy Crusade, and Declare Their True Sentiments on the Subject Now Being Agitated. 1878*, 1878, 5, Americana Collection, Brigham Young University, Provo, Utah; "The Governor's Message," *Woman's Exponent*, January 15, 1886, 125. I have used the titles (such as "Mrs.") only when individuals were referred to in this way in the original document. Also, "As the voice of the women of Utah, the EXPONENT declares, we are neither poor, down-trodden, fettered nor wronged, but on the contrary, rich in the happiness and peace of our homes, upheld and honored in every way, as wives and mother should be, we have no fetters, save the golden chains of affection, and are wronged only by our enemies."

116 *"Mormon" Women on Plural Marriage*, 2; "Proceedings in Mass Meeting," 2. For example, at a mass meeting in 1878 Eliza Snow framed the identity of Mormons, "As saints of the living God, who have been persecuted and driven from our homes from place to place, and now located in the valleys of these mountains." Similarly, in 1870 Bathsheba Smith recounted when she and her family "commenced a long and weary journey through a wilderness and mountains, to seek another home, for a wicked mob had decreed we must leave."

117 *"Mormon" Women on Plural Marriage*, 2.

118 "Ladies' Mass Meeting," 158.

119 "Trials Tend to Strengthen and Purify," *Woman's Exponent*, November 15, 1886, 84.

120 "Trials Tend to Strengthen and Purify," 84.

121 *"Mormon" Women's Protest*, 17.

122 "Proceedings in Mass Meeting," 3.

123 "Ladies, Go and Vote," *Woman's Exponent*, July 15, 1884, 28.

124 Emmeline B. Wells, "Letter to the Sisters at Home: To the Women of Utah, in Mass Meeting Assembled, March 6th, 1886," *Woman's Exponent*, April 1, 1886, 164.

125 "Proceedings in Mass Meeting," 3.

126 Wells, "Letter to the Sisters at Home," 164; Sarah A. Fullmer, "Our Franchise," *Woman's Exponent*, May 15, 1883, 185. Also, Sarah Fullmer said,

> Every society seeks the unity of its members as a necessity to its success; and shall all such be debarred the rights of freedom, or is it because we are women, the weaker sex, that man, proud man, exalted to a little brief authority, seeks to deprive us, the 'poor women' of Utah, of our rights? . . . Because we are one with our husbands in the maintenance of the principles of freedom, do they think that we, as the honorable wives of honorable men, having had the franchise for so long a time, (with a secret ballot)

would not, ere this, have thrown off the yoke if we were in bondage? If (as Senator Edmunds says) we were living under the influence of a Mormon hierarchy, such as he represents, we could at any moment have thrown it off and voted against our brethren.

127 Lewis, "Winning Woman Suffrage." Tiffany Lewis argues that Abigail Scott Duniway, prominent Western women's rights activist, utilized a traditionally masculine frontier myth in support of women's rights.

128 Gustive O. Larson, *The "Americanization" of Utah for Statehood* (San Marino, Calif.: Huntington Library, 1971), 283.

129 Richard S. Van Wagoner, *Mormon Polygamy: A History*, 2nd ed. (Salt Lake City, Utah: Signature Books, 1989), 140; Larson, *"Americanization,"* 263.

130 Larson, *"Americanization,"* 301.

Chapter 4

1 Cott, *Public Vows*, 16, 150; Hendrik Hartog, *Man and Wife in America: A History* (Cambridge, Mass.: Harvard University Press, 2002), 114.

2 Carroll Smith-Rosenberg, "Sex as Symbol in Victorian Purity: An Ethnohistorical Analysis of Jacksonian America," supplement, *American Journal of Sociology* 84 (1978): S220.

3 Tyler, *Freedom's Ferment*, 70; Whitney R. Cross, *The Burned-Over District: The Social and Intellectual History of Enthusiastic Religion in Western New York, 1800–1850* (Ithaca: Cornell University Press, 1950), 3.

4 Charles Grandison Finney, "What a Revival of Religion Is," in *Lectures on Revivals of Religion*, ed. William G. McLoughlin (Cambridge, Mass.: Harvard University Press, 1960), 18; Timothy L. Smith, "Righteousness and Hope: Christian Holiness and the Millennial Vision in America, 1800–1900," *American Quarterly* 31, no. 1 (1979): 24; Charles Hambrick-Stowe, *Charles G. Finney and the Spirit of American Evangelicalism* (Grand Rapids: Eerdmans, 1996), 92. Finney explained that conversion required the "agency" of the sinner because the sinner was required to act in the proper way.

5 Finney, *Lectures on Revivals of Religion*; John C. Spurlock, *Free Love: Marriage and Middle-Class Radicalism in America, 1825–1860* (New York: New York University Press, 1988), 7. Finney argued that a revival was necessary when there was evidence of "complacency" because salvation necessitated constant work (25). Further, that work necessitated self-control. Finney lectured, "Self-denial is a *condition of discipleship*" (45).

6 Nancy Cott, "Passionlessness: An Interpretation of Victorian Sexual Ideology, 1790–1850," *Signs* 4, no. 2 (1978); Barbara Welter, "The Cult of True Womanhood: 1820–1860," *American Quarterly* 18, no. 2 (1966); Smith-Rosenberg, "Sex as Symbol in Victorian Purity," S213. While Welter describes the "cult of true womanhood" as existing between 1820 and 1860, more recent research suggests that these cultural norms persisted throughout much of the nineteenth century and, for some women such as WCTU members, the cultural norms of womanhood provided a rhetorical justification for limited public action.

7 Bizzell, "Chastity Warrants."

8 Passet, *Sex Radicals*, 95.

9 Amy R. Slagell, "The Rhetorical Structure of Frances E. Willard's Campaign

for Woman Suffrage, 1876–1896," *Rhetoric and Public Affairs* 4, no. 1 (2001); Marilley, "Frances Willard."

10 Louise W. Knight, *Citizen: Jane Addams and the Struggle for Democracy* (Chicago: University of Chicago Press, 2005), 73–74, 217–18; William Rounseville Alger, *Friendships of Women* (Boston: Roberts Brothers, 1879), 120.

11 "The Free Love System: Origin, Progress and Position of the Anti-marriage Movement," *New York Daily Times*, September 8, 1855, 2.

12 Juliet H. Severance, *A Discussion of the Social Question between Juliet H. Severance, M.D. and David Jones, Editor of the "Olive Branch"* (Milwaukee: National Advance, 1891), 21, Collection of Leon Kramer, Special Collections, University of Wisconsin–Milwaukee.

13 "Free Love in England and America," *Chicago Tribune*, February 21, 1868.

14 "A Runaway Wife Reclaimed from a Disreputable House," *Chicago Tribune*, January 29, 1868, 2.

15 Aaron S. Hayward, "An Exposition of 'Social Freedom': Monogamic Marriage the Highest Development of Sexual Equality," in *Aaron S. Hayward* (Boston, 1874), 5, Fromkin Memorial Collection, University of Wisconsin–Milwaukee.

16 Hayward, "Exposition of 'Social Freedom,'" 53.

17 This is similar to the way that Republicans used polygamy to amplify the harm of slavery.

18 "Art. V.—the Declaration of Independence and the Republican Party," *DeBow's Review and Industrial Resources, Statistics, etc. Devoted to Commerce, Agriculture, Manufactures* 4, no. 2 (1860): 177.

19 See, e.g., Greeley, "Marriage—Divorce," 155.

20 Hal D. Sears, *The Sex Radicals: Free Love in High Victorian America* (Lawrence: Regents Press of Kansas, 1977), 5.

21 "A Rich Clip," *Liberator*, August 27, 1858. The *Liberator* reported an account of basically the same argument. The *Essex Banner* stated, "They [free lovers] believe in all the disgusting licentiousness of free love, in abolition of marriage, in abolition of slavery, to which creed they could appropriately add abolition of all moral or physical decency." The *Liberator* author responded to this clip from *Banner* by stating, "To believe in free love and abolition of marriage can only be the requisites to prepare the mind to embrace the most radical pro-slavery doctrines." Thus, the authors attempted to make free love the symbol of what they detested—slavery or abolition.

22 Nicola Beisel, *Imperiled Innocents: Anthony Comstock and Family Reproduction in Victorian America* (Princeton: Princeton University Press, 1997), 1.

23 Alyssa Picard, "'To Popularize the Nude in Art': Comstockery Reconsidered," *Journal of the Gilded Age and Progressive Era* 1, no. 3 (2002). Comstock was tremendously popular across social classes (196). "By the end of his career, he had arrested more than 3,700 people and burned over fifty tons of obscene books, 3,984,063 obscene pictures, and 16,900 photographic plates" (195).

24 Anthony Comstock, *Traps for the Young* (New York: Funk & Wagnalls, 1883), ix.

25 Comstock, *Traps for the Young*, 158.

26 Comstock, *Traps for the Young*, 167. For more on the cultural significance of the reference to the Turks and Orientialism, see Said, *Orientalism*.

27 Beisel, *Imperiled Innocents*, 2.

28 Beisel, *Imperiled Innocents*, 76.

29 Kern, *Ordered Love*, 3.

30 Ann Braude, *Radical Spirits: Spiritualism and Women's Rights in Nineteenth-Century America*, 2nd ed. (Bloomington: Indiana University Press, 2001), 4. Tyler, *Freedom's Ferment*, 83. According to Braude, spiritualism is often cited as beginning as a movement in New York in the 1840s as a "religious response to the crisis of faith experienced by many Americans" (4). In 1864 the first National Association of American Spiritualists convention met in Chicago. Braude explains that spiritualism provided a "scientific" faith to many who believed that "contact with the spirits of the dead provided empirical proof of the immortality of the soul" (4).

31 Robert Fogarty, *Special Love / Special Sex: An Oneida Community Diary* (Syracuse: Syracuse University Press, 1994), 4; *Hand-Book of the Oneida Community with a Sketch of Its Founder and an Outline of Its Constitution and Doctrines*, digital ed. (Wallingford, Conn.: Office of the Circular, Wallingford Community, 1867), 3, Oneida Community Collection, Syracuse University Library.

32 Tyler, *Freedom's Ferment*, 195.

33 Tyler, *Freedom's Ferment*, 185.

34 John McKelvie Whitworth, *God's Blueprints: A Sociological Study of Three Utopian Sects* (Boston: Routledge & Kegan Paul, 1975), 89. Whitworth argues that Noyes was unmoved by the religious revivals until he experienced a serious illness.

35 Tyler, *Freedom's Ferment*, 186.

36 Tyler, *Freedom's Ferment*, 186; Kathryn M. Olson, "The Role of Dissociation in Redeeming Knowledge Claims: Nineteenth-Century Shakers' Epistemological Resistance to Decline," *Philosophy & Rhetoric* 28, no. 1 (1995): 48. Followers of Fourier were primarily responsible for bringing French socialism to the United States as a way of reconciling the gap between rich and poor. Fourier's theories gained popularity with some prominent Americans, such as Horace Greeley, who worked to develop phalanxes, communities based on Fourierism. While Americans such as Greeley did not initially understand Fourier's theories of marriage due to apparent exclusions of those theories by English translators, for Fourier marriage reforms were part of a larger mission of reconciling class conflict by attempting to release human goodness. Robert Owen came to the United States from Wales in 1824 to exercise his theories of cooperative communities as a remedy to the social problems of capitalism. In 1824–1825 Owen founded the socialist, utopian community New Harmony in Indiana. According to Spurlock, "Rather than understanding marriage as the consequence of an unwavering and purely private experience of love, Owen viewed marriage as a social product serving the ends of a class-bound society" (26). By 1827 New Harmony had failed due to economic and leadership problems. Nevertheless, New Harmony left a legacy that heavily influenced many future utopian communities, and Robert Owens' son, Robert Dale Owen, remained in the United States, became a state legislator in Indiana, and worked toward reformist goals. The United Society of Believers in Christ's Second Coming, popularly known as the Shakers, were perhaps one of the earliest and best-known utopian communities to challenge traditional conventions of marriage. According to Olson, the Shakers came to the United States in 1774 following the leader Ann Lee, and according to most estimates by 1825 there were over six thousand Shakers in the country. Despite

their emotional passion in worship, the Shakers were most notable because of their self-restraint. They believed that the Bible called for celibacy. Full members were required to dissolve their marriages, live in sex-segregated dorms, and reserve their passion for God. John C. Spurlock, *Free Love: Marriage and Middle-Class Radicalism in America, 1825–1860* (New York: New York University Press, 1988).

37 Tyler, *Freedom's Ferment*, 189.

38 Michael Schudson, *The Good Citizen: A History of American Civic Life* (Cambridge, Mass.: Harvard University Press, 2002), 99.

39 *First Annual Report of the Oneida Association: Exhibiting Its History, Principles, and Transactions to Jan. 1, 1849*, digital ed. (Oneida Reserve: Leonard, 1849), 21, Syracuse University Library, Oneida Community Collection.

40 *First Annual Report*, 30.

41 *First Annual Report*, 28.

42 Whitworth, *God's Blueprints*, 123, 127. This was essentially a Lamarckian conception that the characteristics of parents would be transferred to their children.

43 *First Annual Report*, 32.

44 *Hand-Book of the Oneida Community*, 70–71.

45 "Communism—the Necessity of Preparation," *Circular* 1, no. 46 (1865): 363.

46 *First Annual Report*, 19.

47 *Bible Communism: A Compilation from the Annual Reports and Other Publications of the Oneida Association and Its Branches; Presenting, in Connection with Their History, a Summary View of Their Religious and Social Theories, Brooklyn, NY: Office of the Circular 1853* (New York: AMS Press, 1973), 30.

48 *First Annual Report*, 40.

49 *Bible Communism*, 16. The short book *Bible Communism* explained the day-to-day activities of the group, describing how the women are principally occupied in household affairs, needle-work, &c., except that in summer they mingle freely in the out-door labors of the garden and the farm."

50 *First Annual Report of the Oneida Association*, 6–7.

51 "Communism—the Necessity of Preparation," 363.

52 *Hand-Book of the Oneida Community*, 63–64.

53 Passet, *Sex Radicals*, 77.

54 Sue Zschoche, "Review, *Wash and Be Healed: The Water-Cure Movement and Women's Health* by Susan E. Cayleff," *Signs* 15, no. 2 (1990). Much like a spa, water cure establishments tended to cater to the upper classes. They typically involved drinking and bathing in mineral water, thought to cure a number of illnesses. The water cure was especially popular among women.

55 Passet, *Sex Radicals*, 80.

56 Passet, *Sex Radicals*, 82.

57 "Free Love in Ohio," *Chicago Daily Tribune*, April 15, 1858, 2.

58 Passet, *Sex Radicals*, 81.

59 Joseph Treat, "Socialism—How Do We Come at It: The Whole Thing in One View," *Social Revolutionist*, November 1856, 152.

60 "Another Free-Love Manifesto," *Chicago Press and Tribune*, August 6, 1858, 2.

61 " 'Free Love'—a Reply," *Social Revolutionist* 2, no. 5 (1856): 144.

62 J. H. Cook, "The Human Brain and Its Relations to Human Society," *Social Revolutionist* 2, no. 5 (1856): 132.

63 Vivian Grey, "Sexual Slavery," *Social Revolutionist* 2, no. 5 (1856): 138.
64 Grey, "Sexual Slavery," 137.
65 Grey, "Sexual Slavery," 138.
66 "The Free-Love Settlement at Berlin Heights Ohio," *New York Times*, July 21, 1858, 3. The account from the *Sandusky Register* was reprinted in other papers, including the *New York Times*.
67 "Free Love in Ohio," 2. This was originally published in the *Cleveland Herald* and republished across the country. It was also published in "The Berlin 'Love Cure'—Progress of Free Love in Erie County," *Milwaukee Daily Sentinel*, April 16, 1858, 3.
68 Anne Hunter, "Letter from the Wife of the Founder of the Berlin Free Love Institution," *Chicago Press and Tribune*, July 16, 1858, 2.
69 *New York Times*, November 27, 1857, 3.
70 "News Items," *Saturday Evening Post*, December 5, 1857, 7.
71 "The Free Lovers Again—Bonfire—a Chase after One of the 'Lovers,'" *Chicago Daily Tribune*, December 8, 1857, 2.
72 Passet, *Sex Radicals*, 88.
73 Martin Henry Blatt, *Free Love and Anarchism: The Biography of Ezra Heywood* (Urbana: University of Illinois Press, 1989), 41.
74 Emil F. Ruedebusch, *The Old and the New Ideal*, 2nd ed. (Mayville, Wisc.: by author, 1897), 131–35; Fromkin Memorial Collection, University of Wisconsin–Milwaukee; "Remarks," *Social Revolutionist* 2, no. 5 (1856): 134. The author of "Remarks" argued,

> There is not unanimity amongst those who believe in free love any more than amongst those who believe in free religion. I may specify the different views as follows:—1. Dual, exclusive life-union between those pairs that were born for each other. If unhappiness [results] . . . it is evidence that the parties made a 'mistake;' and so they should be free to seek again for the 'right one.' 2. But one integral sexual love at a time, which, however, is liable to perish even while the parties live, and so there should be freedom for a succession of loves. 3. More loves than one for the same individual, at the same time, but one of these is, or should be a 'pivotal love'—a greater love than the rest. 4. Many loves, at the same time, for one individual, but the physical ultimatum should obtain only for the purpose of conception. 5. The plurality of integral loves, or more than one at the same time, which should receive the physical ultimation in temperance, as the right of the love.

75 Robin E. Jensen, "Sexual Polysemy: The Discursive Ground of Talk about Sex and Education in U.S. History," *Communication, Culture & Critique* 1, no. 4 (2008): 405; Severance, *Discussion of the Social Question*, 16–17. Also, Severance argued, "A Free-lover raises the sexual act on which is based all physical and spiritual life, from the mud and filth with which the ignorance of the past has slimed it over, and elevates it to the very highest pinnacle of the temple, recognizing the sacredness of its mission, as not alone the generator of all physical life, but of spirit life also."
76 William H. Pilcher, "Varietism," *Lucifer, the Light-Bearer* 3, no. 6 (285/1886): 3; "The New Calendar," *Lucifer, the Light-Bearer* 3, no. 18 (285/1886): 2. *Lucifer*

dates the year from January 1, 1601, and they call this dating "the Era of Man, because previous to that time, man as *man* had no rights. The rights all belonged to the gods and to their agents or deputies, kings and priests."

77 Passet, *Sex Radicals*, 15.

78 *The Next Revolution, or Woman's Emancipation from Sex Slavery: No. 2* (Valley Fall, Kans.: Lucifer, 1890), 63, Special Collections, University of Wisconsin–Milwaukee.

79 *Next Revolution*, 14.

80 *Next Revolution*, 3.

81 *Next Revolution*, 7.

82 Mary Gabriel, *Notorious Victoria: The Life of Victoria Woodhull, Uncensored* (Chapel Hill: Algonquin Books of Chapel Hill, 1998), 7.

83 Gabriel, *Notorious Victoria*, 11; Barbara Goldsmith, *Other Powers: The Age of Suffrage, Spiritualism, and the Scandalous Victoria Woodhull* (New York: Alfred A. Knopf, 1998), 51.

84 Gabriel, *Notorious Victoria*, 12–13; Lois Beachy Underhill, *The Woman Who Ran for President: The Many Lives of Victoria Woodhull* (New York: Bridge Works, 1995), 24–25.

85 Goldsmith, *Other Powers*, 70.

86 Gabriel, *Notorious Victoria*, 30; Underhill, *Woman Who Ran for President*, 38.

87 Gabriel, *Notorious Victoria*, 33; Goldsmith, *Other Powers*, 157–58; Underhill, *Woman Who Ran for President*, 47.

88 Goldsmith, *Other Powers*, 191, 212; Underhill, *Woman Who Ran for President*, 64, 86.

89 Jason Jones, "Breathing Life into a Public Woman: Victoria Woodhull's Defense of Woman's Suffrage," *Rhetoric Review* 28, no. 4 (2009); Underhill, *Woman Who Ran for President*, 78, 101–2.

90 Helen Lefkowitz Horowitz, "Victoria Woodhull, Anthony Comstock, and Conflict over Sex in the United States in the 1870s," *Journal of American History* 87, no. 2 (2000); Molly McGarry, "Spectral Sexualities: Nineteenth-Century Spiritualism, Moral Panics, and the Making of the U.S. Obscenity Law," *Journal of Women's History* 12, no. 2 (2000): 13; Underhill, *Woman Who Ran for President*, 221, 29. Woodhull was acquitted because the law did not explicitly include newspapers. This acquittal, in part, motivated Comstock to push for passage of stricter obscenity legislation that came to be known as the Comstock laws.

91 Amanda Frisken, "Sex in Politics: Victoria Woodhull as an American Public Woman, 1870–1876," *Journal of Women's History* 12, no. 1 (2000); idem, *Victoria Woodhull's Sexual Revolution: Political Theater and the Popular Press in Nineteenth-Century America* (Philadelphia: University of Pennsylvania Press, 2004).

92 Underhill, *Woman Who Ran for President*, 259. Underhill called "Tried as by Fire" the "most successful [speech] of her [Woodhull's] career, a distillation of all her speeches on sexual topics, frank, personal, and wise."

93 Victoria Woodhull, *Tried as by Fire; or, the True and the False, Socially. An Oration Delivered by Victoria C. Woodhull, in All the Principal Cities and Towns of the Country during an Engagement of One Hundred and Fifty Consecutive Nights, to Audiences Together Numbering a Quarter of a Million of People* (New York: Woodhull & Claflin, 1874), 4.

94 Woodhull, *Tried as by Fire*, 8.
95 Woodhull, *Tried as by Fire*, 8, 20.
96 Woodhull, *Tried as by Fire*, 32.
97 Woodhull, *Tried as by Fire*, 27.
98 For more information on the connections between Woodhull's free love and evolutionary discourse, see Wendy Hayden, "(R)Evolutionary Rhetorics: Science and Sexuality in Nineteenth-Century Free-Love Discourse," *Rhetoric Review* 29, no. 2 (2010); Cathy Gutierrez, "Sex in the City of God: Free Love and the American Millennium," *Religion and American Culture: A Journal of Interpretation* 15, no. 2 (2005).
99 Woodhull, *Tried as by Fire*, 12.
100 Woodhull, *Tried as by Fire*, 33.
101 Eugenia C. DeLamotte, *Gates of Freedom: Voltairine de Cleyre and the Revolution of the Mind* (Ann Arbor: University of Michigan Press, 2004), 4; Paul Avrich, *An American Anarchist: The Life of Voltairine de Cleyre* (Princeton: Princeton University Press, 1978), 10. Biographer Avrich encapsulated the difficulty of her life when he noted, "Born in poverty in Michigan, she lived in poverty in Philadelphia and died in poverty in Chicago after weeks of agonizing pain. She suffered from chronic physical illness and moral torment. Her life, moreover, was jarred by a series of emotional dislocations which might have destroyed a weaker nature."
102 Avrich, *American Anarchist*, 18–19.
103 Avrich, *American Anarchist*, 30.
104 Avrich, *American Anarchist*, 47.
105 DeLamotte, *Gates of Freedom*, 8.
106 Avrich, *American Anarchist*, 72.
107 DeLamotte, *Gates of Freedom*, 8.
108 DeLamotte, *Gates of Freedom*, 222; Avrich, *American Anarchist*, 158; Catherine Helen Palczewski, "Voltairine de Cleyre: Sexual Slavery and Sexual Pleasure in the Nineteenth Century," *National Women's Studies Association* 7 (1995): 67. DeLamotte and Avrich suggested that de Cleyre delivered this speech in 1890. Palczewski noted that the speech was first delivered 1886. Passet noted that Harman (whom de Cleyre references at the beginning of the speech) was arrested four times (1890, 1892, 1895, and 1906). Thus, I believe that 1890 was probably the actual year that the speech was delivered.
109 Voltairine de Cleyre, "Sex Slavery," in *Selected Works of Voltairine de Cleyre: Pioneer of Women's Liberation*, ed. Alexander Berkman (New York: Revisionist Press, 1972), 344.
110 Nancy Cott, *Public Vows*, 58; Caroline W. Healy Dall, "Pictures of Southern Life for the Drawing Rooms of American Ladies," in *Liberty Bell*, ed. Friends of Freedom (Boston: National Anti-slavery Bazaar, 1851); Eliza Lee Follen, "Women's Work," in *Liberty Bell*, ed. Friends of Freedom (Boston: Massachusetts Anti-slavery Fair, 1842); Leslie J. Harris, "Motherhood, Race, and Gender: The Rhetoric of Women's Antislavery Activism in the *Liberty Bell* Giftbooks," *Women's Studies in Communication* 32, no. 3 (2009).
111 Charlotte H. L. Coues, "Appeal to Mothers," in *Liberty Bell*, ed. Friends of Freedom (Boston: Massachusetts Anti-slavery Fair, 1845); Martha Hempstead, "The

Fugitive," in *Liberty Bell*, ed. Friends of Freedom (Boston: Massachusetts Anti-slavery Fair, 1844).

112 de Cleyre, "Sex Slavery," 346.

113 de Cleyre, "Sex Slavery," 346.

114 Perelman and Olbrechts-Tyteca, *The New Rhetoric*, 415–19.

115 de Cleyre, "Sex Slavery," 347.

116 de Cleyre, "Sex Slavery," 355–56.

117 de Cleyre, "Sex Slavery," 354.

Chapter 5

1 Abraham Lincoln, "Annual Message to Congress, December 1, 1862," in *Collected Works of Abraham Lincoln*, ed. Roy P. Basler (Ann Arbor: University of Michigan Digital Library Production Services, 2001), 537.

2 Dred Scott, Plaintiff in Error, v. John F. A. Sandford, 60 U.S. 393, 407 (1857).

3 Taney was explicit in arguing that, while Native Americans were uncivilized, the condition of black Americans was clearly different because of their connection to slavery.

4 Plessy v. Ferguson, 163 U.S. 16 (1896).

5 William Frank Zornow, *Lincoln and the Party Divided* (Westport, Conn.: Greenwood Press, 1972), 8, 13.

6 John C. Waugh, *Reelecting Lincoln: The Battle for the 1864 Presidency* (New York: Crown, 1997), 203.

7 Waugh, *Reelecting Lincoln*, 11–12.

8 Waugh, *Reelecting Lincoln*, 12.

9 Waugh, *Reelecting Lincoln*, 62, 179.

10 J. M. Bloch, *Miscegenation, Melaleukation, and Mr. Lincoln's Dog* (New York: Schaum, 1958), 8–9.

11 Waugh, *Reelecting Lincoln*, 318–19; Bloch, *Miscegenation, Melaleukation*, 36.

12 Peter Wallenstein, *Tell the Court I Love My Wife: Race, Marriage, and Law—an American History* (New York: Palgrave Macmillan, 2002), 56. According to Wallenstein, Lincoln said, "I do not understand that because I do not want a negro woman for a slave that I must necessarily want her for a wife."

13 Michael Grossberg, *Governing the Hearth: Law and the Family in Nineteenth-Century America* (Chapel Hill: University of North Carolina Press, 1985), 126.

14 George A. Test, *Satire: Spirit and Art* (Tampa: University of South Florida Press, 1991); Wayne C. Booth, *A Rhetoric of Irony* (Chicago: University of Chicago Press, 1974); Robert Hariman, "Political Parody and Public Culture," *Quarterly Journal of Speech* 94, no. 3 (2008); Lisa Gring-Pemble and Martha Solomon Watson, "The Rhetorical Limits of Satire: An Analysis of James Finn Garner's *Politically Correct Bedtime Stories*," *Quarterly Journal of Speech* 89, no. 2 (2003); Don J. Waisanen, "Crafting Hyperreal Spaces for Comic Insights: The *Onion News Network*'s Ironic Iconicity," *Communication Quarterly* 59, no. 5 (2011). Satire and irony are notoriously difficult to define, but both Test (151) and Booth (30) agree that they are closely related concepts. Test also argues that hoax becomes satire when judgment is involved (179).

15 The creation of a new word is one way to deploy definition to shape the terms and frame of a controversy. A contemporary example is "partial birth abortion." This

labeling of the specific abortion procedure changes the shape of the controversy. However, with the example of "miscegenation" I believe that the creation of a new term functioned satirically in contributing to the parody of tone and scientific persona.

16 *Miscegenation: The Theory of the Blending of the Races, Applied to the American White Man and Negro* (New York: H. Dexter, Hamilton, 1864), 1.

17 *Miscegenation*, ii.

18 *Miscegenation*, ii.

19 *Miscegenation*, 9.

20 John S. Haller Jr., *Outcasts from Evolution: Scientific Attitudes of Racial Inferiority, 1859–1900* (Urbana: University of Illinois Press, 1971).

21 Peter S. Onuf, "American Exceptionalism and National Identity," *American Political Thought* 1, no. 1 (2012); Stephen John Hartnett, *Democratic Dissent and the Cultural Fictions of Antebellum America* (Urbana: University of Illinois Press, 2002), 110.

22 *Miscegenation*, 14.

23 *Miscegenation*, 34.

24 *Miscegenation*, 34.

25 *Miscegenation*, 36.

26 "Amalgamation among the Yankees," *Memphis Daily Appeal*, April 3, 1864. This Southern newspaper quoted extensively from this section of the pamphlet to illustrate the "shameless fanatics and cruel bigots" that would destroy the South if given the opportunity.

27 *Miscegenation*, 20.

28 *Miscegenation*, 28.

29 W. H. Hutter and Ray H. Abrams, "Copperhead Newspapers and the Negro," *Journal of Negro History* 20, no. 2 (1935): 134.

30 *Miscegenation*, 43.

31 *Miscegenation*, 52.

32 For more on racial politics of mimesis, see Kirt H. Wilson, "The Racial Politics of Imitation in the Nineteenth Century," *Quarterly Journal of Speech* 89, no. 2 (2003).

33 *Clarksville Weekly Chronicle*, October 20, 1865.

34 S. S. Nicholas, *Conservative Essays Legal and Political* (Philadelphia: J. B. Lippincott, 1865), 30.

35 "The New York News Lecturing Democratic Brethren at the South," *Cleveland Morning Leader*, April 18, 1864. The supposed divide between the passionate and rational also mapped onto assumptions of racial difference. A common assumption was that people of African descent were passionate and emotional. See, e.g., "Amalgamation among the Yankees."

36 "Practical Miscegenation," *Columbia Democrat and Bloomsburg General Advertiser*, July 16, 1864; "Abolitionism in Minnesota—Negro Equality and Miscegenation," *Memphis Daily Appeal*, April 6, 1864.

37 "Choose between Them," *Holmes County Farmer*, August 25, 1864.

38 "Miscegenation," *Ashtabula Weekly Telegraph*, August 6, 1864; Horace Otis, "Miscegenation," *Columbia Democrat and Bloomsburg General Advertiser*, May 7, 1864.

39 See, e.g., "Miscegenation," *Ashtabula Weekly Telegraph*; "Abolitionism in Minnesota—Negro Equality and Miscegenation." Papers such as these argued that miscegenation would eliminate the white race.

40 "The Miscegen Party," *Belmont Chronicle*, April 21, 1864; "The Miscegen Party," *Fremont Journal*, April 15, 1862.

41 "Miscegenational," *Belmont Chronicle*, May 12, 1864.

42 "The Miscegen Party," *Belmont Chronicle*, April 21, 1864; "The Miscegen Party," *Fremont Journal*, April 15, 1862.

43 "The Miscegen Party," *Belmont Chronicle*, April 21, 1864; "The Miscegen Party," *Fremont Journal*, April 15, 1862.

44 Cott, *Public Vows*, 99. According to Cott, "More laws of this sort were passed during the Civil War and Reconstruction than in any comparable short period. Ten states created new bans; eight others reiterated or refined theirs; others kept previous laws in place."

45 B., "Letter from the Capitol City: Society—Frederick Douglass's Marriage—Ballots and Bullets—Funereal—Garfield Memorial," *New York Evangelist*, January 31, 1884; Jane Grey Swisshelm, "Fred Douglass: The Opinion of Jane Grey Swisshelm regarding His Marriage," *Chicago Daily Tribune*, February 2, 1884; "Fred Douglass's Marriage," *New York Times*, January 26, 1884; "Washington. Great Example of Miscegenation. Building Better Than He Knew. The Old Man Eloquent Takes a White Bride. Views of Our Correspondent—Prof. J. M. Gregory Endorsed by the Colored Press Generally—Personals," *Cleveland Gazette*, February 2, 1884.

46 B., "Letter from the Capitol City"; "Items of General News," *Maine Farmer*, January 31, 1884; "Marriage of Frederick Douglass," *New York Times*, January 25, 1884; Junius, "Washington Letter," *Arkansas Mansion*, February 2, 1884. Douglass told reporters that Pitts was forty-six years old.

47 B., "Letter from the Capitol City"; "Frederick Douglass's Marriage," *Independent*, January 31, 1884.

48 Like Douglass, Francis Grimké was the product of an enslaved mother and slaveholding father, but, unlike Douglass, Grimké's father claimed him as his child.

49 Grossberg, *Governing the Hearth*, 127; Cott, *Public Vows*, 40. Grossberg explains that in "the nineteenth century, thirty-eight states and commonwealths had such restrictions at one time or another." According to Cott, "By 1860, when there were thirty-three states, twenty-three state or territorial legislatures had passed similar legislation," and seven more states did so during the Civil War.

50 Henry Clay Whitney, *Marriage and Divorce: The Effect of Each on Personal Status and Property Rights, with a Consideration of Fraudulent Divorces and the Ethics of Divorce for Popular and Professional Use* (Philadelphia: J. E. Potter, 1894), 141; William T. Nelson, *A Treatise on the Law of Divorce and Annulment of Marriage Including the Adjustment of Property Rights upon Divorce, the Procedure in Suits for Divorce, and the Validity and Extraterritorial Effects of Decrees of Divorce*, 2 vols. (Chicago: Callaghan, 1895), 2:647.

51 Tony Pace v. The State of Alabama, 106 U.S. 583 (1883).

52 An Act to Prevent the Intermarriage of White and Negro Races in the District of Columbia, H.R. 4212, 48th Cong. (1884). The measure appears to have been abandoned in committee.

53 "Sundries," *Colman's Rural World* 37, no. 11 (1884); "Items of General News," *Maine Farmer* 52, no. 11 (1884).

54 Kate Masur, *An Example for All the Land: Emancipation and the Struggle over Equality in Washington, D.C.* (Chapel Hill: University of North Carolina Press, 2010), 138, 290n93; Amy Dru Stanley, *From Bondage to Contract: Wage Labor, Marriage, and the Market in the Age of Slave Emancipation* (Cambridge: Cambridge University Press, 1998), 55–57. According to Stanley, the meanings of and implications for marriage of the 1866 Civil Rights Act were debated and inconsistently interpreted.

55 "Fred Douglass: Gen. T. W. Conway Discusses His Marriage—a Harmful Example," *Chicago Daily Tribune*, January 30, 1884.

56 "Fred Douglass's Marriage."

57 "Fred Douglass: Gen. T. W. Conway Discusses His Marriage—a Harmful Example"; R. D'Unger, "Miscegenation: Its Evil Effects Set Forth in Vivid Colors by a Physician," *Chicago Daily Tribune*, February 6, 1884.

58 "Frederick Douglass's Marriage." In a later article the *Independent* claimed that Douglass' marriage was not of public concern, the paper did not support "amalgamation," and Douglass was mostly white anyway. "Editorial Notes," *Independent*, February 21, 1884. Also see Swisshelm, "Fred Douglass."

59 "Washington. Great Example of Miscegenation." The same article stated, "There are colored ladies good enough for Mr. D and Mr. D *is good enough for any lady in the land, colored or white.*" And, "We may date the obliteration of the barbaric racial lines, the demolition of the babel of prejudice from the date of his second marriage. We are Americans all. We are a composite nation. Let us maintain our composite uniformity." Also, another paper commented, "Mr. Douglass is loved, honored and even revered, by all classes of colored people, [and whites too, pretty generally] [*sic*]. There is not a person in all our midst that is mad or chagrined." *Washington Bee*, February 2, 1884.

60 Douglass and Pitts did receive letters of congratulation from friends. These friends appeared to be genuinely happy for the couple, but messages such as these tended to remain private. For examples, see "General Correspondence," Jan.–Jul. 1884, Frederick Douglass Papers, Library of Congress.

61 Swisshelm, "Fred Douglass."

62 Swisshelm, "Fred Douglass."

63 Swisshelm, "Fred Douglass."

64 "The Mistake of His Life," *Grit*, January 26, 1884; "The Life of Frederick Douglass Can Now Be Written," *Western Recorder*, February 1, 1884; R. H. C, "Youngstown. Our Regular Correspondent Again to the Front—Barber Question—the Gazette's Editorial on the Douglass Marriage Generally Indorsed," *Cleveland Gazette*, February 9, 1884. The *Cleveland Gazette* wrote, "The old man forgets that he holds his present position on the strength of his identity with the Negro race."

65 "The Douglass Marriage," *Cleveland Gazette*, February 2, 1884.

66 "Douglass Marriage."

67 "Douglass Marriage."

68 "Douglass Marriage"; "Must We Intermarry?," *People's Advocate*, February 9, 1884.

69 J. A. Sykes, "Fred Douglass' Fatal Leap! His Marriage Ventilated! The Golden Egg Crushed! His Strong Grasp on the Negro Race as a Party Leader Lost Eternally! Between Two Gulfs He Stand! To Face the Coming Storm!," *Savannah Weekly Echo*, February 10, 1884.

70 Sykes, "Fred Douglass' Fatal Leap!" The author also said, "If the law of nature and of decency, enjoins upon the white man the duty to preserve the purity of his race, I hold that it enjoins the same duty upon the colored man, for nature unlike men, makes no distinction in the enforcement of its laws."

71 Africanus, "That Marriage. Some Very Sensible Reasons Why Frederick Douglass Should Have Selected a Wife from His Own Race," *Cleveland Gazette*, February 16, 1884; "Must We Intermarry?" The *People's Advocate* wrote, "Obliterating the color-line by absorption does not meet it [the issue of equality]; it simply rids the country of the Negro—that's all; the prejudice against the Negro remains."

72 "Fred. Douglass Not Denounced. Philadelphia Times," *Washington Bee*, February 2, 1884.

73 "Springfield. Our Regular Correspondent with His Usual Interesting Letter—Fisk Jubilance—Douglass' Marriage—Mattie Lawrence—Notes," *Cleveland Gazette*, February 2, 1884.

74 "Must We Intermarry?"

75 Frederick Douglass, "God Almighty Made but One Race: An Interview Given in Washington, D.C. on 25 January 1884," in *The Frederick Douglass Papers: Series One: Speeches, Debates, and Interviews*, ed. John W. Blassingam and John R. McKivigan, vol. 5 (New Haven: Yale University Press, 1992), 146.

76 Douglass, "God Almighty Made but One Race," 146.

77 Douglass, "God Almighty Made but One Race," 147.

78 Frederick Douglass, "Measuring the Progress of the Colored Race, Boston, Mass., 1886," in *The Frederick Douglass Papers: Series One*, vol. 5, 240.

79 Douglass, "Measuring the Progress," 240.

80 Frederick Douglass, "The Nation's Problem: An Address Delivered in Washington, D.C., on 16 April 1889," in *The Frederick Douglass Papers: Series One*, vol. 5, 411.

81 Ray, *Lyceum and Public Culture*, 123.

82 Douglass, "Nation's Problem," 405.

83 Douglass, "Nation's Problem," 409.

84 Douglass, "Measuring the Progress," 241.

85 These positions are not entirely inconsistent in that Douglass suggested that culture was important in constituting racial difference. However, even as he emphasized the role of culture, he also seemed to represent some racial difference as intrinsic, especially as racial difference intersected with nation.

86 "The Wife of His Youth; and Other Stories of the Color Line," *Zion's Herald*, December 6, 1899.

87 "Literary Notes," *Friends' Intelligencer*, March 3, 1900. These comments reference reviews of *The Wife of His Youth and Other Stories of the Color Line*. Also see *The Chautauquan: A Weekly Newsmagazine*, December 1900.

88 Hamilton Wright Mabie, "Books and Writers: The New Books I.—the Best New Novels," *Outlook*, November 16, 1901, 683.

89 W. D. Howells, "Charles W. Chesnutt's Stories: Atlantic," *Current Literature*, June 1900, 278.

90 Charles W. Chesnutt, "What Is a White Man?," *Independent*, May 30, 1889, 6.

91 Ida B. Wells, "Southern Horrors: Lynch Law in All Its Phases," in *Southern Horrors and Other Writings: The Anti-lynching Campaign of Ida B. Wells, 1892–1900*, ed. Jacqueline Jones Royster (Boston: St. Martins, 1997), 52.

Conclusion

1 Mulford, *The Nation*, 280; "The Late Dr. Elisha Mulford," *New York Times*, December 12, 1885; Matthew J. Lindsay, "Reproducing a Fit Citizenry: Dependency, Eugenics, and the Law of Marriage in the United States, 1860–1920," *Law & Social Inquiry* 23, no. 3 (1998); Grossberg, *Governing the Hearth*, 10, 83–84; *Moyler*, 620, 623. Similar arguments were common, and Lindsay and Grossberg provide several additional examples. Grossberg argues that by the second half of the nineteenth century there was a type of moral panic over the state of marriage. The 1847 *Moyler* decision provides another fairly typical example:

> Marriage is the most important of all the social relations. Upon the strict observance of its duties, by the married pair, depends not only everything which ministers to comfort and happiness, but also to private virtue. A facility of obtaining divorces . . . leads to licentiousness, and the disregard of the offspring of the marriage, and thus saps the very foundation of domestic happiness, and public virtue. Historians trace the decline of public morals, in ancient Rome, to this cause, more than to any other; and it cannot be doubted that the State in its political capacity, has a deep interest in this question.

2 Dorsey, *We Are All Americans*, 14.

3 Stuckey, *Defining Americans*; Beasley, *You, the People.*

4 White, *Legal Imagination.*

5 Wills, *Inventing America.*

6 Black Public Sphere Collective, ed., *The Black Public Sphere: A Public Culture Book* (Chicago: University of Chicago Press, 1995); Robert Asen and Daniel C. Brouwer, eds., *Counterpublics and the State* (Albany: State University of New York Press, 2001).

7 Gerard A. Hauser, *Vernacular Voices: The Rhetoric of Publics and Public Spheres* (Columbia: University of South Carolina Press, 1999).

8 Priscilla Wald, *Constituting Americans: Cultural Anxiety and Narrative Form* (Durham, N.C.: Duke University Press, 1995).

9 Robert Asen, "A Discourse Theory of Citizenship," *Quarterly Journal of Speech* 90, no. 2 (2004); Ray, *Lyceum and Public Culture*; Angela Ray and Cindy Koenig Richards, "Inventing Citizens, Imagining Gender Justice: The Suffrage Rhetoric of Virginia and Francis Minor," *Quarterly Journal of Speech* 93, no. 4 (2007); Cara A. Finnegan and Kang Jiyeon, "'Sighting' the Public: Iconoclasm and Public Sphere Theory," *Quarterly Journal of Speech* 90, no. 4 (2004); Lisa M. Gring-Pemble, "Writing Themselves into Consciousness: Creating a Rhetorical Bridge between the Public and Private Spheres," *Quarterly Journal of Speech* 84, no. 1 (1998): 41; Stuckey, "One Nation."

10 Stuckey, *Defining Americans*, 3.

11 Dorsey, *We Are All Americans.*

12 Schudson, *Good Citizen*. Schudson's focus is on what he labels as the "basic rules

of political practice," and he pays particular attention to modes of "good" citizenship in terms of explicit public engagement, such as voting (7). My study is not inconsistent with Schudson's argument. However, Schudson does not explicitly consider ways of being in family or marriage as enactments of citizenship. Moreover, the "good citizens" in Schudson's analysis were actually "good" male citizens, and my analysis of marriage suggests that citizenship can be seen in less explicit political enactments.

13 Nelson, *National Manhood*; Stuckey, *Defining Americans*, 128. Nelson's argument is important in suggesting that rather than being gender-neutral, citizenship has long been a gendered (and raced) concept in the United States, a concept that functions symbolically in the sense that it is a mythic ideal that is disconnected from the reality of the human experience. Nelson argues that an individual man or boy was expected to meet the "contradictory demands of self, family, market, and national interests *in his own person*" (12). My study illustrates that women faced similar expectations. Too often Americans sustained hyperbolic claims that the future of the nation rested on the shoulders of a mythic ideal of womanhood. For women to behave in accordance with this ideal was an enactment of good citizenship. Marriage was often a site where this ideal was negated. Nelson does not neglect the presence of women. She argues that the symbolic representation of the male subject always entails a symbolic representation of the female subject (and vice versa) (36, 49–50). Nonetheless, my study is valuable in more explicitly considering womanhood and the role of marriage.

14 Roger M. Smith, *Civic Ideals: Conflicting Visions of Citizenship in U.S. History* (New Haven: Yale University Press, 1997). Smith argues that the simultaneous and contradictory forces of liberalism, republicanism, and what he labels as ascriptive inegalitarianism, a political ideology driven by identity, characterize the history of the United States. He argues that the presence of gender inequality meant that even proponents of republicanism and liberalism sustained women's exclusion from full citizenship (110). I extend this analysis to argue that marriage provided a political and ideological frame that ran counter to republicanism and liberalism. Rather than conceptualizing women's citizenship as incomplete or simply absent, I argue that women's citizenship was understood as fundamentally distinct from men's citizenship. Further, beyond configuring women's status as citizens, marriage also participated in shaping understandings of male citizenship. For more on the history of political philosophy and marriage, see Scott Yenor, *Family Politics: The Idea of Marriage in Modern Political Thought* (Waco, Tex.: Baylor University Press, 2012).

15 See, e.g., Michael Warner, *Publics and Counterpublics* (New York: Zone Books, 2005), 23; Nancy Fraser, "Rethinking the Public Sphere: A Contribution to the Critique of Actually Existing Democracy," in *Habermas and the Public Sphere*, ed. Craig Calhoun (Cambridge: MIT Press, 1992); Robert Asen, "Imagining in the Public Sphere," *Philosophy & Rhetoric* 34, no. 4 (2002); Melissa Deem and Bonnie J. Dow, "Scandal, Heteronormative Culture, and the Disciplining of Feminism," *Critical Studies in Mass Communication* 16, no. 1 (1999); Mary Ryan, *Women in Public: Between Banners and Ballots, 1825–1880* (Baltimore: Johns Hopkins University Press, 1990), 3–18; Richard Sennett, *The Fall of Public Man* (New York: W. W. Norton, 1976). Sennett explores the importance of family to public life in the nineteenth century, yet he continues to deploy the language of

public and private to make sense of this relationship. Mary Ryan provides an excellent overview of the instability of the public/private dichotomy. While her approach is to find women in public, she also forces a consideration of the public/private as a social construct.

16 Berlant, *Queen of America*, 2–3, 56; idem, *Female Complaint*.

17 Warner, *Publics and Counterpublics*, 39.

18 Bishop, *Commentaries on the Law of Marriage and Divorce*, 6th ed., 1:3; Siegel, "Rule of Love," 2147. Siegel argues,

> Social contract theorists never applied concepts of individualism to the family with the confidence that they applied them to market and state relationships; instead, with the rise of liberalism, it became commonplace to define the family in terms of its differences from other social relationships. Countless nineteenth-century accounts of the home depict the family as fundamentally distinct from other spheres of social life, a domain in which altruism and other-regard prevailed, rather than self-interested individualism.

19 Grossberg, *Governing the Hearth*, 7; Kerber, *No Constitutional Right*, 10–12. My analysis deviates somewhat from Grossberg's argument. Grossberg argues that what he labels as the Republican Family was characterized by a movement from status to contract in marriage, movement from authority to affection, and entrenchment of separate spheres. Grossberg proceeds to nuance all of these claims. He is clear that male power in the home persisted throughout the nineteenth century, and he concedes that marriage was considered to be more than "mere" contract (21). Part of the seeming inconsistency in Grossberg's argument can be reconciled through a distinction between representation and lived reality. The Republican Family functioned symbolically in the norms and expectations sustained by American public culture, including, as in Grossberg's study, law. The rhetoric of the Republican Family was always gendered, raced, and classed, and that rhetoric created and enforced expectations of *duty* and *freedom* in the American family. Both of these terms, "duty" and "freedom," are ideographs, value terms with nonspecific referents that carry imbedded ideological assumptions. I argue that the concept of republicanism was part of what sustained power hierarchies because arbitrary power persisted, but that power was hidden behind very specific expectations of duty and freedom. Kerber's explanation may be more accurate. She argues, "But republican ideology did not eliminate the political father immediately and completely. It was simultaneously patriarchal and antipatriarchal, holding a liberal ideology of individualism in ambivalent tension with the old ideology of patriarchy" (10). Similarly, Ginzberg argues, "As in other emerging nations, the laws of political rights and obligations in the early republic frequently conflicted with laws underpinning family status. Such contradictions were typically resolved by deferring to traditional and religious conventions of domestic life" (28–29). Lori Ginzberg, *Untidy Origins: A Story of Woman's Rights in Antebellum New York* (Chapel Hill: University of North Carolina Press, 2005). For more on ideographs, see Michael Calvin McGee, "The 'Ideograph': A Link between Rhetoric and Ideology," *Quarterly Journal of Speech* 66, no. 1 (1980): 1–16; Celeste Michelle Condit and John Louis Lucaites, *Crafting Equality: America's Anglo-African Word* (Chicago: University of Chicago Press, 1993).

20 Norbert Elias, *The Civilizing Process*, vol. 2, *Power and Civility*, trans. Edmund Jephcott (New York: Pantheon Books, 1982); Said, *Orientalism*.

21 Marouf Arif Hasian Jr., *The Rhetoric of Eugenics in Anglo-American Thought* (Athens: University of Georgia Press, 1996), 17.

22 John Angus Campbell, "Scientific Revolution and the Grammar of Culture," *Quarterly Journal of Speech* 72, no. 4 (1986): 366; Richard Hofstradter, *Social Darwinism in American Thought* (Philadelphia: University of Pennsylvania Press, 1945), 15; Katie L. Gibson, "Judicial Rhetoric and Women's 'Place': The United States Supreme Court's Darwinian Defense of Separate Spheres," *Western Journal of Communication* 71, no. 2 (2007); Evelleen Richards, "Darwin and the Descent of Woman," in *The Wider Domain of Evolutionary Thought*, ed. Ian Langham (Boston: D. Reidel, 1983), 57–112.

23 Sally Kohlstedt and Mark Jorgensen, "The Irrepressible Woman Question: Women's Responses to Darwinian Evolutionary Ideology," in *Disseminating Darwinism: The Role of Place, Race, Religion, and Gender*, ed. John Stenhouse (Cambridge: Cambridge University Press, 1999), 271; Hofstradter, *Social Darwinism in American Thought*, 26.

24 Hasian, *Rhetoric of Eugenics*, 21; Robin E. Jensen, *Dirty Words: The Rhetoric of Public Sex Education, 1870–1924* (Urbana: University of Illinois Press, 2010), 18.

25 Thomas M. Lessl, *Rhetorical Darwinism: Religion, Evolution, and the Scientific Identity* (Waco, Tex.: Baylor University Press, 2012).

26 Brett Lunceford, "Rhetoric and Religion in Contemporary Politics," *Journal of Contemporary Rhetoric* 2, no. 2 (2012): 19–20.

27 Mackenzie v. Hare et al., Board of Elections of San Francisco, 239 U.S. 299 (1915); Candice Lewis Bredbenner, *A Nationality of Her Own: Women, Marriage, and the Law of Citizenship* (Berkeley: University of California Press, 1998), 2.

28 Bredbenner, *Nationality of Her Own*, 16, 17, 37. The 1855 statute made women the only adults to receive "citizenship derivatively, regardless of the preference of the actual women involved." The courts decided that the laws applied only to women who were otherwise eligible for citizenship, which excluded some races, the immoral, abd the insane.

29 Cong. Globe, 33rd Cong., 1st Sess. 170 (1854). In his justification of the bill to the House, Representative Cutting argued, "And the House will perceive, sir, that there can be no objection to it, because women possess no political rights; and where you confer on her the political character of her husband, it is a relief to the husband, and it aids him in instilling of proper principles in his children, and it cannot interfere with any possible right of political character." The name of the act and nearly all discussion surrounding the act referred to children of US citizens who were born abroad. The inclusion of women in the legislation was rhetorically presented as an afterthought and a convenience to husbands, suggesting that norms of the family government were so natural that they did not warrant debate. Nonetheless, the inclusion of women presented the only controversy over the legislation. Initially, the Senate Judiciary Committee recommended striking out the section of the act referring to wives. However, when brought to debate in the Senate, the Committee amended its recommendation to state that only women who would otherwise qualify for naturalization could become citizens through marriage. Such a recommendation highlights that the primary concern was that only the right kind of women become US citizens.

30 Woman's rights journals tended to frame this legislation as a clear injustice. For example, "Expatriation of American Women," *Suffragist* 4, no. 52 (1916); Chrystal Macmillan, "Nationality of Married Women," *International Women's News* 11, no. 1 (1916); Burnita Shelton Matthews, "The Woman without a Country," *Equal Rights* 1, no. 15 (1923); "Expatriation of Women Citizens," *Suffragist* 2, no. 52 (1914); "American Notes: Naturalisation Laws in U.S.A.," *International Women's News* 10, no. 5 (1916). The Cable Act of 1922 effectively reversed the 1907 Expatriation Act, but some woman's rights activists argued that it did not go far enough because it did not ensure equal citizenship rights. Gordon Mackenzie eventually said that he would apply for US citizenship so that his wife could once again become a citizen.

31 *Expatriation of Citizens and Their Protection Abroad* (1907) 34 Stat. 1228; Cott, *Public Vows*, 143; House Committee on Foreign Affairs, "Expatriation of American Citizens," 59th Cong., 2nd Sess., H.R. Rep. No. 6431 (1907); Secretary of State, "Citizenship of the United States, Expatriation, and Protection Abroad," 59th Cong., 2nd Sess., H.R. Rep. No. 326 (1906). The House Committee on Foreign Affairs framed the most "important" provision of the bill as one to prevent fraudulent claims of citizenship by people who wanted the protection of the United States without having true allegiance to the United States. This legislation was adopted with virtually no debate. Much as in 1855, the citizenship status of women seemed like an afterthought.

32 Case of the Chinese Wife; in re Ah Moy, on Habeas Corpus, 21 F. 785 (1884).

33 Tsoi Sim v. United States, 116 F. 920 (1902).

34 George Anthony Peffer, *If They Don't Bring Their Women Here: Chinese Female Immigration before Exclusion* (Urbana: University of Illinois Press, 1999), 7, 8; Adam McKeown, "Transnational Chinese Families and Chinese Exclusion, 1875–1943," *Journal of American Ethnic History* 18, no. 2 (1999): 80; Emily Ryo, "Through the Back Door: Applying Theories of Legal Compliance to Illegal Immigration during the Chinese Exclusion Era," *Law & Social Inquiry* 31, no. 1 (2006): 116. According to Peffer, the Page Act of 1875 prohibited the entry of Chinese women into the United States for "immoral" or "lewd" purposes. The reality of Chinese prostitution is difficult to discern. While there certainly were Chinese prostitutes, some reports indicate that numbers may have been inflated in order to increase anti-Chinese sentiment in the United States. As Chinese women's entry into the United States came to be limited to wives of merchants, there were frequent reports of fraudulent wives, women who claimed to be married but were really prostitutes or women who married pimps in order to stay in the United States. One of the most publicized cases was that of the "20 Chinese wives." These Chinese women were detained under the accusation that they were clearly prostitutes who were fraudulently claiming to be wives, but Peffer challenges that assumption. Indeed, it was difficult, if not impossible, to prove that one did not intend to be a prostitute after entering the United States. Regardless of the reality, the public rhetoric judged these women to be prostitutes, which fit into the cultural assumption of sexual immorality of the Other. This rhetorical logic is part of what contributed to adoption of the Chinese Exclusion Acts. McKeown argues that the limited immigration of Chinese women is likely due to a number of factors beyond the Page Act, including a general fear of the Chinese and a belief that Chinese immigration threatened to harm the country.

35 Ardeshir Ruttonji Wadia, *The Ethics of Feminism: A Study of the Revolt of Woman* (London: G. Allen & Unwin, 1923); Heber Leonidas Hart, *Woman Suffrage: A National Danger* (London: T. Murby, 1909); Maddux, "When Patriots Protest"; Catherine H. Palczewski, "The Male Madonna and the Feminine Uncle Sam: Visual Argument, Icons, and Ideographs in 1909 Anti-Woman Suffrage Postcards," *Quarterly Journal of Speech* 91, no. 4 (2005). Books such as Wadia's and Hart's argued that women's newfound rights irrevocably changed the family and, thus, the nation. Maddux and Palczewski argue that, especially prior to 1917, the perceived threat to family was an important trope in the antisuffrage arguments.

36 See, e.g., Sheila M. Webb, "The Woman Citizen: A Study of How News Narratives Adapt to a Changing Social Environment," *American Journalism* 29, no. 2 (2012): 9–36; Slagell, "Rhetorical Structure"; E. Michele Ramsey, "Inventing Citizens during World War I: Suffrage Cartoons in *The Woman Citizen*," *Western Journal of Communication* 64, no. 2 (2000).

37 Cott, *Public Vows*, 209, 211. Cott also cites a California case from the 1990s that drew on the logic of coverture to argue that a wife had an obligation to care for her husband.

38 Address by President Roosevelt before the National Congress of Mothers, 5.

39 United States v. Windsor, No. 12-307 slip op. (U.S. June 26, 2013).

Bibliography

Archival Collections

The following archival collections have been consulted for the material in this work: Americana Collection, Brigham Young University, Provo, Utah; Chicago History Museum Research Center, Chicago, Ill.; Church History Library, Salt Lake City, Utah; Collection of Leon Kramer, Special Collections, University of Wisconsin–Milwaukee; Frances Willard Memorial Library and Archives, Evanston, Ill.; Frederick Douglass Papers, Library of Congress, Washington, D.C.; Fromkin Memorial Collection, University of Wisconsin–Milwaukee; Illinois Humane Society Records, University of Illinois–Chicago; Oneida Community Collection, Syracuse University Library; Schroeder Collection, Wisconsin Historical Society, Madison; Special Collections, University of Wisconsin–Milwaukee; Theodore Roosevelt Collection, Houghton Library, Harvard University; Tom Perry Special Collections, Brigham Young University Library, Provo, Utah.

Court Decisions

The following court decisions have been discussed in the course of this work: *Case of the Chinese Wife; in re Ah Moy, on Habeas Corpus*, Circuit Court, D. California 21 F. 785 (1884); *Close v. Close*, 24 N.J. Eq. 338 (1874); *David v. David*, 27 Ala. 222, 225 (1855); *Dred Scott, Plaintiff in Error, v. John F. A. Sandford*, 60 U.S. 393 (1857); *Farnham v. Farnham*,

73 Ill. 497 (1874); *Foley v. Foley*, 61 Ill. App. 577 (1895); *Gordon v. Potter*, 17 Vt. 348 (1845); *Henderson v. Henderson*, 88 Ill. 248, 250 (1878); *Hoshall v. Hoshall*, 51 Md. 72 (1879); *Lander, Jr. v. Seaver*, 32 Vt. 114 (1859); *Mackenzie v. Hare et al., Board of Elections of San Francisco*, 239 U.S. 299 (1915); *Martin v. Robson*, 65 Ill. 129 (1872); *Moyler v. Moyler*, 11 Ala. 620 (1847); *Pace v. The State of Alabama*, 106 U.S. 583 (1883); *Plessy v. Ferguson*, 163 U.S. 16 (1896); *Poor v. Poor*, 8 N.H. 307 (1836); *Reed, Appellant v. Reed, Respondent*, 4 Nev. 395 (1868); *Reynolds v. United States*, 98 U.S. 145 (1878); *Skinner, Appellee, Petitioner v. Skinner, Appellant, Defendant*, 5 Wis. 449, 452 (1856); *State v. Jones*, 95 N.C. 588 (1886); *State v. Rhodes*, 61 N.C. 453 (1868); *State v. Richard Oliver* 70 N.C. 60 (1874); *State v. Simpson Pettie* 80 N.C. 367 (1879); *Tsoi Sim v. United States*, Circuit Court of Appeals, Ninth Circuit, 116 F. 920 (1902); *United States v. Windsor*, No. 12-307 slip op. (U.S. June 26, 2013); *Ward v. Ward*, 103 Ill. 477 (1882); *Williams, Plaintiff in Error v. Edward L. Williams and Elizabeth M. Williams, Defendants in Error*, 1 Colo. App. 281 (1892).

Sources

Agonistes. *Doctrine of Divorce*. Albany, 1857.

Alger, William Rounseville. *Friendships of Women*. Boston: Roberts Brothers, 1879.

"American Notes: Naturalisation Laws in U.S.A." *International Women's News* 10, no. 5 (1916): 73.

Amsterdam, Anthony, and Jerome Bruner. *Minding the Law*. Cambridge, Mass.: Harvard University Press, 2000.

Anderson, Benedict. *Imagined Communities*. Rev. ed. New York: Verso, 1991.

Anderson, Karrin Vasby. " 'Rhymes with Rich': 'Bitch' as a Tool of Containment in Contemporary American Politics." *Rhetoric and Public Affairs* 2, no. 4 (1999): 599–623.

Anthony, Susan B., and Ida Husted Harper. *The History of Woman Suffrage*. Vol. 4. Rochester, N.Y.: Susan B. Anthony, 1902.

Aristodemou, Maria. *Law and Literature: Journeys from Her to Eternity*. New York: Oxford University Press, 2000.

Asen, Robert. "A Discourse Theory of Citizenship." *Quarterly Journal of Speech* 90, no. 2 (2004): 189–211.

———. "Imagining in the Public Sphere." *Philosophy & Rhetoric* 34, no. 4 (2002): 345–67.

Asen, Robert, and Daniel C. Brouwer, eds. *Counterpublics and the State*. Albany: State University of New York Press, 2001.

Avrich, Paul. *An American Anarchist: The Life of Voltairine de Cleyre*. Princeton: Princeton University Press, 1978.

Basch, Norma. *Framing American Divorce: From the Revolutionary Generation to the Victorians*. Berkeley: University of California Press, 1999.

Beasley, Vanessa B. *You, the People: American National Identity in Presidential Rhetoric*. College Station: Texas A&M University Press, 2004.

Beecher, Catherine E. *A Treatise on Domestic Economy, for the Use of Young Ladies at Home and at School*. Rev. ed. New York: Harper & Brothers, 1854.

Beisel, Nicola. *Imperiled Innocents: Anthony Comstock and Family Reproduction in Victorian America*. Princeton: Princeton University Press, 1997.

Berlant, Lauren. *The Female Complaint: The Unfinished Business of Sentimentality in American Culture*. Durham, N.C.: Duke University Press, 2008.

———. *The Queen of America Goes to Washington City: Essays on Sex and Citizenship*. Durham, N.C.: Duke University Press, 1997.

Bible Communism: A Compilation from the Annual Reports and Other Publications of the Oneida Association and Its Branches; Presenting, in Connection with Their History, a Summary View of Their Religious and Social Theories. Brooklyn, NY: Office of the Circular 1853. New York: AMS Press, 1973.

A Bill to Discourage Polygamy in Utah by Granting the Right to Suffrage to the Women of That Territory. 1st, H.R. 64. L. Tom Perry Special Collections. Brigham Young University Library, Provo, Utah (1869).

Bishop, Joel Prentiss. *Commentaries on the Law of Marriage and Divorce: With the Evidence, Practice, Pleading, and Forms: Also of Separation without Divorce and of the Evidence of Marriage in All Issues*. 5th ed. 2 vols. Vol. 1. Boston: Little, Brown, 1873.

———. *Commentaries on the Law of Marriage and Divorce: With the Evidence, Practice, Pleading, and Forms: Also of Separation without Divorce and of the Evidence of Marriage in All Issues*. 6th ed. 2 vols. Boston: Little, Brown, 1881.

Bizzell, Patricia. "Chastity Warrants for Women Public Speakers in Nineteenth-Century American Fiction." *Rhetoric Society Quarterly* 40, no. 4 (2010): 385–401.

Black, Edwin. *Rhetorical Questions: Studies of Public Discourse*. Chicago: University of Chicago Press, 1992.

Black Public Sphere Collective, ed. *The Black Public Sphere: A Public Culture Book*. Chicago: University of Chicago Press, 1995.

Blackstone, William. *Commentaries on the Laws of England, in Four Books*. 12th ed. Vol. 1. London: A. Strahan and W. Woodfall, for T. Cadell, 1793–1795.

Blackwell, Alice Stone. "The Divorce Question." *Woman's Column* 12, no. 21 (1899): 1.

Blackwell, Antoinette Brown. "Speech of Rev. Antoinette Brown [Blackwell]." In *Man Cannot Speak for Her*, vol. 2, *Key Texts of the Early Feminists*, edited by Karlyn Kohrs Campbell, 202–14. Westport, Conn.: Praeger, 1989.

Blatt, Martin Henry. *Free Love and Anarchism: The Biography of Ezra Heywood*. Urbana: University of Illinois Press, 1989.

Bloch, J. M. *Miscegenation, Melaleukation, and Mr. Lincoln's Dog*. New York: Schaum, 1958.

"Book Notices." *American Catholic Quarterly Review* 16, no. 62 (1891): 428.

"Book Notices." *American Law Review* 1, no. 4 (1867): 729.

Booth, Wayne C. *A Rhetoric of Irony*. Chicago: University of Chicago Press, 1974.

Bosmajian, Haig. *Metaphor and Reason in Judicial Opinions*. Carbondale: Southern Illinois University Press, 1992.

Braude, Ann. *Radical Spirits: Spiritualism and Women's Rights in Nineteenth-Century America*. 2nd ed. Bloomington: Indiana University Press, 2001.

Bredbenner, Candice Lewis. *A Nationality of Her Own: Women, Marriage, and the Law of Citizenship*. Berkeley: University of California Press, 1998.

Brooks, Peter. *The Melodramatic Imagination*. New Haven: Yale University Press, 1976.

Browne, Stephen H. *Angelina Grimké: Rhetoric, Identity, and the Radical Imagination*. East Lansing: Michigan State University Press, 2000.

Buchanan, James. "State of the Union Address." 1857.

———. "State of the Union Address." 1858.

Campbell, John Angus. "Scientific Revolution and the Grammar of Culture." *Quarterly Journal of Speech* 72, no. 4 (1986): 351–76.

Campbell, Karlyn Kohrs. "Gender and Genre: Loci of Invention and Contradiction in the Earliest Speeches by U.S. Women." *Quarterly Journal of Speech* 81, no. 4 (1995): 479–95.

———. *Man Cannot Speak for Her*. Vol. 1, *A Critical Study of Early Feminist Rhetoric*. Westport, Conn.: Praeger, 1989.

———, ed. *Man Cannot Speak for Her*. Vol. 2, *Key Texts of the Early Feminists*. Westport, Conn.: Praeger, 1989.

"Can a Married Woman Maintain an Action of Tort against Her Husband for a Tort Committed during Coverture?" *Yale Law Journal* 22, no. 3 (1913): 250–55.

Carlier, Auguste. *Marriage in the United States*. Translated by B. Joy Jeffries. 3rd ed. Boston: De Vries, Ibarra, 1867.

Carlson, A. Cheree. "Creative Casuistry and Feminist Consciousness: The Rhetoric of Moral Reform." *Quarterly Journal of Speech* 78, no. 1 (1992): 16–32.

———. "The Role of Character in Public Moral Argument: Henry Ward Beecher and the Brooklyn Scandal." *Quarterly Journal of Speech* 77, no. 1 (1991): 38–52.

Chandler, Lucinda B. "Justice and Judicial Murder." *Woman's Tribune* 5, no. 42 (1888): 6.

Chesnutt, Charles W. "What Is a White Man?" *Independent*, May 30, 1889, 5–6.

"Chicago Metropolitan Population." In *The Encyclopedia of Chicago*, edited by James R. Grossman, Ann Durkin Keating, and Janice L. Reiff, 1005–45. Chicago: University of Chicago Press, 2004.

Chused, Richard. *Private Acts in Public Places*. Philadelphia: University of Pennsylvania Press, 1994.

A Citizen of Massachusetts. *The Mormon Problem. A Letter to the Massachusetts Members of Congress on Plural Marriage: Its Morality and Lawfulness*. Boston: James Campbell, 1882. Schroeder Collection. Wisconsin Historical Society, Madison.

Clapp, Elizabeth. *Mother of All Children: Women Reformers and the Rise of the Juvenile Courts in Progressive Era America*. University Park: Pennsylvania State University Press, 1998.

"Communism—the Necessity of Preparation." *Circular* 1, no. 46 (1865): 362–63.

Comstock, Anthony. *Traps for the Young*. New York: Funk & Wagnalls, 1883.

Condit, Celeste Michelle, and John Louis Lucaites. *Crafting Equality: America's Anglo-African Word*. Chicago: University of Chicago Press, 1993.

Cook, J. H. "The Human Brain and Its Relations to Human Society." *Social Revolutionist* 2, no. 5 (1856): 131–33.

Coontz, Stephanie. *Marriage, A History: From Obedience to Intimacy, or How Love Conquered Marriage.* New York: Viking, 2005.

Cott, Nancy. "Passionlessness: An Interpretation of Victorian Sexual Ideology, 1790–1850." *Signs* 4, no. 2 (1978): 219–36.

———. *Public Vows: A History of Marriage and the Nation.* Cambridge, Mass.: Harvard University Press, 2000.

Coues, Charlotte H. L. "Appeal to Mothers." In *Liberty Bell,* edited by Friends of Freedom, 3–8. Boston: Massachusetts Anti-slavery Fair, 1845.

Cowley, Charles. *Browne's Divorce and Its Consequences.* Lowell, Mass.: Penhallow Printing [1877?].

Cradlebaugh, John. "Mormon Horrors! Judge Cradlebaugh's Speech in Congress in 1863. Terrible Arraignment of the Blood-Stained Mormon Church. Graphic Account of the Mountain Meadows Massacre. Blood Atonement Openly Preached by Brigham Young and His Apostles. A Reeking, Filthy, Bloody Scar on the Nation. Let No Tool Stand in the Way of Wiping It Out." *Supplement to the Salt Lake Tribune* [1863?]. Church History Library, Salt Lake City, Utah.

Cross, Whitney R. *The Burned-Over District: The Social and Intellectual History of Enthusiastic Religion in Western New York, 1800–1850.* Ithaca: Cornell University Press, 1950.

Dall, Caroline W. Healy. "Pictures of Southern Life for the Drawing Rooms of American Ladies." In *Liberty Bell,* edited by Friends of Freedom, 24–47. Boston: National Anti-slavery Bazaar, 1851.

Darwin, Charles. *The Descent of Man.* Amherst, N.Y.: Prometheus Books, 1998.

"Declaration of Sentiments and Resolutions." In *Man Cannot Speak for Her,* vol. 2, *Key Texts of the Early Feminists,* edited by Karlyn Kohrs Campbell, 33–39. Westport, Conn.: Praeger, 1989.

de Cleyre, Voltairine. "Sex Slavery." In *Selected Works of Voltairine de Cleyre: Pioneer of Women's Liberation,* edited by Alexander Berkman, 342–58. New York: Revisionist Press, 1972.

Deem, Melissa, and Bonnie J. Dow. "Scandal, Heteronormative Culture, and the Disciplining of Feminism." *Critical Studies in Mass Communication* 16, no. 1 (1999): 86–94.

DeLamotte, Eugenia C. *Gates of Freedom: Voltairine de Cleyre and the Revolution of the Mind.* Ann Arbor: University of Michigan Press, 2004.

DeWitt, Robert, ed. *Report of the Beardsley Divorce Case.* New York: Robert M. DeWitt, 1860.

Dickenson, Anna. "Whited Sepulchres." In Angela Ray, *The Lyceum and Public Culture in the Nineteenth-Century United States*, 221–38. East Lansing: Michigan State University Press, 2005.

Dorsey, Leroy G. *We Are All Americans, Pure and Simple: Theodore Roosevelt and the Myth of Americanism*. Tuscaloosa: University of Alabama Press, 2007.

Douglass, Frederick. "God Almighty Made but One Race: An Interview Given in Washington, D.C. on 25 January 1884." In *The Frederick Douglass Papers: Series One: Speeches, Debates, and Interviews*, edited by John W. Blassingam and John R. McKivigan, vol. 5, 145–47. New Haven: Yale University Press, 1992.

———. "Measuring the Progress of the Colored Race, Boston, Mass., 1886." In *The Frederick Douglass Papers: Series One: Speeches, Debates, and Interviews*, edited by John W. Blassingam and John R. McKivigan, vol. 5, 238–46. New Haven: Yale University Press, 1992.

———. "The Nation's Problem: An Address Delivered in Washington, D.C., on 16 April 1889." In *The Frederick Douglass Papers: Series One: Speeches, Debates, and Interviews*, edited by John W. Blassingam and John R. McKivigan, vol. 5, 403–26. New Haven: Yale University Press, 1992.

Dow, Bonnie J., and Mari Boor Tonn. "Feminine Style and Political Judgement in the Rhetoric of Ann Richards." *Quarterly Journal of Speech* 79, no. 3 (1993): 286–302.

DuBois, Ellen Carol. " 'The Pivot of the Marriage Relation': Stanton's Analysis of Women's Subordination in Marriage." In *Elizabeth Cady Stanton, Feminist as Thinker: A Reader in Documents and Essays*, edited by Ellen Carol DuBois and Richard Candida Smith, 82–92. New York: New York University Press, 2007.

Duffey, Mrs. E. B. *The Relations of the Sexes*. New York: Estill, 1876.

Edwards, Rebecca. "Pioneers at the Polls: Woman Suffrage in the West." In *Votes for Women: The Struggle for Suffrage Revisited*, edited by Jean H. Baker, 90–101. New York: Oxford University Press, 2002.

Elias, Norbert. *The Civilizing Process*. Vol. 2, *Power and Civility*. Translated by Edmund Jephcott. New York: Pantheon Books, 1982.

Eliason, Eric. "Curious Gentiles and Representational Authority in the City of the Saints." *Religion and American Culture: A Journal of Interpretation* 11, no. 2 (2001): 155–90.

Ertman, Martha M. "Race Treason: The Untold Story of America's Ban on Polygamy." *Columbia Journal of Gender and Law* 19 (2010): 287–366.

Evans, Mrs. E. E. "At Sea with the Mormons, from the Notebook of a Gentile Traveler." *Herald of Health* 17, no. 1 (1871): 13–16.

"Expatriation of American Women." *Suffragist* 4, no. 52 (1916): 4.

"Expatriation of Women Citizens." *Suffragist* 2, no. 52 (1914): 3.

Finnegan, Cara A., and Kang Jiyeon. " 'Sighting' the Public: Iconoclasm and Public Sphere Theory." *Quarterly Journal of Speech* 90, no. 4 (2004): 377–402.

Finney, Charles Grandison. "What a Revival of Religion Is." In *Lectures on Revivals of Religion*, edited by William G. McLoughlin, 9–23. Cambridge, Mass.: Harvard University Press, 1960.

First Annual Report of the Oneida Association: Exhibiting Its History, Principles, and Transactions to Jan. 1, 1849. Digital ed. Oneida Reserve: Leonard, 1849. Oneida Community Collection. Syracuse University Library.

Fogarty, Robert. *Special Love / Special Sex: An Oneida Community Diary*. Syracuse: Syracuse University Press, 1994.

Follen, Eliza Lee. "Women's Work." In *Liberty Bell*, edited by Friends of Freedom, 6–13. Boston: Massachusetts Anti-slavery Fair, 1842.

Fox, Richard Wightman. *Trials of Intimacy: Love and Loss in the Beecher-Tilton Scandal*. Chicago: University of Chicago Press, 1999.

Frank, Henriette Greenbaum, and Amalie Hofer Jermone, eds. *Annals of the Chicago Woman's Club: For the First Forty Years of Its Organization 1876–1916*. Chicago: Chicago Woman's Club, 1916.

Fraser, Nancy. "Rethinking the Public Sphere: A Contribution to the Critique of Actually Existing Democracy." In *Habermas and the Public Sphere*, edited by Craig Calhoun, 109–42. Cambridge: MIT Press, 1992.

" 'Free Love'—a Reply." *Social Revolutionist* 2, no. 5 (1856): 144–46.

Freeman, Elizabeth. *The Wedding Complex: Forms of Belonging in Modern American Culture*. Durham, N.C.: Duke University Press, 2002.

Frisken, Amanda. "Sex in Politics: Victoria Woodhull as an American Public Woman, 1870–1876." *Journal of Women's History* 12, no. 1 (2000): 89–111.

———. *Victoria Woodhull's Sexual Revolution: Political Theater and the Popular Press in Nineteenth-Century America*. Philadelphia: University of Pennsylvania Press, 2004.

Gabriel, Mary. *Notorious Victoria: The Life of Victoria Woodhull, Uncensored*. Chapel Hill: Algonquin Books of Chapel Hill, 1998.

Ganz, Melissa J. "Wicked Women and Veiled Ladies: Gendered

Narratives of the Mcfarland-Richardson Tragedy." *Yale Journal of Law & Feminism* 9 (1996): 255–303.

Gibson, Katie L. "Judicial Rhetoric and Women's 'Place': The United States Supreme Court's Darwinian Defense of Separate Spheres." *Western Journal of Communication* 71, no. 2 (2007): 159–75.

Ginzberg, Lori. *Untidy Origins: A Story of Woman's Rights in Antebellum New York.* Chapel Hill: University of North Carolina Press, 2005.

Gladstone, W. E., Joseph P. Bradley, and Senator Joseph N. Dolph. "The Question of Divorce." *North American Review* 149, no. 397 (1889): 641–52.

Goldsmith, Barbara. *Other Powers: The Age of Suffrage, Spiritualism, and the Scandalous Victoria Woodhull.* New York: Alfred A. Knopf, 1998.

Gordon, Linda. *Heroes of Their Own Lives: The Politics and History of Family Violence, Boston 1880–1960.* New York: Viking, 1988.

———. "Putting Children First: Women, Maternalism, and Welfare in the Early Twentieth Century." In *U.S. History as Women's History*, edited by Linda K. Kerber, Alice Kessler-Harris, and Kathryn Kish Sklar, 63–86. Chapel Hill: University of North Carolina Press, 1995.

Gordon, Sarah Barringer. *The Mormon Question: Polygamy and Constitutional Conflict in Nineteenth-Century America.* Chapel Hill: University of North Carolina Press, 2002.

Grant, Ulysses S. "State of the Union Address." 1871.

Greeley, Horace. "Marriage—Divorce." In *Love, Marriage, and Divorce and the Sovereignty of the Individual,* 154–57 and 163–67. New York: Source Book Press, 1972.

Grey, Vivian. "Sexual Slavery." *Social Revolutionist* 2, no. 5 (1856): 137–38.

Gring-Pemble, Lisa M. "Writing Themselves into Consciousness: Creating a Rhetorical Bridge between the Public and Private Spheres." *Quarterly Journal of Speech* 84, no. 1 (1998): 41–62.

Gring-Pemble, Lisa, and Martha Solomon Watson. "The Rhetorical Limits of Satire: An Analysis of James Finn Garner's *Politically Correct Bedtime Stories.*" *Quarterly Journal of Speech* 89, no. 2 (2003): 132–53.

Griswold, Robert L. "Law, Sex, Cruelty, and Divorce in Victorian America, 1840–1900." *American Quarterly* 38, no. 5 (1986): 721–45.

———. "Sexual Cruelty and the Case for Divorce in Victorian America." *Signs* 11, no. 3 (1986): 529–41.

Grossberg, Michael. *Governing the Hearth: Law and the Family in Nineteenth-Century America*. Chapel Hill: University of North Carolina Press, 1985.

Gutierrez, Cathy. "Sex in the City of God: Free Love and the American Millennium." *Religion and American Culture: A Journal of Interpretation* 15, no. 2 (2005): 187–208.

Hafetz, Jonathan L. "'A Man's Home Is His Castle?': Reflections on the Home, the Family, and Privacy during the Late Nineteenth and Early Twentieth Centuries." *William and Mary Journal of Women and the Law* 8 (2002): 175–242.

Haller, John S. Jr. *Outcasts from Evolution: Scientific Attitudes of Racial Inferiority, 1859–1900*. Urbana: University of Illinois Press, 1971.

Hambrick-Stowe, Charles. *Charles G. Finney and the Spirit of American Evangelicalism*. Grand Rapids: Eerdmans, 1996.

Hand-Book of the Oneida Community with a Sketch of Its Founder and an Outline of Its Constitution and Doctrines. Digital ed. Wallingford, Conn.: Office of the Circular, Wallingford Community, 1867. Oneida Community Collection. Syracuse University Library.

Hardy, B. Carmon. *Solemn Covenant: The Mormon Polygamous Passage*. Urbana: University of Illinois Press, 1992.

Hariman, Robert. "Political Parody and Public Culture." *Quarterly Journal of Speech* 94, no. 3 (2008): 247–72.

Harris, Leslie J. "Law as Father: Metaphors of Family in Nineteenth-Century Law." *Communication Studies* 61, no. 5 (2010): 526–42.

———. "Motherhood, Race, and Gender: The Rhetoric of Women's Antislavery Activism in the *Liberty Bell* Giftbooks." *Women's Studies in Communication* 32, no. 3 (2009): 293–319.

Harris, Leslie J., and Mike Allan. "The Paradox of Authentic Identity: Mormon Women and the Nineteenth-Century Polygamy Controversy." In *Reason and Social Change*, edited by Robert Rowlands, 340–47. Washington, D.C.: National Communication Association, 2011.

Hart, Heber Leonidas. *Woman Suffrage: A National Danger*. London: T. Murby, 1909.

Hartnett, Stephen John. *Democratic Dissent and the Cultural Fictions of Antebellum America*. Urbana: University of Illinois Press, 2002.

———. "Fanny Fern's 1855 *Ruth Hall*, the Cheerful Brutality of Capitalism, and the Irony of Sentimental Rhetoric." *Quarterly Journal of Speech* 88, no. 1 (2002): 1–18.

Hartog, Hendrik. "Lawyering, Husbands' Rights, and 'the Unwritten Law' in Nineteenth-Century America." *Journal of American History* 84, no. 1 (1997): 67–96.

———. "Lecture: Marital Exits and Marital Expectations in Nineteenth-Century America." *Georgetown Law Journal* 80 (1991): 95.

———. *Man and Wife in America: A History*. Cambridge, Mass.: Harvard University Press, 2000.

Hasian, Marouf. "Critical Legal Rhetorics: The Theory and Practice of Law in a Postmodern World." *Southern Communication Journal* 60, no. 1 (1994): 44–56.

———. *The Rhetoric of Eugenics in Anglo-American Thought*. Athens: University of Georgia Press, 1996.

Hasian, Marouf, Celeste Michelle Condit, and John Louis Lucaites. "The Rhetorical Boundaries of 'the Law': A Consideration of the Rhetorical Culture of Legal Practice and the Case of the 'Separate but Equal' Doctrine." *Quarterly Journal of Speech* 82, no. 4 (1996): 323–42.

Haskell, D. C. *Mormonism and Polygamy: An Address Delivered by D. C. Haskell, of Kansas, at Central Music Hall, Chicago, June 8th, 1881, before the National Convention of the American Home Missionary Society*. Lawrence, Kans.: Republican Journal Steam Printing, 1881. Schroeder Collection. Wisconsin Historical Society, Madison.

Hauser, Gerard A. *Vernacular Voices: The Rhetoric of Publics and Public Spheres*. Columbia: University of South Carolina Press, 1999.

Hayden, Wendy. "(R)Evolutionary Rhetorics: Science and Sexuality in Nineteenth-Century Free-Love Discourse." *Rhetoric Review* 29, no. 2 (2010): 111–28.

Hayes, Rutherford B. "State of the Union Address." 1879.

———. "State of the Union Address." 1880.

Hayward, Aaron S. "An Exposition of 'Social Freedom': Monogamic Marriage the Highest Development of Sexual Equality." Boston, 1874. Fromkin Memorial Collection. University of Wisconsin–Milwaukee.

Hempstead, Martha. "The Fugitive." In *Liberty Bell*, edited by Friends of Freedom, 209–14. Boston: Massachusetts Anti-slavery Fair, 1844.

Hickox, George A. *Legal Disabilities of Married Women in Connecticut*. Hartford: Case, Lockwood & Brainard, 1871.

Hofstradter, Richard. *Social Darwinism in American Thought*. Philadelphia: University of Pennsylvania Press, 1945.

Horowitz, Helen Lefkowitz. "Victoria Woodhull, Anthony Comstock, and Conflict over Sex in the United States in the 1870s." *Journal of American History* 87, no. 2 (2000): 403–34.

Howells, W. D. "Charles W. Chesnutt's Stories: Atlantic." *Current Literature*, June 1900, 277–78.

Hutter, W. H., and Ray H. Abrams. "Copperhead Newspapers and the Negro." *Journal of Negro History* 20, no. 2 (1935): 131–52.

"Illinois Humane Society Annual Reports, 1879–1899." Illinois Humane Society Records. University of Illinois–Chicago.

"In the Supreme Court of Pennsylvania, 1858. Williams and Wife vs. Coward and Wife." *American Law Register* 6, no. 5 (1858): 315.

Iversen, Joan Smyth. *The Antipolygamy Controversy in U.S. Women's Movements, 1880–1925: A Debate on the American Home*. New York: Garland, 1997.

Jensen, Robin E. *Dirty Words: The Rhetoric of Public Sex Education, 1870–1924*. Urbana: University of Illinois Press, 2010.

———. "Sexual Polysemy: The Discursive Ground of Talk about Sex and Education in U.S. History." *Communication, Culture & Critique* 1, no. 4 (2008): 396–415.

Johnson, Nan. *Gender and Rhetorical Space in American Life, 1866–1910*. Carbondale: Southern Illinois University Press, 2002.

———. "Reigning in the Court of Silence: Women and Rhetorical Space in Postbellum America." *Philosophy and Rhetoric* 33, no. 3 (2000): 221–42.

Jones, Jason. "Breathing Life into a Public Woman: Victoria Woodhull's Defense of Woman's Suffrage." *Rhetoric Review* 28, no. 4 (2009): 352–69.

Kaplan, E. Ann. *Motherhood and Representation: The Mother in Popular Culture and Melodrama*. New York: Routledge, 1992.

Keetly, Dawn. "From Anger to Jealousy: Explaining Domestic Homicide in Antebellum America." *Journal of Social History* 42, no. 2 (2008): 269–97.

Kerber, Linda. *No Constitutional Right to Be Ladies: Women and the Obligations of Citizenship*. New York: Hill & Wang, 1998.

———. *Women of the Republic: Intellect and Ideology in Revolutionary America*. Chapel Hill: University of North Carolina Press, 1980.

Kern, Louis J. *An Ordered Love: Sex Roles and Sexuality in Victorian Utopias—the Shakers, the Mormons, and the Oneida Community*. Chapel Hill: University of North Carolina Press, 1981.

Knight, Louise W. *Citizen: Jane Addams and the Struggle for Democracy*. Chicago: University of Chicago Press, 2005.

Kohlstedt, Sally, and Mark Jorgensen. "The Irrepressible Woman Question: Women's Responses to Darwinian Evolutionary Ideology." In *Disseminating Darwinism: The Role of Place, Race, Religion, and Gender*, edited by John Stenhouse, 267–93. Cambridge: Cambridge University Press, 1999.

Korobkin, Laura Hanft. *Criminal Converstaions: Sentimentality and Nineteenth-Century Legal Stories of Adultery*. New York: Columbia University Press, 1998.

Koven, Seth, and Sonya Michel. "Introduction: Mother Worlds." In *Mothers of a New World: Maternalist Politics and the Origins of Welfare States*, edited by Seth Koven and Sonya Michel, 1–41. New York: Routledge, 1993.

Kraditor, Aileen S. *The Ideas of the Woman Suffrage Movement 1890–1920*. New York: Anchor Books, 1971.

Ladd-Taylor, Molly. *Mother-Work: Women, Child Welfare, and the State, 1890–1930*. Urbana: University of Illinois Press, 1994.

Lane, Marion S., and Stephen L. Zawistowski. *Heritage of Care: The American Society for the Prevention of Cruelty to Animals*. Westport, Conn.: Praeger, 2008.

Larson, Gustive O. *The "Americanization" of Utah for Statehood*. San Marino, Ca.: Huntington Library, 1971.

Larson, Stan. Introduction to *Prisoner for Polygamy: The Memoirs and Letters of Rudger Clawson at the Utah Territorial Penitentiary, 1884–87*, edited by Stan Larson, 1–34. Urbana: University of Illinois Press, 1993.

Leff, Michael. "Things Made by Words: Reflections on Textual Criticism." *Quarterly Journal of Speech* 78, no. 2 (1992): 223–31.

Leff, Michael, and Ebony A. Utley. "Instrumental and Constitutive Rhetoric in Martin Luther King Jr.'s 'Letter from Birmingham Jail.'" *Rhetoric and Public Affairs* 7, no. 1 (2004): 37–52.

Lessl, Thomas M. *Rhetorical Darwinism: Religion, Evolution, and the Scientific Identity*. Waco: Baylor University Press, 2012.

Lewis, Robert M. *From Traveling Show to Vaudeville*. Baltimore: Johns Hopkins University Press, 2003.

Lewis, Tiffany. "Winning Woman Suffrage in the Masculine West: Abigail Scott Duniway's Frontier Myth." *Western Journal of Communication* 75, no. 2 (2011): 127–47.

Lincoln, Abraham. "Annual Message to Congress, December 1, 1862." In *Collected Works of Abraham Lincoln*, vol. 5, edited by Roy P. Basler, 518–37. Ann Arbor: University of Michigan Digital Library, 2001.

Lindsay, Matthew J. "Reproducing a Fit Citizenry: Dependency, Eugenics, and the Law of Marriage in the United States, 1860–1920." *Law & Social Inquiry* 23, no. 3 (1998): 541–85.

Long, Jos. R. "Tinkering with the Constitution." *Yale Law Journal* 24, no. 7 (1915): 573–89.

Lunceford, Brett. "Rhetoric and Religion in Contemporary Politics." *Journal of Contemporary Rhetoric* 2, no. 2 (2012): 19–29.

Mabie, Hamilton Wright. "Books and Writers: The New Books I.—the Best New Novels." *Outlook*, November 16, 1901, 681–85.

Macmillan, Chrystal. "Nationality of Married Women." *International Women's News* 11, no. 1 (1916): 2–3.

Maddux, Kristy. "When Patriots Protest: The Anti-suffrage Discursive Transformation of 1917." *Rhetoric and Public Affairs* 7, no. 3 (2004): 283–310.

Marilley, Suzanne M. "Frances Willard and the Feminism of Fear." *Feminist Studies* 19, no. 1 (1993): 123–46.

"Married Women's Act. Coverture. Statute of Limitations. Bliler v. Boswell, 59 Pac. Rep. 798 (Wyo.). Feme Covert." *Yale Law Journal* 9, no. 6 (1900): 279.

Mason, Jeffrey. *Melodrama and the Myth of America*. Bloomington: Indiana University Press, 1993.

Masur, Kate. *An Example for All the Land: Emancipation and the Struggle over Equality in Washington, D.C.* Chapel Hill: University of North Carolina Press, 2010.

Matthews, Burnita Shelton. "The Woman without a Country." *Equal Rights* 1, no. 15 (1923): 117–18.

McConacie, Bruce A. *Melodramatic Formations*. Iowa City: University of Iowa Press, 1992.

McGarry, Molly. "Spectral Sexualities: Nineteenth-Century Spiritualism, Moral Panics, and the Making of the U.S. Obscenity Law." *Journal of Women's History* 12, no. 2 (2000): 8–29.

McGee, Michael Calvin. "The 'Ideograph': A Link between Rhetoric and Ideology." *Quarterly Journal of Speech* 66, no. 1 (1980): 1–16.

McKeown, Adam. "Transnational Chinese Families and Chinese Exclusion, 1875–1943." *Journal of American Ethnic History* 18, no. 2 (1999): 73–110.

Medhurst, Martin. "The First Amendment vs. Human Rights: A Case Study in Community Sentiment and Argument from Definition." *Western Journal of Speech Communication* 46, no. 1 (1982): 1–19.

Miscegenation: The Theory of the Blending of the Races, Applied to the American White Man and Negro. New York: H. Dexter, Hamilton, 1864.

Morin, Karen M., and Jeanne Kay Guelke. "Strategies of Representation, Relationship, and Resistance: British Women Travelers and Mormon Plural Wives, Ca. 1870–1890." *Annals of the Association of American Geographers* 88, no. 3 (1998): 436–62.

"Mormon Life." *Oneida Circular* 8, no. 15 (1871): 119–20.

'Mormon' Women on Plural Marriage. Fifteen Hundred 'Mormon' Ladies Convene in the Salt Lake Theatre, to Protest against the Misrepresentations of the Ladies Engaged in the Anti-polygamy Crusade, and Declare Their True Sentiments on the Subject Now Being Agitated. 1878. Americana Collection. Brigham Young University, Provo, Utah.

'Mormon' Women's Protest. An Appeal for Freedom, Justice and Equal Rights. The Ladies of the Church of Jesus Christ of Latter-Day Saints Protest against the Tyranny and Indecency of Federal Officials in Utah, and against Their Own Disfranchisement without Cause. Full Account of Proceedings at the Great Mass Meeting, Held in the Theater, Salt Lake City, Utah. 1886. Schroeder Collection. Wisconsin Historical Society, Madison.

Morrill, Justin S. *Utah Territory and Its Laws—Polygamy and Its License; Delivered in the House of Representatives, February 23, 1857.* Washington, D.C.: Office of the Congressional Globe, 1857.

Mulford, Elisha. *The Nation: The Foundations of Civil Order and Political Life in the United States.* New York: Hurd and Houghton, 1870.

Munson, C. LaRue, and William D. Crocker. "The Divorce Question in the United States." *Yale Law Journal* 18, no. 6 (1909): 387–98.

The National Divorce Reform League: An Abstract of Its Annual Reports. Montpelier: Vermont Watchman and State Journal Press, 1885.

Nelson, Dana D. *National Manhood: Capitalist Citizenship and the Imagined Fraternity of White Men.* Durham, N.C.: Duke University Press, 1998.

Nelson, William T. *A Treatise on the Law of Divorce and Annulment of Marriage Including the Adjustment of Property Rights upon Divorce, the Procedure in Suits for Divorce, and the Validity and Extraterritorial Effects of Decrees of Divorce.* 2 vols. Chicago: Callaghan, 1895.

"The New Calandar." *Lucifer, the Light-Bearer* 3, no. 18 (285/1886): 2.

"The Next Revolution, or Woman's Emancipation from Sex Slavery: No. 2." Valley Fall, Kans.: Lucifer, 1890. Special Collections. University of Wisconsin–Milwaukee.

Nicholas, S. S. *Conservative Essays Legal and Political*. Philadelphia: J. B. Lippincott, 1865.

Nichols, Jeffrey. *Prostitution, Polygamy, and Power: Salt Lake City, 1847–1918*. Urbana: University of Illinois Press, 2002.

"Notes on Books and Booksellers." *American Literary Gazette and Publishers' Circular* 9, no. 1 (1867): 4–11.

Nugent, Walter. "Demography: Chicago as a Modern World City." In *The Encyclopedia of Chicago*, edited by James R. Grossman, Ann Durkin Keating, and Janice L. Reiff, 233–37. Chicago: University of Chicago Press, 2004.

Olson, Kathryn M. "The Controversy over President Reagan's Visit to Bitburg: Strategies of Definition and Redefinition." *Quarterly Journal of Speech* 75, no. 2 (1989): 129–51.

———. "The Role of Dissociation in Redeeming Knowledge Claims: Nineteenth-Century Shakers' Epistemological Resistance to Decline." *Philosophy & Rhetoric* 28, no. 1 (1995): 45–68.

O'Neill, William L. "Divorce in the Progressive Era." *American Quarterly* 17, no. 2 (1965): 203–17.

Onuf, Peter S. "American Exceptionalism and National Identity." *American Political Thought* 1, no. 1 (2012): 77–100.

Owen, Robert Dale. "Divorce." In *Love, Marriage, and Divorce and the Sovereignty of the Individual*, 149–53. New York: Source Book Press, 1972.

Palczewski, Catherine Helen. "The Male Madonna and the Feminine Uncle Sam: Visual Argument, Icons, and Ideographs in 1909 Anti-Woman Suffrage Postcards." *Quarterly Journal of Speech* 91, no. 4 (2005): 365–94.

———. "Voltairine de Cleyre: Sexual Slavery and Sexual Pleasure in the Nineteenth Century." *National Women's Studies Association* 7 (1995): 54–68.

Passet, Joanne E. *Sex Radicals and the Quest for Women's Equality*. Urbana: University of Illinois Press, 2003.

Peeples, Jennifer A., and Kevin M. DeLuca. "The Truth of the Matter: Motherhood, Community and Environmental Justice." *Women's Studies in Communication* 29, no. 1 (2006): 59–87.

Peffer, George Anthony. *If They Don't Bring Their Women Here: Chinese Female Immigration before Exclusion*. Urbana: University of Illinois Press, 1999.

Perelman, Ch., and L. Olbrechts-Tyteca. *The New Rhetoric: A Treatise on*

Argumentation. Translated by John Wilkinson and Purcell Weaver. Notre Dame: University of Notre Dame Press, 1971.

Picard, Alyssa. "'To Popularize the Nude in Art': Comstockery Reconsidered." *Journal of the Gilded Age and Progressive Era* 1, no. 3 (2002): 195–224.

Pilcher, William H. "Varietism." *Lucifer, the Light-Bearer* 3, no. 6 (285/1886): 3.

Pleck, Elizabeth. *Domestic Tyranny: The Making of Social Policy against Family Violence from Colonial Times to the Present*. New York: Oxford University Press, 1987.

Poauillac, Myriam. "Near West Side." In *The Encyclopedia of Chicago*, edited by James R. Grossman, Ann Durkin Keating, and Janice L. Reiff, 563–64. Chicago: University of Chicago Press, 2004.

Pond, James Burton. *Eccentricities of Genius: Memories of Famous Men and Women of the Platform and Stage*. London: Chatto & Windus, 1901.

Postlewait, Thomas. "From Melodrama to Realism: The Suspect History of American Drama." In *Melodrama: The Cultural Emergence of a Genre*, edited by Michael Hays and Anastasia Nikolopoulou, 39–60. New York: St. Martin's Press, 1996.

Pratt, Belinda Marden. "Defense of Polygamy by a Lady of Utah, in a Letter to Her Sister in New Hampshire." Edited by Schroeder Collection/Wisconsin Historical Society. 1854. Schroeder Collection. Wisconsin Historical Society, Madison.

Pratt, Orson. "Discourse." 1869. Schroeder Collection. Wisconsin Historical Society, Madison.

Pratt, Orson, and J. P. Newman. *The Bible and Polygamy: Does the Bible Sanction Polygamy?* Salt Lake City, Utah: Deseret News Steam Printing, 1874. Schroeder Collection. Wisconsin Historical Society, Madison.

"Proceedings in Mass Meeting of the Ladies of Salt Lake City to Protest against the Passage of Cullom's Bill, January 14, 1870." 1870. Church History Library, Salt Lake City, Utah.

"Protective Agency for Women and Children Annual Reports." 1887–1905, Chicago History Museum.

Ramsey, E. Michele. "Inventing Citizens during World War I: Suffrage Cartoons in *The Woman Citizen*." *Western Journal of Communication* 64, no. 2 (2000): 113–47.

Ray, Angela. *The Lyceum and Public Culture in the Nineteenth-Century United States*. East Lansing: Michigan State University Press, 2005.

Ray, Angela, and Cindy Koenig Richards. "Inventing Citizens, Imagining Gender Justice: The Suffrage Rhetoric of Virginia and Francis Minor." *Quarterly Journal of Speech* 93, no. 4 (2007): 375–402.

Reed, Henry. *Bigamy and Polygamy, Review of the Opinion of the Supreme Court of the United States, Rendered at the October Term, 1878, in the Case of George Reynolds, Plaintiff in Error, v. The United States, Defendant in Error.* New York, 1897. Wisconsin Historical Society, Madison.

"Remarks." *Social Revolutionist* 2, no. 5 (1856): 134–35.

Richards, Evelleen. "Darwin and the Descent of Woman." In *The Wider Domain of Evolutionary Thought*, edited by Ian Langham, 57–112. Boston: D. Reidel, 1983.

Riley, Glenda. *Divorce: An American Tradition.* New York: Oxford University Press, 1991.

Ruedebusch, Emil F. *The Old and the New Ideal.* 2nd ed. Mayville, Wisc.: by author, 1897. Fromkin Memorial Collection. University of Wisconsin–Milwaukee.

Ryan, Mary. *Women in Public: Between Banners and Ballots, 1825–1880.* Baltimore: Johns Hopkins University Press, 1990.

Ryo, Emily. "Through the Back Door: Applying Theories of Legal Compliance to Illegal Immigration during the Chinese Exclusion Era." *Law & Social Inquiry* 31, no. 1 (2006): 109–46.

Said, Edward W. *Orientalism.* New York: Vintage Books, 1979.

Schiappa, Edward. *Defining Reality.* Carbondale: Southern Illinois University Press, 2003.

Schudson, Michael. *The Good Citizen: A History of American Civic Life.* Cambridge, Mass.: Harvard University Press, 2002.

"Scrapbook." 1899–1900. Illinois Humane Society Records. University of Illinois–Chicago.

Sears, Hal D. *The Sex Radicals: Free Love in High Victorian America.* Lawrence: Regents Press of Kansas, 1977.

Sennett, Richard. *The Fall of Public Man.* New York: W. W. Norton, 1976.

Severance, Juliet H. *A Discussion of the Social Question between Juliet H. Severance, M.D. and David Jones, Editor of the "Olive Branch."* Milwaukee: National Advance, 1891. Collection of Leon Kramer. Special Collections. University of Wisconsin–Milwaukee.

Siegel, Reva B. "The Modernization of Marital Status Law: Adjudicating Wives' Rights to Earnings, 1860–1930." Symposium on Divorce and Feminist Legal Theory. Special issue, *Georgetown Law Journal* 82 (1994): 2127–211.

———. "'The Rule of Love': Wife Beating as Prerogative and Privacy." *Yale Law Journal* 105 (1996): 2117–207.

———. "She the People: The Nineteenth Amendment, Sex Equality, Federalism, and the Family." *Harvard Law Review* 115 (2002): 947–1046.

Slagell, Amy R. "The Rhetorical Structure of Frances E. Willard's Campaign for Woman Suffrage, 1876–1896." *Rhetoric and Public Affairs* 4, no. 1 (2001): 1–23.

Smith, Roger M. *Civic Ideals: Conflicting Visions of Citizenship in U.S. History*. New Haven: Yale University Press, 1997.

Smith, Timothy L. "Righteousness and Hope: Christian Holiness and the Millennial Vision in America, 1800–1900." *American Quarterly* 31, no. 1 (1979): 21–45.

Smith-Rosenberg, Carroll. "Sex as Symbol in Victorian Purity: An Ethnohistorical Analysis of Jacksonian America." Supplement, *American Journal of Sociology* 84 (1978): S212–47.

Spinney, Robert G. *City of Big Shoulders: A History of Chicago*. DeKalb: Northern Illinois University Press, 2000.

Spurlock, John C. *Free Love: Marriage and Middle-Class Radicalism in America, 1825–1860*. New York: New York University Press, 1988.

Stanley, Amy Dru. *From Bondage to Contract: Wage Labor, Marriage, and the Market in the Age of Slave Emancipation*. Cambridge: Cambridge University Press, 1998.

Stanton, Elizabeth Cady. "Address of Mrs. E. C. Stanton." In *Man Cannot Speak for Her*, vol. 2, *Key Texts of the Early Feminists*, edited by Karlyn Kohrs Campbell, 191–202. Westport, Conn.: Praeger, 1989.

———. "Divorce versus Domestic Warfare (1890)." In *Elizabeth Cady Stanton, Feminist as Thinker: A Reader in Documents and Essays*, edited by Ellen Carol DuBois and Richard Candida Smith, 254–63. New York: New York University Press, 2007.

Stanton, Elizabeth Cady, Susan Brownell Anthony, and Matilda Joslyn Gage. *History of Woman Suffrage*. Vol. 1. New York: Fowler & Wells, 1881.

Stenhouse, Mrs. T. B. H. (Fanny Warn). *An Englishwoman in Utah: A Life's Experience in Mormonism*. London: Samson Low, Marston, Searle, & Rivington, 1882. Church History Library. Salt Lake City, Utah.

———. *Tell It All: The Tyranny of Mormonism or an Englishwoman in Utah*. Sussex: Centaur Press, 1971.

Stimson, F. J. "National Unification of Law." *Harvard Law Review* 7, no. 2 (1893): 92–106.

Stowe, Harriet Beecher. "Preface." In Mrs. T. B. H. (Fanny Warn) Stenhouse, *Tell It All: The Tyranny of Mormonism or an Englishwoman in Utah,* iii. 1875; repr. Sussex: Centaur Press, 1971.

Stuckey, Mary E. *Defining Americans: The Presidency and National Identity*. Lawrence: University Press of Kansas, 2004.

———. "One Nation (Pretty Darn) Divisible: National Identity in the 2004 Conventions." *Rhetoric and Public Affairs* 8, no. 4 (2005): 639–56.

Test, George A. *Satire: Spirit and Art*. Tampa: University of South Florida Press, 1991.

Tiffany, Walter C. *Handbook on the Law of Persons and Domestic Relations*. St. Paul: West Publishing, 1896.

Tonn, Mari Boor. "Militant Motherhood: Labor's Mary Harris 'Mother' Jones." *Quarterly Journal of Speech* 82, no. 1 (1996): 1–21.

Treat, Joseph. "Socialism—How Do We Come at It. The Whole Thing in One View." *Social Revolutionist*, November 1856, 152–57.

Tucker, J. Randolph. "Polygamy. Speech of Hon. J. Randolph Tucker, of Virginia. In the House of Representatives." Washington, D.C.: Franklin Printing House, 1887. Schroeder Collection. Wisconsin Historical Society, Madison.

Turner, Kathleen J. "Introduction: Rhetorical History as Social Construction." In *Doing Rhetorical History: Concepts and Cases*, edited by Kathleen J. Turner, 1–15. Tuscaloosa: University of Alabama Press, 1998.

Tyler, Alice Felt. *Freedom's Ferment: Phases of American Social History from the Colonial Period to the Outbreak of the Civil War*. New York: Harper & Row, 1944.

Tyler, Ransom H. *Commentaries on the Law of Infancy: Including Guardianship and Custody of Infants, and the Law of Coverture, Embracing Dower, Marriage and Divorce, and the Statutory Policy of the Several States in Respect to Husband and Wife*. Albany: W. Gould, 1869.

Underhill, Lois Beachy. *The Woman Who Ran for President: The Many Lives of Victoria Woodhull*. New York: Bridge Works, 1995.

Van Wagoner, Richard S. *Mormon Polygamy: A History*. 2nd ed. Salt Lake City, Utah: Signature Books, 1989.

Vonnegut, Kristin S. "Poison or Panacea? Sarah Moore Grimké's Use of the Public Letter." *Communication Studies* 46 (1995): 73–88.

Wadia, Ardeshir Ruttonji. *The Ethics of Feminism: A Study of the Revolt of Woman*. London: G. Allen & Unwin, 1923.

Waisanen, Don J. "Crafting Hyperreal Spaces for Comic Insights: The

Onion News Network's Ironic Iconicity." *Communication Quarterly* 59, no. 5 (2011): 508–28.

Wald, Priscilla. *Constituting Americans: Cultural Anxiety and Narrative Form*. Durham, N.C.: Duke University Press, 1995.

Wallace, Irving. *The Twenty-Seventh Wife*. New York: Simon & Schuster, 1961.

Wallenstein, Peter. *Tell the Court I Love My Wife: Race, Marriage, and Law—an American History*. New York: Palgrave Macmillan, 2002.

Warner, Michael. *Publics and Counterpublics*. New York: Zone Books, 2005.

Waugh, John C. *Reelecting Lincoln: The Battle for the 1864 Presidency*. New York: Crown, 1997.

Webb, Sheila M. "The Woman Citizen: A Study of How News Narratives Adapt to a Changing Social Environment." *American Journalism* 29, no. 2 (2012): 9–36.

Weisbrod, Carol, and Pamela Sheingorn. "Reynolds v. United States: Nineteenth-Century Forms of Marriage and the Status of Women." *Connecticut Law Review* 10 (1977–1978): 828–58.

Wells, Ida B. "Southern Horrors: Lynch Law in All Its Phases." In *Southern Horrors and Other Writings: The Anti-lynching Campaign of Ida B. Wells, 1892–1900*, edited by Jacqueline Jones Royster, 49–72. Boston: St. Martins, 1997.

Welter, Barbara. "The Cult of True Womanhood: 1820–1860." *American Quarterly* 18, no. 2 (1966): 151–74.

White, James Boyd. *Heracles' Bow*. Madison: University of Wisconsin Press, 1985.

———. *The Legal Imagination*. Chicago: University of Chicago Press, 1985.

Whitney, Henry Clay. *Marriage and Divorce: The Effect of Each on Personal Status and Property Rights, with a Consideration of Fraudulent Divorces and the Ethics of Divorce for Popular and Professional Use*. Philadelphia: J. E. Potter, 1894.

Whittaker, David. "Early Mormon Polygamy Defenses." *Journal of Mormon History* 11, no. 1 (1984): 43–63.

Whitworth, John McKelvie. *God's Blueprints: A Sociological Study of Three Utopian Sects*. Boston: Routledge & Kegan Paul, 1975.

Willard, Frances E. "Tenth Annual Address." In *Minutes of the National Woman's Christian Temperance Union at the Sixteenth Annual Meeting*, 92–163. Chicago: Woman's Christian Temperance Union, 1889. Frances Willard Memorial Library and Archives, Evanston, Ill.

Wills, Garry. *Inventing America: Jefferson's Declaration of Independence*. New York: Vintage Books, 1979.

Wilson, Kirt H. "The Racial Politics of Imitation in the Nineteenth Century." *Quarterly Journal of Speech* 89, no. 2 (2003): 89–108.

Woodhull, Victoria. *Tried as by Fire; or, the True and the False, Socially. An Oration Delivered by Victoria C. Woodhull, in All the Principal Cities and Towns of the Country during an Engagement of One Hundred and Fifty Consecutive Nights, to Audiences Together Numbering a Quarter of a Million of People*. New York: Woodhull & Claflin, 1874.

Woolsey, Theodore Dwight. *Essay on Divorce and Divorce Legislation, with Special Reference to the United States*. New York: C. Scribner, 1869.

Wright, Carroll D. *A Report on Marriage and Divorce in the United States, 1867–1886*. Washington, D.C.: Government Printing Office, 1889.

Yenor, Scott. *Family Politics: The Idea of Marriage in Modern Political Thought*. Waco: Baylor University Press, 2012.

Young, Ann Eliza. *Wife No. 19, or The Story of a Life in Bondage, Being a Complete Expose of Mormonism, and Revealing the Sorrows, Sacrifices and Sufferings of Women in Polygamy*. New York: Arno Press, 1972.

Zaeske, Susan. *Signatures of Citizenship: Petitioning, Antislavery, and Women's Political Identity*. Chapel Hill: University of North Carolina Press, 2003.

Zarefsky, David. "Definitions." In *Argument in a Time of Change: Definitions, Frameworks, and Critiques*, edited by James F. Klumpp, 1–11. Annandale, Va.: National Communication Association, 1997.

———. "Echoes of the Slavery Controversy in the Current Abortion Debate," In *Argument in Controversy*, 89–95. Annandale, Va.: National Communication Association, 1991.

———. "Four Senses of Rhetorical History." In *Doing Rhetorical History: Concepts and Cases*, edited by Kathleen J. Turner, 19–32. Tuscaloosa: University of Alabama Press, 1998.

———. "Strategic Maneuvering through Persuasive Definitions: Implications for Dialectic and Rhetoric." *Argumentation* 20, no. 3 (2006): 399–416.

Zornow, William Frank. *Lincoln and the Party Divided*. Westport, Conn.: Greenwood Press, 1972.

Zschoche, Sue. "Review, Wash and Be Healed: The Water-Cure Movement and Women's Health by Susan E. Cayleff." *Signs* 15, no. 2 (1990): 414–16.

Index